Professional Training Institution

2803 St. Joseph Ave Suite B
PO Box 6302
Evansville, IN 47720
Phone 812.422.4068 • info@ptischool.com

This publication is designed to provide accurate and authoritative information regarding the subject matter covered. It is sold with the understanding that the publisher is not engaged in rendering legal, accounting, or other professional services. If legal advice or other expert assistance is required, the services of a competent professional should be sought.

Any laws and regulations cited in this publication have been edited and summarized for clarity sake.

We have tried to provide the most accurate and useful information possible. However, the content of this publication may be affected by changes in law or industry practice and information may become outdated.

Table of Contents

Chapter 1

Insurance Basics for Property and Casualty

The basics lay the foundation for the material that will be discussed in later chapters. This chapter introduces the language of the insurance industry. This material is tested on specifically, but it is also woven throughout the policies and questions concerning the policies. The better you know and understand the basics, the better prepared you will be for the exam.

Being familiar with the basic terms and concepts of the insurance industry is the first step in understanding the products of the industry, as well as the industry itself. But, it is not just memorizing definitions; it is the **comprehending** of these terms and concepts and being able to understand them in the context of their use. For a student new to the insurance industry, learning the terms and how to use them properly is much like learning a new language. Without a full knowledge of the language, even the simplest concepts can be confusing. Once one has a full grasp of the language and the concepts represented, then understanding begins to fall into place.

Meet the Browns

Meet the All-American family, the Browns: Grant, his wife Holly and their two kids Doug and Maria. The Browns are just like you and me, living in a fast paced world where unfortunately, accidents happen. Speeding down the expressway trying to get to work before the boss discovers that you are late turns into an automobile pile up. Stepping away from the kitchen with supper on the stove turns into a small kitchen fire. The Browns live in a nice, suburban home. Grant drives a thirty minute commute every day to work. They own a boat and take it out on the lake on the weekends. Each member of the Brown family has what we call **exposures** (being subject to a loss). A synonym for the term exposure is vulnerability. Because the Browns own a boat, they could experience a loss on their boat; therefore they are exposed to boat owners claims.

An antonym of the word exposure is protection. In the Brown's case, they can purchase a boat owners insurance policy to provide them financial protection from a loss. However, before we dive into the definition of insurance, we must first cover a few terms.

The Very Basics

As stated above, the Browns are **exposed** to boat owner claims since they own a boat. There is no guarantee that the Browns will ever experience a loss or file a claim on their boat, but it *could happen.* The chance that *it could happen* is known as **risk.** Every person lives with risk. **Risk is defined as the "chance or possibility of a loss."** Risk is all about statistics and numbers. Insurance companies use the law of large numbers to determine an applicant's risk. What are the chances that the Browns will have a house fire resulting in a total loss this year? The insurance company will come up with an answer to this question and that number, along with some other factors, will determine how much premium the Browns will pay on their Homeowners Policy.

Note: The "Law of large numbers" basically says that the more numbers used in a statistic, the more accurate the statistic will be.

Understanding Risk

Risk has now been defined as the "possibility or chance of a loss." There are two different types of risk; one type is insurable, while the other is not. The first type is referred to as a **"pure risk."** In a pure risk, there is only a possibility of loss. If this happens, there is no opportunity for financial gain. Death, sickness, and your house burning down are examples of pure risks. These are the types of risks individuals always try to avoid. The second type of risk is called a **"speculative risk."** With a speculative risk, an individual has the chance to gain or lose. The individual may voluntarily choose to take this risk because there is a chance of coming out ahead. Investments and gambling are both examples of speculative risks. **The insurance companies never insure speculative risks; they only insure pure risks.**

Managing Risk

Risk is a part of life. Some risks are greater than others and may pose a greater threat to an individual. Managing risk is an important part of a person's life. Take Grant and Holly for example. Grant and Holly can manage their risk in several different ways. Risk may be:

1. **Avoided** – If Grant chooses not to expose himself to the risk, the risk can be avoided. Some risk can be realistically avoided, but others cannot. For

example, Grant may choose not to own a boat and as a result, he has avoided the chance of experiencing a boat loss. However, homeowner and auto risks are harder to avoid.

2. **Reduced** – By reducing the risk, the chance of it occurring is less. Holly could choose not to drive during rush hour to lessen her chance of an automobile accident. A business could install a sprinkler system. The sprinklers will not prevent a fire from starting, but can reduce damages in the event of a fire.

3. **Retained** – When Grant retains the risk or a portion of the risk, he is willing to pay for the loss, when and if it occurs. Grant may say, "I'm not going to buy insurance on my boat. If I experience a loss, I'll just pay for it out of my own pocket. I'll take the chance and save my money that I would have spent on premiums." Another way Grant can retain some risk is by use of a **deductible**. If he has a $1,000 deductible on his homeowners policy, he is responsible for the first $1,000 of damages before the insurance policy pays.

4. **Shared** – When a risk is shared, Holly assumes a portion of the risk in relationship to her invested portion. An industry may join together to assume its own risk.

5. **Transferred** – Transference means that Grant takes the risk he is personally responsible for and transfers it to another party, who then assumes the risk. Insurance is the most common way to transfer risk. **When Grant purchases an insurance policy, he is transferring risk from himself to the insurance company.**

Peril

A peril is defined as a **cause of a loss**. In Property and Casualty Insurance, there are many perils. A few examples are: a house fire, theft to a business, and an automobile accident. When the Browns lost their home, they lost it to the peril of fire.

Hazards

Hazards increase the chance of a loss. A hazard makes the risk more likely to occur. For example, ice on the road during a winter storm creates a more hazardous driving situation. The ice increases the risk or likelihood of an auto accident. In our example, the ice is the hazard; the accident is the peril. The end result is the loss. There are three different types of hazards:

1. **Physical hazard** – These hazards are physical in nature. You can see, touch, or smell them. The ice in the above example is a physical hazard.

2. **Moral** – A moral hazard is based on a person's values and ethics. A policyholder might attempt to create a loss on purpose in order to take advantage of the insurance company. This increases the chance that a company may have to pay a claim.

3. **Morale** – A morale hazard deals more with carelessness or irresponsibility. Someone who always drives fast or texts while driving may increase the chance of a loss.

Loss

Loss is defined as the **disappearance or decrease in value** of a piece of property. When the Browns experienced a fire in their home, their kitchen was totally destroyed. Their home is no longer worth as much as it was prior to the fire. Some of the items in the kitchen were completely destroyed and have lost all value. The Browns have experienced a loss.

There are two types of loss:

- **Direct loss**
- **Indirect or consequential loss**

A direct loss is a **physical** loss. It is tangible. If the Browns experience a house fire, the damage to their household possessions and their home are considered direct losses. These losses can be seen, touched, and smelt. When most people think of a loss, this is the type that typically comes to mind.

Indirect loss is a **financial** loss that is a **result or consequence** of a direct loss. While their home is being repaired, the Browns must live in a hotel for a few weeks, eat meals out, and do their laundry at the laundromat. These are examples of indirect loss. Expenses that the Browns now have *because* of the house fire (direct loss). Another term for indirect loss is consequential loss (think of the financial loss being a consequence of the direct/physical loss).

What is Insurance?

Now that a foundation of basic concepts has been laid, we can now look at the definition of insurance. In its simplest form, **insurance is defined as the**

transference of risk. In a Homeowners Policy, the insured's risk is a loss of property value. If the Brown's house were to burn to the ground, they would experience a loss of great value. It is this risk that the Browns are concerned about. Replacing their home and meeting their financial obligation to the mortgage company is a greater loss than the Browns are comfortable with. Insurance takes that large uncertain financial risk and for a relatively minimal fee, passes the responsibility to the insurer. Once the insurer accepts the risk, it then spreads that risk among other insureds (other policyholders) with like exposure. The insurer will collect premiums from all of its policyholders, but only a small number will have a claim in a given year. Insurance then becomes the "many" paying for the "few." If Grant and Holly are properly insured and experience a house fire resulting in a total loss, the insurance then pays the Browns for the loss. The Browns have transferred the financial risk of losing their home to the insurance company.

Property Insurance (Two Party Contracts)

Property insurance is a two party contract in which the insured (first party) purchases protection from the insurer (second party) against loss to property from a covered peril. The property insured could be a building or the possessions in the building. The property could be at a fixed location or it might be covered wherever the owner takes it. Contracts that provide protection that follow the property wherever it goes are typically called marine insurance policies or floaters.

Casualty Insurance (Third Party Contracts)

Casualty insurance is a policy that includes liability insurance. Liability insurance is a three party contract that protects the insured against negligent damage done to another party. The three parties are the insured, insurer, and injured third party. Benefits from this policy will be paid directly to the damaged third party; the insured never collects on a liability policy. It protects the insured from lawsuits and the potential of a lawsuit.

Property	Liability
• Covers my stuff • Two Party Insurance	• Covers my responsibility to others • Three Party Insurance

Personal vs Commercial

There are two other ways to classify insurance. Not only could it be property or liability, it could also be personal or commercial. **Personal insurance** provides protection for your personal needs. **Commercial insurance** is used to protect a business and its exposures.

Insurable Interest

Insurable interest is defined as the financial interest that an individual has in the property. In Property and Casualty Insurance, insurable interest is determined at the time of the loss. It does not matter the amount the property was purchased for, it only matters what the financial value of the property was at the time of the loss. If Holly Brown inherited a house from her father, she would have a financial interest in the building. It does not matter that she did not invest in the property. The property has value. If it is damaged or destroyed, value is lost. When the property is damaged, the insurer will determine the value of the loss at that time.

Indemnification

The purpose of insurance is to indemnify or **make the insured whole**, no more, no less. If the insured carries the right type and amount of insurance, then the objective of indemnification will be met. After a loss occurs and the insurance pays the claim, the customer should be brought back to the financial state he/she enjoyed prior to the loss. **Insurance should not allow the insured to make a profit**, but rather it should make the insured whole. If the insured were allowed to profit from a loss, it would encourage fraud and abuse.

Limit of liability

Another word for liability is responsibility. When the policy talks about the "limit of liability," it is referring to the policy's limit of responsibility. This is the most the policy will pay for the given situation. How much a policy will pay is based upon the limit of protection chosen by the insured or provided in the policy. **The policy will always pay the lesser of the limit of liability or the value of the loss**. The policy objective is to indemnify the insured up to the limit of liability.

OCCURRENCE LIMITS

An occurrence limit is a maximum limit within a policy and is based upon each time the policy is used. This is **the most the policy will pay for any one occurrence.** The policy will still indemnify the insured up to the value of the loss or the occurrence limit, whichever is less.

AGGREGATE LIMITS

An aggregate limit is **the most that the policy will pay within a policy year.** Once this limit is reached, the policy will pay no more until a new policy year is reached. How would a policy with a $100,000 Occurrence Limit and a $300,000 Aggregate Limit perform? If the first claim in the policy year resulted in a $120,000 loss, the policy would limit the benefit to the Occurrence Limit of $100,000. The remaining coverage for the balance of the year would be $200,000.

Insureds

One of the most important definitions in the insurance policy is the definition of the insured. The **insured** is the party that the policy is designed to protect against a loss. There are several different types of insureds.

1. **Named Insured** - The first type of insured is the one that is specifically named on the Declaration Page of the policy. When Grant and Holly bought their Homeowners Policy, both of their names were listed on the Declaration Page of the policy. They would both be named insureds.

2. **Insured by Definition** – Doug and Maria are the children living in the household. They are not specifically named as insureds, but they are defined in the policy as covered insureds.

3. **Additional Insured** – An Additional Insured is a party that is added by request onto the policy to be insured. Since the Browns have a mortgage on their home, the bank has an insurable interest in the house. The bank will want to be listed as an Additional Insured. This will then protect their interest in the home.

4. **First Named Insured** – The First Named Insured is the first insured listed on the Declaration Page. This is a designation that will be used on commercial policies to designate the individual that will be given the rights of the policy. The First Named Insured is the "contact" person that the insurance company will work with.

Common Elements within the Insurance Concept

Exclusions

Every policy will come with a list of exclusions. Most will have multiple lists within the policy. An **exclusion** is a peril or issue that **will not be covered** by the policy. Sometimes knowing the exclusions is more important than knowing what is covered. These lists may seem to be overwhelming, but there are some general concepts that will help us understand the types of things that will be excluded in a policy.

CATASTROPHIC

Insurers will always exclude perils that are catastrophic in nature. Examples might include nuclear, war, and flood. When these perils occur, they affect such a large number of insureds at one time that it is financially impossible for an insurer to assume the risk.

COVERED ELSEWHERE

Sometimes an insurer will exclude something because it is better covered elsewhere. Elsewhere could be in another part of the policy or in another policy all together. For example, the automobile will be excluded under the Homeowners Policy because there is a separate policy designed to specifically cover the auto.

EXCLUDED BUT AVAILABLE

Some areas are initially excluded in the policy, only to be added back in through the use of an **endorsement.** Earthquake and motorcycles are examples of issues initially excluded; however, for an additional fee, these can be added back in through an endorsement or rider.

PREDICTABLE LOSSES

A risk is the chance of a loss. Sometimes it is not a chance, it is a sure thing. A loss will happen; it is just a matter of time. Most property policies exclude **inherent vice**. Inherent vice is normal wear and tear on pieces of property. Mechanical breakdown is not something that might happen, over time it is something that will happen.

Note: Endorsements or riders are changes made to a policy. They can increase, decrease or make neutral changes in the coverages of the policy.

Liberalization Clause

The **Liberalization Clause** is a clause found in most policies. It allows the insurer to extend broader legislated or regulated coverages to a current policy. Coverage can only be modified if the **change does not affect the premiums**. The state regulatory bodies will always allow an insurer to better their coverage, especially if there is no additional cost to the customer. Companies would utilize this to keep products current and up to date as legislative changes occur.

Assignment

Assignment means to "assign" or to give a right to another party. This may be used in a commercial policy when one party purchases a business from another. Insurance needs to be maintained even though the business is switching hands. This may be done by assigning the policy to the new owner and making them the new "first named insured." We will see that this can only be done with the insurance company's permission. The insurer always wants to approve who they are insuring.

Cancellation and Nonrenewal

The main difference between cancellation and nonrenewal is timing. **Cancellation** is when the policy coverage ends prior to the expiration date on the policy. If the insurance company would choose not to renew the policy at the end of the policy period, the policy would end due to **nonrenewal.**

Policy premiums are paid in advance. But, what happens when the insurance policy is cancelled midterm? What happens with the unearned premium? It depends on which party cancels the policy. In the example below, a payment has been made of $1,000. Halfway through the year, the policy is being cancelled. If the cancellation is being initiated by the insured, the premium will be refunded on a **short rate** basis. It was the expectation of the insurance company to keep the policy throughout the entire policy period. Since the insured requested the cancellation, now the insurance company has unexpected expenses in order to fulfill the insured's request. They have to update their files and mail a refund check. The state will allow the insurer to charge a small fee for administrative expenses.

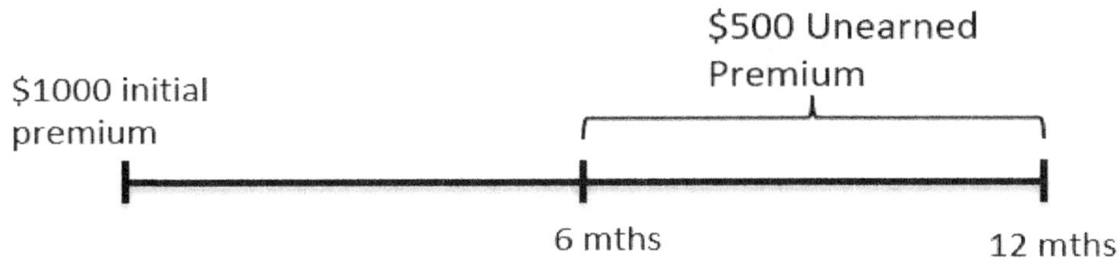

If the insurance company chooses to cancel the policy, the premium due will be refunded on a **pro rata** basis. Since it is the insurer that is initiating the cancellation, the customer should not be financially penalized. A full proportion of the unearned premium must be refunded. In the above example, this would mean that a full $500 of the unearned premium must be refunded. **The insurer cannot cancel a policy at any time.** There are state laws in place to protect the insured. The insurer can only cancel the policy for a limited number of reasons. Also, the insured must be notified in advance of the cancellation. Coverage cannot be ended without proper notification.

Certificate of Insurance

A **certificate of insurance** is written evidence showing that an insurance policy has been issued. The certificate will indicate the limits of insurance and the type of coverage provided. Certificates may be used by contractors to show that they are properly insured. A certificate may also be required by lenders to show that the property is adequately covered with a homeowners policy.

Accidents and Occurrences

A covered event will either be defined as an accident or an occurrence. Coverage could be dependent upon which term is used in the policy. An **accident** is a **sudden and unexpected** event resulting in damage or injury. An **occurrence has a broader definition**. This definition includes an accidental event along with an event that is continuous or on going. With occurrence, time is the factor; damage was created over time. Two cars colliding would meet both the definition of an accident and an occurrence. Mold building up over time is not an accident, but it would be considered an occurrence since there was no accident and the damage was created over time.

Countersignature

When a policy is issued, the state (Department of Insurance) may require a **countersignature** in order to validate the insurance policy. A countersignature is a signature by a licensed resident agent or representative of the company.

Types of Insurers

Lloyds

Lloyd's is a company that insures by **spreading risk over a group of investors.** Lloyd's of London is the original Lloyd's. Although Lloyd's is not considered to be an insurance company (because an insurance company assumes risk and spreads that risk over its group of insureds), they do insure. The Lloyd's assumes risk and spreads the risk over a group of investors. They specialize in unique, hard to insure situations. Because of the unique nature of the need, there may not be the large numbers needed to properly spread the risk among others with the same need. The Lloyd's will use investors, who assume the risk individually, to properly spread the risk.

Stock Company

Stock companies are insurance companies owned by stockholders or shareholders. When a stock company makes a profit, the company may pay out that profit in the form of a dividend to the stockholders, who are the owners. The policyholder does not normally participate in receiving any divisible surplus that the company may have earned. Because the policyholder does not usually receive a dividend, both the product and company are referred to as **nonparticipating**. Stock companies do not generally pay dividends to the policyholder.

Mutual Company

Mutual companies are companies owned by its policyholders. Since each policyholder has an ownership interest in the company, when the company makes a profit, it pays it out to the policyholder as a divisible surplus. When the divisible surplus is paid out, it is paid out as a dividend to the policy owner. Since the policy owner is receiving the dividend, this is referred to as a **participating** product or company.

The dividend from a participating product is defined as a **return of premium**. The policyholder previously paid a premium to the insurance company in exchange for coverage. If the insurance company has a favorable experience throughout the year, the insurance company will not need as much of that premium as it expected earlier in the year. Thus, the company sends back to the insured a portion of the premium paid at the beginning of the year. The **gross premium** of the insurance contract is determined by three sources: risk, interest and expenses. The formula for the gross premium is:

Gross Premium = Risk – Interest + Expenses

When an insurance company has favorable experience in any of the above areas, then the company may declare a dividend. For example, if fewer people had claims than the company expected in the current year, the company may not need as much as it collected and as a result has a divisible surplus. If the company's investment returns are better than expected or expenses are lower than anticipated, a similar result could occur. Since the dividend is actually a return of the policyholder's premium and this premium was paid with previously taxed money, **any dividend returned to the policyholder will not be taxed**.

Also, keep in mind that since dividends are based upon three areas that cannot be precisely predicted, **the agent cannot guarantee a dividend** will be paid in the future. Dividends can be projected, but never guaranteed.

Self Insurers

Self-Insurers retain their own risk. If a business is large enough, it is possible that they may be able to set aside the premiums they would normally pay to an insurance company for their own future needs. Businesses will typically limit their exposure to a manageable amount. Any excess risk could then be transferred to an insurance company for a limited premium.

Risk Retention Groups

Risk Retention Groups are group self-insurance programs. Industries or group with similar liability exposures can come together to insure themselves.

Federal and State Governments

Federal and State Governments will sometimes provide insurance protection programs. When the insurance industry is not able to adequately insure the public, the government will generally step in and provide protection. Flood is excluded by all property policies, but coverage can be purchased through a federal government program. Most states provide high risk pool policies that provide high risk coverage. Examples include the FAIR plan for property and the "Second Injury Fund" for work related injuries.

Reinsurance

Reinsurance is a form of insurance between insurers. Occasionally an insurance company (**ceding company**) will need to spread its risk beyond its own policyholder base. If a risk is larger than the company is comfortable with, the ceding company may seek out a reinsurer (**assuming company**). Reinsurance is when one insurer, for consideration, assumes the risk or part of the risk of another insurer. The concept of insurance is based upon being able to spread risk among large numbers. Reinsurance allows an insurance company to limit its exposure to a manageable amount. This allows risks of all sizes to be assumed.

A **reinsurance treaty** is the agreement between the ceding and the assuming company.

Other ways of Classifying Companies

Domestic insurer is an insurer organized **under the laws of that state.** It will have its home office in the state and be regulated by that state.

Foreign insurer is an insurer organized **under the laws of another state.** This home office will be located out of state. The other state will be responsible for the oversight of that company.

Alien insurer is organized **under the laws of another country**. This company is from another country.

An **authorized (admitted) insurer** has been **approved** by the state Insurance Commissioner to do business in the state. In order for an insurer to do business in a state, it must first be issued a **certificate of authority** by that state's Commissioner. The certificate shows that the company has submitted a sound plan of operation to the Commissioner and the Commissioner has deemed the general character of the insurer is acceptable.

An **unauthorized (non-admitted) insurer** is one that **has not been approved** by the Commissioner to do business in the state.

Terms to Know

Exposure
Risk
Insurer
Insured
Pure Risk
Speculative Risk
Deductible
Peril
Hazard
Physical Hazard
Moral Hazard
Morale Hazard
Loss
Direct Loss
Indirect/Consequential Loss
Property Insurance/ 2 Party Insurance
Casualty Insurance/ Liability Insurance/ 3 Party Insurance
Personal Lines
Commercial Lines
Insurable Interest
Indemnification/Indemnify
Limit of Liability
Occurrence Limit
Aggregate Limit
Named Insured
Additional Insured

First Named Insured
Exclusions
Endorsements/ Riders
Inherent Vice
Liberalization
Assignment
Cancellation
Non-Renewal
Short Rate Refund
Pro Rata Refund
Certificate of Insurance
Accident
Occurrence
Counter Signature
Lloyd's
Stock Company/Nonparticipating
Mutual Company/Participating
Gross Premium
Dividend
Self-Insurers
Risk Retention Group
Reinsurance
Domestic Insurer
Foreign Insurer
Alien Insurer
Authorized/Admitted Insurer
Unauthorized/ Non admitted Insurer

Practice Exam

1. Which term is defined as "the chance of a loss?"
    a. Risk
    b. Peril
    c. Hazard
    d. Loss
2. What is the principle of indemnity?
    a. The requirement to meet the needs of the insured
    b. The requirement to provide complete benefits
    c. Restore to the original financial condition of the insured
    d. Restored to the financial condition prior to the loss
3. An insurance company is able to insure:
    a. A pure risk only
    b. A speculative risk only
    c. Either a pure or speculative risk
    d. Neither the pure or speculative risk
4. What is the difference between indirect and direct losses?
    a. Indirect losses are covered by insurance, direct are not
    b. Indirect is physical in nature, direct is financial
    c. Indirect is consequential, direct is due to a physical peril
    d. Indirect losses are never covered, Direct are covered
5. If an insured experiences a loss due to a peril covered by the policy, the claim will be paid by the insurance company. A peril is defined as:
    a. The chance of a loss
    b. Increases the chance of a loss
    c. The cause of a loss
    d. Uncertainty that leads to loss

6. Ice on the road increases the chance of an auto accident. The ice is an example of:
    a. Peril
    b. Risk
    c. Exposure
    d. Hazard
7. Which of the following statements is FALSE?
    a. An indirect loss is a financial loss resulting from a direct loss
    b. Direct loss and consequential loss are interchangeable terms
    c. Loss is the disappearance or decrease in value
    d. A direct loss is a physical loss
8. The transfer of risk is:
    a. Insurance
    b. Hazard
    c. Peril
    d. Risk
9. Which of the following statements is FALSE?
    a. Casualty/Liability insurance is three party insurance
    b. Personal insurance provides coverage for personal needs
    c. Commercial insurance provides coverage for business needs
    d. Commercial insurance is two party insurance
10. In Property & Casualty insurance, when must insurable interest exist?
    a. At the time of the sale and time of the loss
    b. At the time of the sale
    c. At the time of the loss
    d. At the time of the beneficiary's death
11. When the insurance company makes the insured whole, no more, no less, this is the concept of:
    a. Insurable Interest
    b. Adverse Selection
    c. Insurance
    d. Indemnification

12. If the insurer cancels a policy, how will unearned premium be refunded?
    a. Pro rata
    b. Short rate
    c. Non-renewal
    d. Retroactive
13. An event that happens over a period of time or suddenly is:
    a. An accident
    b. An occurrence
    c. Liberalization
    d. Inherent vice
14. In which situation would an insurable interest exist?
    a. Property to be closed on in the next day
    b. Property owned, but of no financial value
    c. Land inherited from distant relatives
    d. Land soon to be inherited
15. What is a certificate of insurance?
    a. Proof of insurance
    b. The cover page of the insurance policy
    c. The insurance policy
    d. Certification for insurance sales
16. Which of the following would not be considered an insured?
    a. Individual listed on the declaration page
    b. Individual described by definition
    c. Mortgage company added by endorsement
    d. A domestic partner of 10 years
17. Which of the following is an example of a morale hazard?
    a. Chance of lightning striking a home
    b. Ice on the sidewalks
    c. Misrepresenting pertinent underwriting information
    d. Lack of property maintenance

Answer key: 1.a 2.d 3.a 4.c 5.c 6.d 7.b 8.a 9.d 10.c 11.d 12.a 13.b 14.c 15.a 16.d 17.d

Chapter

2

Contract Law and Underwriting

A contract is defined as an agreement between two parties. Agreements can be verbal or in writing. The policy the insurance company issues are legal binding contracts and as such, must meet the requirements of contract law.

Elements of a Legal Contract

A legal contract is basically an agreement between two parties. It may be verbal or formalized in writing. The insurance policy is a legal and binding contract. As such, it must meet certain legal requirements. All contracts consist of four legal elements:

- Competent parties (Legal Capacity)
- Legal purpose
- Offer and acceptance (Agreement)
- Consideration

In order to understand the insurance transaction and the product itself, an understanding of each of these concepts is useful.

Competent Parties

In a legal binding contract, each party must be legally competent. To be legally competent means to be accountable under the law. Examples of those who **would not be competent** include: one who is intoxicated or under the influence of drugs, mentally unstable, or under the legal age to transact business. Incompetent parties could not be held responsible for an agreement they entered into.

Legal Purpose

The intent of the contract itself must be for a legal purpose. A contract for an illegal purpose cannot be enforced in a court of law.

Offer and Acceptance (Agreement)

In order for agreement to occur, one party must make an offer and the other party must accept the offer. When both have happened, agreement has occurred.

The offer can be made by either party, but **the offer is most typically made by the applicant.** It is an offer to buy. The applicant makes the offer with a completed application and payment into the plan (premium). The transaction is between the company and the applicant. The agent is not a party to the contract; therefore, the agent does not make an offer. The agent may present the plan or may assist the applicant in making the offer to the company, but this is not considered an offer. The offer is distinguished by the consideration. **The first party to offer full "consideration" as part in the transaction makes the offer.**

When the other party agrees to accept the first party's consideration in exchange for its own consideration, acceptance has occurred. **Agreement then results when an offer is made and accepted.**

Counter Offer

Counter offers occur when an applicant submits an application and premium (his/her full consideration), but the company rejects the offer as submitted. Perhaps in the underwriting process the company discovers that the applicant has multiple claims. As a result, the company is not willing to accept the business as applied. The company will then reject the original offer and come back with a new offer. The new offer may say that the company will cover the applicant, but for a higher premium than was submitted. This new offer is made by the company and is called a counter offer. Once the applicant agrees to the alteration in terms or the additional premium, the offer has been accepted.

Consideration

In the insurance transaction contract, consideration is defined as **something of value exchanged** between each party of the contract. For a contract to be legally binding, each party must give to the other "something of value." In the insurance transaction the applicant gives two things of value:

- **Premium**, and
- **Information on the application**

In exchange for the applicant's consideration, the company gives the **promise to pay** as stated in the policy.

Doctrine of Utmost Good Faith & the Doctrine of Reasonable Expectation

Utmost Good Faith is a concept of trust. In an insurance transaction, each party (the insurer and the insured) must exhibit a certain amount of trust in the other party. The insurance company will trust that the insured will share the information needed to underwrite the policy and that he/she will pay future premiums to maintain coverage. The insured must trust that the company will follow through with the intent of the contract if a claim occurs in the future.

The **Doctrine of Reasonable Expectation** says that the insured should be able to expect the insurance company to fulfill their obligation in a reasonable way. The policy benefits should be interpreted in a way that a reasonable person would expect and understand.

Defining Truth

Warranties – A warranty is **a promise or a guarantee**. In Property and Casualty insurance, the statements made on the application are **not** considered warranties. In Property and Casualty, a warranty is a condition of coverage. If the client does not maintain the warranty, coverage will not exist.

A business might purchase crime insurance. The insurer may ask the business to secure (or warrant) an alarm system in order to limit claims. With a Yacht policy the insurer might require (or warrant) the policyholder to plot a planned trip. In property and casualty a warranty is a condition of coverage. If the client does not maintain the warranty, coverage will not exist.

Representation – The statements on the application are considered representations. A representation is **the truth to the best of the applicant's knowledge**. It is what the applicant believes to be true. The insured can only be held accountable for the knowledge he/she has.

Misrepresentation – A misrepresentation is a **mistruth or lie**. If the insured lies about information that is considered material, the policy could be voided. A **material statement** is something that had the insurance company been aware of, the information would have affected how or if the policy was issued. In other words, it is important information to the underwriting process.

Concealment – Concealment is the **hiding or withholding of the truth**. Whereas this is not a direct lie (misrepresentation), it does mean that the customer is holding back information that may be important to the insurer.

The main difference between concealment and a misrepresentation has much to do with how an agent asks the questions to the applicant. If an agent asks direct questions (How many automobile accidents have you had in the past five years?), the customer's answer is either the truth or it is a misrepresentation. If the agent's questions are vague (Have you had any accidents lately?), this opens the door to all kinds of vague answers and the opportunity for the applicant to conceal important information. Grant could tell the agent about his speeding ticket last month without mentioning that he had a DUI the month before. Grant has not lied; he just has not told all of the truth.

Fraud always includes three elements in its definition. First, it always includes the element of misrepresentation. Second, it is done with intent. Third, it is done for the purpose of taking advantage of another. Fraud is always illegal. It could be committed by an insured when trying to collect for a claim that never occurred. It also could be committed by an agent when trying to get money out of a client. Either way, it is an illegal act.

A **Fiduciary** is someone who is responsible for someone else's finances. Mishandling money is always a violation of an agent's fiduciary responsibilities.

When Does Coverage Start? Interim Insuring Agreements

Based upon contract law, a contract does not go into effect until after the agreement is complete. Agreement is not complete until the offer has been accepted and each party has exchanged consideration. In the insurance transaction, this would mean the policy would not go into effect until after the money is paid, the application is submitted, the policy is issued and the policy is delivered. This total process may take over a month to complete. In our industry, this may not be acceptable. The client expects coverage as soon as the premium is paid. The unexpected will happen eventually. The agent will have cases when a client buys a product and experiences a loss within days of purchasing the policy. Thus, there is a need for the **interim insuring agreement**.

An **interim insuring agreement is an agreement for the company to provide coverage on the client while still completing the underwriting process**. The purpose of the agreement is to speed up the effective date prior to the contract law situation. There are several different agreements that a company may use. The method most commonly used in property and casualty is the **binding receipt or binder.**

Binders are temporary immediate coverage. Agents can issue binders in verbal or written form. Binders can be used to provide new coverage or change existing coverage. If Grant applies for an auto policy, and his agent tells him "you're covered;" the agent has issued a verbal binder and coverage exists.

Binders can end in three ways:

- **Cancelled**- The insurer can cancel the binder. If during the underwriting process the insurer discovers Grant has a suspended driver's license and therefore decides not to issue him an auto policy, the company will cancel the binder. The insurer must give Grant at least **one days' notice** of cancellation.

- **Replaced** by the policy- In many cases, the binder is replaced once the policy is issued. Binders are designed to be temporary for this purpose. Binders provide coverage from the date of the application until the effective date of the policy.

- **Expire**- Binders are temporary. If a binder is written, it will have an expiration date listed. If a policy is not issued before this expiration date, the binder will end. This is the least common of the three options.

Unique Characteristics of an Insurance Contract

We earlier stated that the insurance policy is a legal binding contract. As a result, it must meet some standard characteristics of a contract. This industry is unique in many different ways. In fact, the policies (contracts) issued have characteristics specific to the insurance industry. The following is a list of some of this industry's unique characteristics:

Personal – Even though most people would think that a property policy is insuring the property described in the policy, this is not accurate. What the insurance company is insuring is the individual's financial interest in the property. We don't promise to make the property whole. We promise to make the insured whole. Insurance is a personal contract because the insurer is insuring the person, not the property.

Conditional – The insurance contract comes with conditions that will be spelled out in the policy. For example, certain events must occur before the insurance company will pay its claims. Fires must happen or auto accidents must occur before the policy will pay out its benefits.

Unilateral – The insurance contract is considered to be a unilateral contract. Only one party in the contract can be held to a promise. **The insurer makes a promise to pay** if a claim occurs. The policyholder is not obligated to pay a premium.

Adhesion – One party (the insurer) is responsible for the wording of the contract. Since the contract is written by the insurance company with no input allowed from the insured, if the contract wording is "**ambiguous**" or unclear, any challenge would be interpreted by the courts in favor of the insured.

Aleatory – An aleatory contract is a contract of **unequal exchange**. One party stands to receive more than the other. In insurance, the insured may pay premiums for years and never file a claim. On the other hand, the insured could file a claim immediately after paying the first premium.

Parts of the Policy

There are different sections of the insurance policy that you will need to be familiar with. The acronym DICED will help you remember the parts of the insurance policy.

- Declarations Page: Contains all of the details
- Insuring Clause: Heart of the policy; promise to pay
- Conditions: Rules and responsibilities
- Exclusions: Anything NOT covered
- Definitions: Glossary of terms

D-The **Declarations** Page has all of the **details.** **Who** is insured? **What** property is covered? **Where** is this property covered? **When** is the coverage effective? **How much** insurance? On the Declarations Page, you will find the insured's name, the property address or the type of vehicle covered, the policy period, and the amount of insurance. Please note, this is **the only part of the policy** where the insured's name will be listed. Everywhere else in the policy, the customer will be referred to as "the insured."

I-The **insuring clause** is the heart of the policy. It is the **promise** that the policy is based upon. It will include the four P's

- **P**arties – in generic form (insurer and insured)
- **P**roperty – in generic form (property address is listed on the Declaration Page)
- **P**erils – cause of losses (fire, lightning, explosion, etc.)
- **P**romise – We the insurer, promise to pay the insured for damage done to the property listed in the declarations as a result of fire, lightning, explosion, etc.

C- The **conditions** section lists all of the rules, rights, duties, obligations and responsibilities of both the insured and insurer. This is the section of the policy that will include things like "Duties after a loss clause," "Mortgage clause," "Liberalization clause" and many more conditions that we will see in later material.

E- The **exclusions** section is the list of perils **not covered** by the insurance policy. Although a peril may be listed here in the exclusions section, the customer may be covered if additional endorsements were purchased and added onto the policy.

D- The **definitions** section is the fifth component and is a glossary of terms used within the policy.

Other Contract Terms

Waiver – Waiver means to **voluntarily give up a known right**. The insurance company has the right to collect the premium in a timely fashion. If a policyholder paid a premium beyond the acceptable time period, the company would have the right to cancel coverage. If the company chose to accept this late premium without consequence, then the company has waived its right to cancel and reinstate by accepting the late payment.

Estoppel – Estoppel means **to be legally stopped** from being able to enforce one's legal right. In the above example, the company chose to accept the late payment without consequence. If this happens year after year, then a precedent has been established. If a claim occurred between the premium due date and the date that the policyholder normally paid a premium, the company might have normally had the right to refuse the payment of that claim due to nonpayment of premium. However, the court could force the company to pay since its history shows that it had accepted late payments and all indications are that it would have accepted this one also, had there not been a claim.

Insurance Law and the Agent/Producer

An agent is defined as the **representative of a principal** (insurance company). This makes you, the agent, an extension of your insurance company. This agreement is established through the **agency agreement**. The agency agreement is the contract between you and your insurance company.

Note: an "agent" is the representative of his/her company. A "broker" represents the interest of his/her client.

You, as an agent, also need to understand your responsibility with your insurance company. Because you are considered an extension of your principal, the **agent's knowledge is deemed to be the knowledge of the company**. If an applicant discloses material underwriting information to the agent, the agent has the responsibility to disclose it to the company.

You also need to understand that your actions and statements may extend the company's liability or responsibility to the client. If an agent were to imply or state that coverage exists when the contract states otherwise, the company could find that it is liable for a claim which it should never have been responsible for. You, as the agent, must understand your role, relationship and responsibility with your principal.

Powers of Agency

As a representative of your insurance company, you will have certain powers or authorities. When discussing the "powers of agency," there are three different categories of power:

- **Expressed** – These are the powers and authorities expressed in the agency agreement. They are clearly spelled out as the powers that you have when representing your insurance company. For example, the agent may have the power to use company material and name.

- **Implied** – These powers are not spelled out or expressed by the company, however the powers are allowed and may even be expected by the company. The company is aware of what the agent is doing and does nothing to deter the agent. The company may even encourage the agent to continue these actions. For example, the company may not tell the agent to assist the client with claims, but allows the agent to do so, since it is good business for the company and the agent.

- **Apparent** – This authority, unlike the two previous ones, is not a "real" authority. Due to the licensing authority with the state and with the company, the first two are considered "real." Apparent authority **looks "real" from the client's perspective**, but it does not actually exist as a "real" authority. For example, a client enters an insurance office to purchase an insurance policy. The person behind the desk at this office designated as an insurance office may not be licensed and would not have the "real" authority of a licensed agent. But to all appearances, this person may look licensed. Insurance companies and agencies must be careful about what this person says and does with the client.

  When an insurance company provides company material, applications, or brochures to an unlicensed person, a **presumption of agency** may exist. This could also occur when an unlicensed person is explaining coverage or acting as an agent without proper licensing. Presumption of agency is the appearance of agency from the client's perspective.

Underwriting Basics

The underwriting process involves the company **gathering and evaluating the information** of a prospective insured in order to determine the applicant's risk. Once the underwriter understands the risk involved, he/she must decide to **accept or reject** the risk. If the risk is accepted, it must then be **classified for rating.**

Note: Adverse Selection is the selection of risks that are higher or more likely to have a claim. When a company selects a disproportionate amount of high risks this creates an adverse situation for the company which will force the company to increase their rates. Adverse selection creates a negative situation for the company and the customer and must be avoided at all costs.

Why is Underwriting necessary?

There is a direct relationship between the risk assumed by the company and the premium charged to the customer. Each insurance company prices its product based upon the risk assumed. If the risk is greater than expected or priced, the company could find it difficult, if not impossible, to meet its financial obligation to the client. In order to meet the needs of the client, the company must work within its established risk parameters. **The primary responsibility for underwriters is to select risks** their companies are designed to handle.

Sources of Insurability Information

In order to properly evaluate the risk, the first step is to gather the relative information. The insurance company has many sources to gather information from:

Application – One of the first and most obvious sources of information is the application itself. It includes personal, medical and other insurance information. The application is the written "offer" signed and made by the prospective insured. If there is a mistake on the application and it needs corrected, it is the applicant who is responsible for the correction. Even though the agent is involved in the presentation of the product, the application is the applicant's statement of information and **an agent may not change the information** that has been stated by the applicant. **The applicant will designate the correction by initialing any change made** on the application.

If an application is submitted without complete information, it is the responsibility of the company to obtain the missing information if it is important. **If the application is approved and accepted without complete information, the applicant cannot be held responsible for that information after the policy is issued**. An applicant cannot be accused of misrepresentation or concealment if the question was never answered on the application in the first place. The company may request the information prior to issuance or may reject the coverage if the information is not obtained. For this reason, agents need to see that the application is completed as required.

The agent and the applicant are both required to sign the application. These signatures are important to the application process. When the applicant signs the application, he/she is stating that the information given is his/her representation of the truth. The applicant's signature may also be necessary to properly gather information for underwriting purposes. When you as the agent sign the application, you state that you have asked the questions on the application and the answers are true and complete to the best of your knowledge. Both parties have a responsibility to the information on the application.

Agent/Producer's reports – The agent's report allows the agent to share information and observations with the insurance company concerning the applicant.

Credit reports – Sometimes the company will include the individual's credit report in the underwriting process. The **"Fair Credit Reporting Act"** is federal legislature designed to protect consumer information.

- The act requires that the applicant knows who is gathering the information
- The applicant has the right to see the information in order to verify its accuracy
- The applicant has the right to have any misinformation corrected if necessary.

Inspection reports – A report concerning the financial, moral, physical or any other relevant information concerning the applicant.

The Law of Large Numbers

The **law of large numbers** is a concept that states the more numbers used to establish a statistic, the more accurate the statistic will be. The chance of heads turning up in a coin toss is 50/50. Tossing a coin twice and getting heads both times would not be a surprise. The statistic would be much more accurate after one hundred tosses.

This concept is critical to the concept of insurance. Because the insurance companies have access to statistics on large numbers of our population, they can adequately predict an insured's chance of an auto accident or the chance that a house might burn to the ground. The law of large numbers is used to adequately predict and anticipate risk. It is the first step in establishing a rate for the product.

Selection and Classification Factors

Once the underwriter has gathered and evaluated the information concerning the applicant, it is time to accept or reject the application. If the risk falls within the parameters of what the company is able to accept, the underwriter may choose to accept the business. Once the decision is made to accept the business, the risk has to be classified.

It is possible that after reviewing the information gathered, the underwriter has determined that the applicant is a greater risk than the insurance company can accept. Instead of accepting and categorizing the risk, the underwriter may choose to **reject** or **decline the risk**. If this occurs, the offer made by the applicant will be rejected and the premium submitted will be returned.

Premiums

Gross premium

Gross premium is the **premium the applicant pays**. It is the full, total or gross amount paid. There are three factors that make up the gross premium.

- **Risk** – Risk was defined earlier as the chance of a loss. When each policyholder pays a premium payment to the company, a portion of that payment has to be available to pay the claims that will result that year. This is the risk factor of the premium. Every policyholder pays a small amount into the company and a few will take out a large amount for the claims experienced.

- **Interest** – The premium is always paid in advance. This means that the company will have use of this money prior to paying out the claims that they will be responsible for throughout the year. The more interest earned on the money prior to using it to pay claims, the more it will reduce the amount that the company will need to collect from the policyholder.

- **Expenses** – Companies must collect enough to cover operating expenses. The company has office space to pay for, payroll, utilities, advertising, and many other responsibilities in order to do business. This is sometimes charged in the form of a "load" fee.

Gross premium is sometimes expressed as a formula. The formula for gross premium is:

Gross Premium = Risk – Interest +Expenses

Net Premium

Net premium is the **true cost of insurance**. Net premium includes both risk and interest, but does not take into account expenses; therefore, the formula for net premium is:

Net Premium = Risk – Interest

A company may offer additional amounts of insurance on a net basis. The expense of adding or changing coverage could be limited on an existing insured.

Premium Modes

The mode of premium is how often or frequent the payments will be made. Most premiums are calculated on an annual basis. Sometimes, the client may choose to break the payments down into smaller, more frequent amounts. For example, a policyholder could choose to pay quarterly instead of annually. The more often the payment is made, the more expensive it will be over the year. For example, an annual payment of $1,000 broken down into two payments (semi-annual) might cost $550 per payment or $1100 a year. If that payment was broken down quarterly, the payment might cost $300 every 3 months.

There are two reasons why the payment will cost more for the policyholder if the payment is broken down:

- Loss of interest or investment opportunity – The company calculated an annual premium it expected to receive up front, in advance of its claim responsibilities. This gave them the opportunity to invest, which in turn would have reduced the payment. That opportunity is gone and must be made up by charging a higher rate.

- Added expenses – Because the payment is broken down, more expenses will result. Now a statement must be generated more often, processed and mailed. This takes time, manpower and supplies. This added expense will result in a higher rate.

Terms to Know

- Contract
- Competent Parties
- Legal Purpose
- Agreement (Offer and Acceptance)
- Consideration
- Counter offer
- Doctrine of Utmost Good Faith
- Doctrine of Reasonable Expectations
- Warranties
- Representation
- Misrepresentation
- Material Statement
- Concealment
- Fraud
- Fiduciary
- Interim Insuring Agreement
- Binding Receipt (Binders)
- Conditional
- Unilateral
- Adhesion
- Aleatory
- Declarations
- Insuring clause
- Conditions
- Exclusions
- Waiver
- Estoppel
- Agency Agreement
- Agent
- Broker
- Expressed
- Implied
- Apparent
- Adverse Selection
- Agent/Producer's Report
- Fair Credit Reporting Act
- Law of Large Numbers
- Gross Premium
- Net Premium

Acronyms to Know

CLOC- Elements of a Contract

Competent parties, Legal Purpose, Offer and Acceptance (Agreement), Consideration

DICED- Parts of the Policy

Declarations, Insuring clause, Conditions, Exclusions, Definitions

4 P's- Insuring clause: Parties, Perils, Property, Promise

Practice Exam

1. Which of the following is not an essential component of a legal binding contract?
    a. Competent Parties
    b. Consideration
    c. Agreement
    d. Counter Offer
2. What are the essential components of a contract?
    a. Competent parties, Legal purpose, Offer + Acceptance = Agreement, Consideration
    b. Competent parties, Legal purpose, Offer, Counteroffer
    c. Counteroffer, Legal purpose, Agreement, Consideration
    d. Consideration, Legal capacity, Agreement, Counteroffer
3. Who typically makes the offer in an insurance transaction?
    a. The applicant
    b. The agent
    c. The insurer
    d. The policyholder
4. In order for agreement to occur, both parties must exchange consideration. What is the applicant's consideration?
    a. Promise to pay
    b. Premium
    c. Information on the application
    d. Premium and information on the application
5. A promise or guarantee is defined as:
    a. Representation
    b. Misrepresentation
    c. Warranty
    d. Concealment

6. The answers the applicant gives on the application are called:
    a. Misrepresentations
    b. Representations
    c. Warranties
    d. Concealment
7. When a client withholds important information crucial to the underwriting process, it is called:
    a. Misrepresentation
    b. Concealment
    c. Fraud
    d. Representation
8. Which of the following statements is FALSE?
    a. Binders can only be issued in written form
    b. Binders are temporary immediate coverage
    c. Binders can end by being cancelled, replaced by policy, or they can expire
    d. The insurer has the right to cancel the binder
9. Which of the following would be found in the conditions section of the insurance policy?
    a. Explanation of the insureds duties after a loss
    b. Description of things that would not be covered
    c. The promise that the policy is based upon
    d. Explanations and details of the property and limitations
10. All the following are sources of underwriting information, except:
    a. Application
    b. Producer's report
    c. Credit reports
    d. Certificate of insurance

11. Which part of the policy contains all of the details specific to the insured?

    a. Exclusions
    b. Conditions
    c. Declarations Page
    d. Insuring clause

12. The insuring clause is the heart of the policy. It contains the 4 P's. What are the 4 P's?

    a. Parties, Property, Perils, Policy
    b. Parties, Property, Perils, Promise
    c. Property, Promise, Premium, Perils
    d. Policy, Perils, Property, Promise

13. In the law of agency, the agent represents:

    a. The insured
    b. The broker
    c. The principal
    d. The insurance agency

14. The Fair Credit Reporting Act is designed to protect:

    a. Agent information
    b. Industry information
    c. Consumer information
    d. Public information

15. Underwriters use which law to accurately predict losses?

    a. Law of Adverse Selection
    b. Law of Large Numbers
    c. Law of Underwriting
    d. Law of Accurate Predictions

Answers: 1.d 2.a 3.a 4.d 5.c 6.b 7.b 8.a 9.a 10.d 11.c 12.b 13.c 14c 15.b

Chapter

3

Basics of Two Party Coverage

Property insurance is sometimes referred to as "two party" insurance. The first party is the insurance and the second is the insured. The customer purchases a policy to protect his/her property. Property insurance is designed to cover property of all types under multiple situations. The policy can cover fixed property, transportable property, commercial or personal.

Property

A property policy is designed to cover various types of property. **Buildings** need to be insured against a variety of risks. Buildings could include homes, garages and commercial buildings. **Contents** coverage would provide protection for the personal and commercial items within the building. This would include furnishings, machinery, inventory, and a wide variety of other items. Property policies can be designed to cover these items on premises only or worldwide.

Cause of Loss Forms (Peril Protection)

Earlier a peril was defined as a "**cause of loss**." Fire and wind are both examples of perils. A Cause of Loss Form defines which perils would be covered within a given policy. The more perils covered, the more effective the protection. There are two types of Cause of Loss Forms; named and open peril (all risk).

Named Peril – A named peril form is a form that lists the perils that are to be covered in the Insuring Clause. If the perils are not named in the Insuring Clause, then it would not be covered. There are two named peril policies: the **Basic** and the **Broad**

Forms. The difference between the two is the number of perils covered. The Broad form includes more perils than the Basic. These forms are progressive. If the peril is in the Basic, it would also be included in the Broad. The Broad just adds perils to the Basic.

Open Peril or All Risk – Open Peril and All Risk are interchangeable terms. An open peril policy covers everything, except that which is excluded. In order to determine what this policy would cover, you would look at the exclusion section of the policy. If the peril is listed in the exclusions, then it is not covered. If it is not listed, then it is covered. This is the best coverage that could be purchased. There are many odd events that insurance companies cannot fathom, thus they are covered.

Basic Cause of Loss Form

The Basic Cause of Loss Form is a named peril form. The following perils are listed under the Basic Form.

Fire & Lightning

Extended Coverages

- Riot
- Explosion
- Vehicles
- Civil Commotion
- Smoke
- Hail
- Aircraft
- Windstorm
- Volcano

Vandalism And Malicious Mischief

Commercial Adds:

- Sprinkler Leakage
- Sinkhole Collapse

Fire and Lightning were the foundation of the original Fire Policy. The fire peril would also include the results of fire. In other words, it would include water and physical damage caused by the fire department while extinguishing the fire. Coverage is limited to **hostile fires** (fires that are not intended or are out of control). It would not include damage done by a **friendly fire** (fire used as intended, like in a fireplace or on a stove).

As policies became more competitive, the Extended Coverages were created and added to the Basic Policy. Today they are built into the policy automatically.

Volcano damage includes **above ground affects only**. This would include ash, lava and the force of the explosion. In personal lines, a new event must be an event separated by **72** hours (3 days), if not it would be considered the same event. In commercial, it must be separated by **168** hours (7 days).

Broad Cause of Loss Form

Fire & Lightning

Extended Coverages

- Riot
- Explosion
- Vehicles
- Civil Commotion
- Smoke
- Hail
- Aircraft
- Windstorm
- Volcano

Vandalism And Malicious Mischief

W.I.F.

- Weight of Ice, Snow or Sleet
- Intentional Water
    - Accidental discharge or overflow,
    - Freezing, and
    - Accidental tearing apart,cracking or bulging
- Falling Objects

Collapse

Commercial Adds:

- Sprinkler Leakage
- Sinkhole Collapse

The Broad Form is also a named peril policy. It will cover everything covered in the Basic, plus it will add some additional perils.

The policy will not mention "**intentional water,**" this is just an easy way to categorize several of the coverages added into the Broad Form. Intentional water is water brought in by man, through pipes and appliances, which is now out of control (a burst water pipe). It does not include freezing, unless the insured has used reasonable means to protect the pipes by maintaining heat or draining pipes.

Collapse is added into the Broad Form. It is different than the other perils in that it has some specific limitations and definition. Collapse is defined as an **abrupt** falling down (sudden and unexpected). It does not include leaning or "in danger of collapse." The property must be damaged to the point of being **uninhabitable**. Collapse acts as an extension of the named perils. Otherwise, it will only be covered if it is due to hidden decay, insect or vermin damage. It also includes weight of people, equipment, personal property or rain.

Special Cause of Loss Form

Open or All Risk

- Covers everything except that which is excluded
- The exclusions determine what perils are covered

With Open Peril coverage, the **burden of proof is on the insurer**. The insurer must clarify what is not covered in the exclusions. If it is not specified clearly, then it will be covered. Open Peril and All Risk are interchangeable terms. Special is not interchangeable. It is the name of the form. It means that open coverage is included within the policy. Not everything in the policy may be covered on an all risk basis.

Valuation – Claim Settlement

Valuation is the method that the policy will use in order to determine the amount of the loss. Valuation is determined at the time of the loss. This is when the insured has lost value. It has nothing to do with what the property was worth at the time it was acquired. When a claim is filed, the valuation within the policy will determine how the claim is to be settled. Depending on the policy purchased, there may be more than one form of valuation used in the policy.

Actual Cash Value (ACV) is **Replacement cost minus Depreciation**. Replacement cost is what it would currently cost to replace the item with a new one.

Depreciation takes into account the wear, tear and age of the product. Actual Cash Value might be used to insure furniture or automobiles.

Replacement Cost – Depreciation = Actual Cash Value

Replacement cost replaces damaged property with **like kind and quality**, without a deduction for depreciation. This might be used to insure a house or be added by endorsement to enhance coverage on contents.

Functional Replacement Cost is a form of valuation in which the insurer will replace using less expensive, but **functionally equivalent materials**. This valuation would be used on older construction that has used older and obsolete materials. Plaster might be replaced with drywall. The old knob and tube wiring will be replaced with better up to date wiring.

Stated value is when the insurer provides coverage for an item for a specific dollar amount that is stated in the policy. The amount scheduled or stated is the maximum amount that will be paid for loss to the item. In the Homeowners policy, $1,500 is the stated amount for watercraft. This is the most the policy will pay for a canoe used in the backyard lake.

Agreed value is when the insured and insurer agree at the time of the policy's inception on the amount of coverage that will be provided for a specific item. In the event of a total loss, this is the amount that will be paid. The amount is usually established with an appraisal and must be current and up to date. It is usually **used for difficult to value items** like jewelry and furs. It is used when **scheduling** coverage.

Fair market value is a valuation commonly used on older homes. The homes are insured for the amount that they would **sell for in today's market**. This valuation is used when the replacement cost is greater than the market value on the home.

Salvage value is the value the insurer can get by selling property that they have collected after paying the customer its full current value or totally the property.

Cost Containment Tools

Deductibles

A deductible is the amount of risk **retained** by the insured. It is the amount that the insured pays before coverage becomes available. Its primary purpose is to **control over utilization** or over usage. The deductible eliminates costly and trivial claims. The secondary advantage is that it reduces the cost for the insured. On an insurance policy, the higher the deductible is, the lower the premium will be. The insurance company can charge the insured less in premium if the insured is willing to retain a larger part of the risk by having a higher deductible.

Coinsurance

The coinsurance clause is a provision designed to encourage the insured to purchase and maintain adequate insurance limits. It is a percentage, typically 80% or 90% of replacement cost. It is commonly used when insuring a building.

The clause provides an **incentive** to the insured for meeting the requirement and a **penalty** if the requirement is not met. The incentive is **full replacement cost coverage for partial losses,** if the coinsurance clause is met and maintained. A house worth $200,000 and a coinsurance clause of 80% would require a minimum limit of $160,000. If the limit was met and a kitchen fire resulted in $10,000 worth of damage, the kitchen would be fully covered. If the house burned to the ground, the policy would only pay $160,000. To get replacement for total losses the insured needs to carry adequate limits.

The penalty for not carrying adequate limits is:

$$\frac{\text{Amount Carried}}{\text{Replacement Cost X Coinsurance Percentage}}$$

In the above example, if the homeowner only carried $120,000 instead of the $160,000 needed to cover partial losses, the claim would pay:

$120,000 / $160,000 times the loss of $10,000 = $7,500. If the homeowner wanted full replacement cost coverage for the partial loss, the insured should have carried at least $160,000 ($200,000 X 80%) of coverage. Remember this only applies to partial losses. Coverage ends when the claim reaches the limit purchased. If the insured wants full replacement cost for a total loss, then he/she needs to carry the full $200,000 limit on the home.

Common Property Provisions

The provisions are the rules and regulations within the policy. All policies will come with provisions. Some of the common provisions that may be found in a property policy would include:

Proof of Loss

In order for a claim to be paid to the insured, a **proof of loss** statement must first be submitted to the company. The proof of loss statement is a sworn statement provided by the insured, describing the loss and the date of occurrence. It is typically used for first party losses. The claim process may begin without the proof of loss statement, but eventually it must be submitted in writing before the claim is paid.

Appraisal and/or Arbitration Clause

Although these two clauses are technically different, they are very similar in their purposes and in how they will work. Both are designed to address differences of opinion between the insurer and insured. Both are designed to bring the two parties to agreement by avoiding the litigation process. The primary difference between these two clauses is when they are used. The **Appraisal Clause** is used when there is a disagreement as to the amount of the claim. The **Arbitration Clause** is used when there is a difference of opinion between the insurer and the insured.

When the insurer does not agree with the decision made by the insured, they have several options. They could attempt to settle their differences in court, but this could be costly and time consuming. These clauses are designed to provide an alternative to litigation.

Each party will be responsible for finding and paying for their representative (appraiser or arbitrator). The two representatives will get together and attempt to come to an agreement that satisfies each party. If they cannot come to agreement, **the two representatives will find and agree upon a third.** This third representative will be paid equally by both parties. He/she will then act as umpire. When **two out of three professionals agree**, this will be settlement.

Right of Salvage

When an insurance company pays a claim for a total loss, the insurer has the right to salvage the property. **Right to salvage** applies when an insurer has paid for a total loss. The insurer then has **the right to claim title or ownership of the damaged property**. If they choose to claim the property, they may then sell the property in order to recoup a portion of their loss.

Abandonment

Just because the insurer has the right to salvage property, this does not mean that the insured has the right to abandon property to the insurer. The insurance company will take the property, if they determine that it has some value to them. But, if they do not salvage, the insured maintains responsibility for the property.

Additional Coverages

Under the Additional Coverages section of the policy, extra coverages are added to the policy for no additional expense. This section adds protection that is typically expected by the insured or just makes sense. Examples of these additional coverages might include: debris removal, fire department, or reasonable repairs. These coverages are built into the policy and do not have to be requested or added by endorsement. These coverages have separate limits and are typically separate from the normal policy limits. This means the additional coverages pay over and above the normal policy limits.

Extensions of Coverage

Coverage Extensions appear to be very similar to the Additional Coverages. Like Additional Coverages, Coverage Extensions pay over and above policy limits and they have no additional cost. The main difference between the two is that Extensions of Coverage are **not automatic**. These coverages have to be **qualified for by meeting the policy coinsurance requirement**. Extensions are typically found in **commercial** property policies.

Vacancy/Unoccupancy

The difference between vacancy and unoccupancy is an important distinction. Vacant homes tend to have an increased risk and insurers are hesitant to cover them.

Vacancy – Vacancy implies that the building is **empty** or **uninhabited**. The longer the building has been vacant, the more concerned the insurer may be to insure the property. Insurers typically will have an issue with the property if it is vacant for over **60 days**. Coverage is either limited after 60 days or a company may cancel coverage due to vacancy.

Unoccupancy – Unoccupancy means that there are items in the building and it is **habitable**, but no one is home at the time. The insured may be in Florida for the winter or at work for the day but they are **expected to return**. The insurance company will typically cover a building that is unoccupied.

Common Property Conditions

Conditions and provisions are the rules in the policy that the insurer and insured have agreed to abide by in the contract. The following is a list of further conditions commonly found in a property policy.

Concealment, Misrepresentation or Fraud

If a policyholder conceals, misrepresents or commits fraud involving a material fact, coverage will be affected. Under the older forms, a policy could be voided as if it never existed. Newer forms state that coverage will not apply to a loss. One way or another, if an insured hides or lies about something important, coverage will probably not exist.

Control of Property

Control of Property states that if a loss occurs by someone other than the insured or someone under the care of the insured, coverage will apply even if it was an act of negligence. The insured cannot be responsible for the acts of others, not under their control.

Insurance under Two or More Coverages

This condition simply states that if the insured is covered for a loss by two or more policies, the insured will not receive more than the actual amount of the loss. This is based upon the concept of indemnity. The insurance company's goal is to make the insured whole, ideally no more or less. If the insured could profit from a claim, they would have an incentive to create a claim. How the insurance company will handle two or more coverages is spelled out in another condition, "Other Insurance."

Other Insurance

Now that the contract makes it clear that the insurer will not over indemnify the insured, the next consideration is to determine how the insurer will pay the claim.

Pro Rata – When two policies exist of the same type and on the same property, they may pay on a Pro Rata basis. Pro Rata means **"proportionate rate."** Each company will pay the claim based upon their proportion of coverage carried on the property.

If Company A provided coverage up to $100,000 and Company B provided $200,000 on the same property, then both companies would pay a portion of the claim. There is a total of $300,000 worth of coverage between the two. Company A provides 1/3 of the overall coverage. Company B provides 2/3 of the coverage. Company A would pay 1/3 of the claim and Company B would pay 2/3 of the claim. This gives the insured 100% coverage between the two companies. If the coverages are **concurrent**, or similar in nature, coverage should be adequate.

Note: Nonconcrancy – separate policies written on the same risk but with different coverages

One problem with the above example is if both companies have deductibles on their coverage. If so, the insured would be required to pay the deductible for each policy.

Primary/Secondary – Depending on the coverages, a policy may be declared primary or secondary. If the policy is primary, it will pay as if it is the only coverage available. The secondary policy will then step in after the first has paid, and pay what may be left over from the first. Again, the insured will not receive any more than the value of the loss between the two.

Excess – In some cases, coverage may be available through a service agreement or coverage specific to that property. In these cases, a general property policy may declare itself as excess to the policy designed to meet the specific needs of the property in question.

Legal action

The insured may not bring action against the insurance company until after all policy terms and conditions have been complied with. If legal action is brought against the company, it must be brought within the time period stipulated by the state, typically 2 years.

Liberalization

The Liberalization clause allows the insured to broaden the language in the policy in order to provide better coverage for the insured, as long as there is **no additional cost**. This allows insurers to add coverage and broaden interpretations without issuing new policies.

No Benefit to the Bailee

A bailee is someone who has temporary **custody of another's property**. In commercial, it might include a repair person who has custody of the customers' property. In personal, it might be the neighbor who has borrowed a lawn mower and is keeping it in their garage.

No Benefit to the Bailee says that if a claim is paid on property in the care of a bailee, **payment of the claim will go to the owner** of the property. The policy will not let the bailee profit on the loss of another's property. The policy will protect the bailee by making payment to the bailor (the owner of the property).

Policy Period

The policy period begins on the **effective date**. It is the time that coverage applies on the property. The effective date will be listed in the declarations.

Coverage Territory

The coverage territory is the location **where** coverage is in force. For example, on a personal auto policy, the insurer may only cover the insured if he drives in the United States, its territories or Canada. If Doug goes on vacation in Mexico, and drives a vehicle, he would not be covered.

Subrogation

Subrogation is when one party passes on his right to recovery to another party. For example; Joe is cutting a tree down in his yard. He negligently drops the tree onto the roof of Sam's house. Sam has the right to sue Joe and hold him responsible for the damages to his roof. Instead, Sam files a claim with his policy and it pays based upon a falling object. Now that Sam has been reimbursed for his loss and made whole, he no longer has a right to sue for damages. Since the company has experienced a loss due to Joe's negligence, Sam's right to sue has passed to them. The company can now hold Joe responsible for the damage that they have sustained.

Insured's Duties in the Event of a Loss

Once a loss has occurred, **the insured will have certain duties and responsibilities** that they will be required to fulfill. This conditions section of the policy will list these conditions. Duties will typically include:

- Provide prompt notice to the company representative
- If theft is involved, notify policy or credit card company
- Protect the property from further damage
- Cooperate with the insurer in the investigation of the claim
- Prepare an inventory of damaged property and make it available for inspection if appropriate
- Submit the proof of loss statement timely and in proper form

Mortgage Holders Rights

A mortgage holder has an insurable interest in the property that is being used as collateral for a loan. Because they have an insurable interest, they can require that insurance be provided and they have certain rights as an additional insured.

When a policy is written on "real" property (non-movable), any mortgagee will want to be listed on the policy as an additional insured. Once listed, the Mortgage Clause will provide coverage and reimbursements based upon their order of interest. In addition to this right, the mortgagee will pick up some additional rights. The bank has the right to:

- Bring suit against others to recover damage
- Pay policy premiums
- Submit their own proof of loss

The mortgagees' rights are separate from the insured. Even if the insured commits arson, the mortgagee may file a separate claim to recover their interest. Mortgagees may only collect up to their insurable interest at the time of the claim.

Loss Payment options

The insurance company has the duty to indemnify the insured for the covered loss. It is up to the insurer to determine how that will be done. The Loss Payment condition states the different methods that the insurer could use to indemnify the insured.

- Make a payment for the value of the loss
- Pay for repair of damaged property
- Replace the property
- Replace or repair property with like kind or quality

Obviously, the insurer will choose whatever method makes the most financial sense to them.

Terms to know

- Contents
- Peril
- Named Peril
- Open Peril/ All Risk
- Basic Form
- Broad Form
- Special Form
- Valuation
- Actual Cash Value
- Replacement Cost
- Depreciation
- Functional Replacement Cost
- Stated Value
- Agreed Value
- Fair Market Value
- Co-Insurance
- Proof of Loss
- Appraisal
- Arbitration
- Right of Salvage
- Abandonment
- Additional Coverages
- Extensions of Coverage
- Vacancy
- Unoccupancy
- Concealment
- Misrepresentation
- Fraud
- Other Insurance
- Pro Rata
- Nonconcurrency
- Primary/Secondary
- Excess
- Legal Action
- No Benefit to the Bailee
- Policy Period
- Effective Date
- Coverage Territory
- Subrogation
- Insured's Duties in Event of a Loss
- Mortgage Holders Rights
- Loss Payment Options

Numbers to Know

Volcano- 72 hours Personal / 168 hours Commercial

Vacancy- 60 Days

Legal Action- 2 years

Appraisal- 2 out of 3 is Settlement

Formulas to Know

Actual Cash Value = Replacement Cost – Depreciation

Co-Insurance = Did carry/Should carry, or

Amount carried/ Replacement Cost x Co-insurance %

Acronyms to Know

ACV- Actual Cash Value

RC- Replacement Cost

Practice Exam

1. Falling objects is a named peril on which form?

    a. Broad

    b. Basic

    c. Special

    d. All Risk

2. Which type of policy covers everything except what is excluded?

    a. Named Peril

    b. Basic Form

    c. Broad Form

    d. Open Peril/ All Risk

3. After a small house fire, the insurer chooses to replace the materials using less expensive, but functionally equivalent materials. Which form of valuation was used?

    a. Replacement cost

    b. Actual Cash Value

    c. Functional Replacement Cost

    d. Fair Market Value

4. The formula for Actual Cash Value (ACV) is:

    a. Replacement Cost + Depreciation

    b. Stated Value – Depreciation

    c. Replacement Cost – Depreciation

    d. Agreed Value – Depreciation

5. Insurers give an incentive for insureds to keep adequate limits on their homeowners policies. Which term describes this?
    a. Deductible
    b. Coinsurance
    c. Arbitration
    d. Appraisal
6. Which of the following statements is FALSE?
    a. After a loss, the insured is required to protect the property from further damage
    b. Coverage territory is the location where coverage is in force
    c. With No Benefit to the Bailee, payment is made to the bailee
    d. The policy period begins on the effective date

Use the following information for the questions7

Market value is $120,000

Replacement cost is $100,000

Bob carries $60,000 in insurance

Small kitchen fire loss $10,000

7. In order to meet an 80% coinsurance requirement, how much insurance should Bob carry?
    a. $100,000
    b. $60,000
    c. $80,000
    d. $50,000
8. Replacement cost is defined as:
    a. Current value minus depreciation
    b. Current value of property covered
    c. Amount that the property was purchased for
    d. Amount the property would sell for

9. Which Property Provision is free, automatic, and pays above and beyond the policy's limits?
    a. Co-insurance
    b. Right of Salvage
    c. Extensions of Coverage
    d. Supplementary Coverages
10. If a building is vacant over __ days, coverage may be limited or cancelled.
    a. 60
    b. 30
    c. 90
    d. 120
11. Which Property Provision gives the insurer the right to claim ownership of the damaged property?
    a. Arbitration
    b. Abandonment
    c. Right of salvage
    d. Additional coverages
12. Of the following perils, which is listed on the Basic Form?
    a. Weight of snow
    b. Water pipe burst
    c. Volcano
    d. Collapse
13. To pass ones right of recovery to another party, is called:
    a. Subrogation
    b. Arbitration
    c. Liberalization
    d. Legal Action
14. With the Other Insurance Property Condition, the insurer will not over indemnify the insured. Which is NOT an option for Other Insurance?
    a. Pro Rata
    b. Excess
    c. Primary/Secondary
    d. No Benefit to the Bailee

15. Who pays for the "umpire" under the appraisal clause?
    a. It is shared equally between the insured and the insurer
    b. It is the responsibility of the insurer to pay
    c. It is the responsibility of the insured to pay
    d. It is not paid by either party, but is a responsibility of the state
16. Which form of valuation is used on hard to value items like jewelry or antiques?
    a. Functional replacement cost
    b. Fair market value
    c. Agreed value
    d. Appraised value
17. The feature that allows the insured to retain part of the risk and discourages over utilization of the policy is:
    a. A deductible
    b. The co-insurance clause
    c. The right of salvage clause
    d. The right to abandon
18. A policy that lists the covered perils in the insuring clause would be described as a/n:
    a. Open peril policy
    b. Named peril policy
    c. Stated value policy
    d. All risk policy

Answer key: 1,a 2,d 3,c 4,c 5,b 6,c 7,c 8,a 9,d 10,a 11,c 12,c 13,a 14,d 15,a 16,c 17,a 18,b

Chapter

4

Basics of Third Party Coverage

Casualty insurance, also known as liability insurance, is third party insurance. This form of insurance protects the insured if he/she damages someone else or someone else's property. There are many casualty insurance policies available providing personal or commercial needs.

Third – Party Contracts

Casualty/Liability policies are third-party contracts. Simply meaning, there are three parties involved in the contract:

- The First Party – The insureds, anyone covered by the policy
- The Second Party – The insurer, insurance company
- The Third Party – The one injured or the one who had property damaged due to the insured's negligence

Liability Coverage

Purpose

Liability coverage is the primary coverage in casualty/liability insurance. This coverage will be triggered when **the insured has caused damage to a third party or a third party's property and, due to that damage, is legally liable to give financial compensation to the third party**. When the insured is legally liable, he/she is responsible for the damages. The purpose of the liability coverage is for the insurer to **pay for the damages in place of the insured,** when the insured is legally liable to make financial compensation. A lost lawsuit may result in a high financial cost and with casualty/liability insurance **the chance of the financial loss is transferred from the insured to the insurer**.

Note: Liability pays in place of the insured. It never pays to the insured.

Coverage

There are casualty/liability policies to cover the **personal needs or commercial needs of the customer**. Personal liability policies will cover insureds in most daily living situations. Commercial liability policies will cover insureds for most business exposures. It is important to offer the policy that best meets the needs of the insured.

Policies can cover these four types of damages: **bodily injury, property damage, personal injury, and advertising injury**. When looking at a policy, it is important to know whether all or only some of these damages are covered.

Casualty/liability policies will **only cover tort law**. These policies **do not cover criminal issues or intentional acts**. For example, if Joe injures another person intentionally, his insurance policy will not pay the claim; he is responsible for his actions of intent. Tort law is civil and will deal with issues between both individuals and businesses.

Financial Compensation

Compensatory Damage

Compensatory damages are the financial obligations the insured must pay due to the damage done to the third party. The amount paid is **intended to financially compensate** the third party for the damage done by the insured. Compensatory damages **will be covered** by liability policies.

- **Economic (Special/Specific) Damages** – A type of compensatory damage that is intended to compensate the third party for financial costs due to the insured's negligence. These damages will compensate medical expenses, property repairs, and other expenses that have a **specific dollar amount** to the cost.

- **Noneconomic (General) Damages** – A type of compensatory damage that is intended to compensate the third party for damage done due to the insured.

This will cover damages that **do not have a specified dollar amount**. The primary damage that noneconomic damages cover is **pain and suffering**.

Punitive Damages

Punitive damages are **meant to punish the insured** for the damages he/she has caused to the third party. These damages have been given to the insured by judgment for his/her actions as a result of gross negligence. Gross negligence is an extreme disregard for the safety of others. Punitive damages **will not be covered** by liability policies.

Aggregate Limits/Occurrence Limits

Aggregate Limits

The aggregate limit is the **maximum amount** of coverage available for the liability coverage **over the course of the policy year**. The most a liability policy will pay for all claims that occur within a year's time is equal to the aggregate limit. Once the policy renews for the next year, then the aggregate limit will reset.

A casualty/liability policy may have an aggregate limit of $500,000. If the insured, over the course of the policy year, is sued for a total amount which exceeds the $500,000 aggregate limit, then the casualty liability policy **will not pay for any of the excess amount over the $500,000.** This limit does not affect the individual claims; this is the limit for the policy year.

Occurrence Limits

The occurrence limit is the **most the insurance company will cover in a single claim** for a liability policy. If the amount owed by the insured is greater than the occurrence limit, then the insurer will cover up to the occurrence limit, regardless of the total aggregate limit, and the insured will be liable for the rest in that claim. If the aggregate limit is less than the occurrence limit when the coverage is needed, then the occurrence limit will be reduced to the amount remaining in the aggregate limit.

A casualty/liability policy does not just have an aggregate limit **or** occurrence limit, it has both. In the above example, the policy had a $500,000 aggregate limit to use for the entire policy year. The same policy may have a $100,000 occurrence limit. The occurrence limit is the allotted amount for each individual claim. Therefore, the insurer will pay no more than $100,000 for each claim the insured has, even though the aggregate limit is higher.

For example, the insured of this policy has had multiple claims within the policy year. The insured has had claims of $30,000, $15,000, and $50,000. Since all claims happened within the policy year, the aggregate limit has been reduced to $405,000. The occurrence limit will be $100,000 if another claim occurs.

Negligence Must Be Established

To have the liability coverage pay, **it must be proven that the insured was negligent**, also termed as at fault. **If the insured is not at fault, then he/she will not be legally liable to give financial compensation to the third party.** This means that the liability coverage would not be needed for this lawsuit. The insured will be negligent if the insured admits to being at fault in a **settlement** outside of court or through **judgment** in a lawsuit. Once the insured's negligence is established, the liability coverage will be used.

Note: tort law deals with civil issues, not criminal issues.

Negligence

Negligence means the **failure to use reasonable care**. An insured can be declared negligent in one of two ways. Either the insured will admit negligence outside of court and make a **settlement** or a judge will declare the insured negligent as a **judgment**. When a settlement or judgment declares the insured negligent, then the insurer will step in and pay the claim in place of the insured. A **liability policy never pays any funds to the insured**. It pays the injured third party in place of the insured. The injured third party is the party that has damages.

Liability policies will pay when the insured is negligent according to tort law. In order to be covered, this must, particularly, be an unintentional act. The liability policy **will not cover intentional acts**. Consequentially, liability policies will pay for **accidents** and **occurrences**. An accident is defined as **a sudden and unexpected event** outside of the insured's control. Occurrences are defined as more expansive than an accident. The occurrence will cover events that are **sudden and unexpected, but also continuous exposures or series of acts** resulting in injury or damage.

Note: Reasonable Care is the degree of care or concern that a reasonable person would have taken under all known circumstances.

Establishing Negligence

To establish negligence, whether it is by settlement or judgment, a process must be used to see if reasonable care was or was not used. There must be a legal duty owed to another party that has been breached, which leads to the third party receiving damages due to the insured.

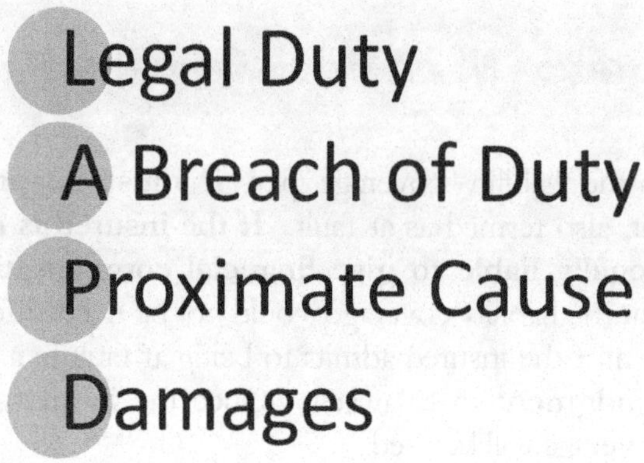

Legal Duty

People have an expectation, and in turn expect others to use reasonable care in day to day life scenarios. When trying to establish if the insured was negligent, the first step is to decide if there was a legal duty owed and what was the legal duty owed to society.

Sally just got a puppy from the pet shop and named it Turbo. Society now expects Sally to take care of the dog. She may need to put up a fence at her home so the dog cannot get out of the yard. Sally also needs to train the dog not to jump on people or bite people. This is the legal duty Sally now owes to society.

A Breach of Duty

The legal duty owed to society is expected to be upheld. When there has been a failure to uphold the legal duty, there has been a breach of duty.

Sally has worked with Turbo for a couple weeks now, but the puppy chews on everything Sally owns and also digs in her yard. The fence does well to keep Turbo in, but one day on her way to work, Sally left the gate open. Turbo quickly discovered this and ran out of the yard to roam the neighborhood while Sally was at work. The legal duty Sally owes to society has now been breached.

Proximate Cause

A breached legal duty alone does not make one negligent. The breach must lead to a third party receiving damage; bodily injury, property damage, personal injury, or advertising injury. That damage must also be tied to the insured. If it is determined the insured caused or could have prevented the breach of duty and it results in a third party's injury, then the insured will be negligent. The proximate cause will link the insured to the cause of the damage.

Since Sally left for work without checking the latch on the gate, the dog was able to leave the yard. If Luke, a neighbor, was bit by Turbo, then a chain of events would need to be established to prove how this happened. This originating chain of events is the **proximate cause**. The end result is that damage was done to Luke, but the beginning of the cause for the damage goes back to Sally's mishap with the gate.

Damage

If there is no damage done, then there is no potential lawsuit. A legal duty that is breached can be fixed before damage occurs. However, **when there is damage, there is a potential lawsuit.** Damage can consist of bodily injury, property damage, personal injury, or advertising injury.

When Turbo was roaming the neighborhood, he saw Luke jogging across the street. Since Turbo loves to chase things, he runs after Luke. Turbo eventually caught up with Luke and bit him. Luke now has bodily injury from the bite and Sally has a potential lawsuit.

No Fault Benefits

The primary protection in liability insurance is for the insurance company to pay, in place of the insured, when the insured is held legally liable for the damage done. That is the liability coverage portion of the policy. However, liability insurance will also provide other types of coverage in addition to this primary function. These types of coverages are the no fault benefits in a liability policy.

No fault benefits will pay without negligence being established. In most cases, these benefits are used to prevent a bigger claim. Some of the benefits may be used to help the insured while in the lawsuit. There are two key no fault benefits to focus on: medical payments and additional coverages.

Medical Payments

Medical Payments are used as a **preventive** measure. The casualty/liability policy provides a certain amount of money to be used for any medical expenses that arise when the third party is injured. As a no fault benefit, medical payments will be used **before a settlement or judgment** determines the insured as negligent. The hope is that the third party will drop any charges against the insured, if the medical expenses have been covered and paid for.

This **does not guarantee** that the charges will be dropped. There are no strings attached; if the third party wants to seek further compensation for the damage, the insured may still be held negligent and be expected to pay more. In this case, the liability coverage will still cover the insured if found negligent, and **any medical payments given to be preventive will count towards the final compensation amount.**

Both **personal lines** and **commercial lines** offer medical payments coverage within the casualty/liability policy. In a personal lines policy, medical payments may be used within **3 years after the accident**. If it is a commercial lines policy, medical payments may only be used within **1 year after the accident**.

Additional Coverages (Supplementary Payments)

No matter which line of insurance is being looked at, **all additional coverages are free, automatic, over and above**. The coverages provided, however, differ from property to casualty. In casualty/liability policies, legal defenses, bail bonds, prejudgment interests, and loss of wages are additional coverages available for the insured.

Legal Defense

The insurer will pay for the legal defense and fees regardless if the insured is at fault or not. Since the defense will be paid regardless of fault, this is a no fault benefit.

The insurer will pay as long as the insurer has money at stake in the lawsuit. This expense is not a part of the aggregate or occurrence limits of the policy, since it is a part of the additional coverages. It is paid over and above the original limits.

When the insurer pays for legal defense and fees, they will build a defense for the insured. Below are some of the defenses used in a liability policy:

Comparative Fault

Comparative fault is used as a way to **share the blame** between the insured and the third party **when both parties are at fault**. This defense is based off a percentage of fault and will change the amount of recovery the third party can receive due to that percentage.

If the insured is 70% at fault and the third party is 30%, then the insured will pay 70% of the damages instead of 100%. Whichever party is majority at fault will pay the claim.

Assumption of Risk

Assumption of risk is used to say that the third party **knew the risk before the damage** occurred. Many times this is seen when people sign up for dangerous events like sky diving, bungee jumping, or white water rafting. The company has the guests sign a form that says they know the risk going into the event.

Assumption of risk does not prevent the third party from suing, but it builds a strong defense if the third party was injured in an expected way due to that event, especially if not following proper instruction. For example, if a third party goes bungee jumping and jumps before the instructor gives the okay then the cords could get tangled and hurt the bungee jumper. Assumption of risk would be a good defense to use because the bungee jumper knew ahead of time he could get hurt if not following instructions.

Intervening Cause

This defense is used to point the direction of **blame to someone other than the insured**. The original chain of events, the proximate cause, points to the insured for the cause of the damage. Intervening cause will step into this chain of events to point the blame elsewhere. It is not the insured's fault, it is someone else's.

If in the previous example of Turbo biting Luke, it was discovered that Sally did indeed latch the gate. But, Luke opened the gate and let Turbo out and then as a result got bit. Now Sally could argue that Luke was the originating cause of the damages and it had nothing to do with Sally being negligent.

Statute of Limitations

This defense is used to say that the third party has taken **too long to file the claim**. If this defense is given, then it is to say that the claim brought against the insured is no longer relevant and should have been dealt with sooner.

Contributory Negligence

This defense says that if the injured third party contributes at all towards the damage then the lawsuit may be thrown out. The plaintiff **must prove that the insured is 100% at fault** and that the third party did not contribute at all. If that cannot be proven, then it will bar recovery.

Miscellaneous Issues

Strict Liability

Strict liability is when a company may be liable for the **distribution of a product** that may have some flaws, which may cause **bodily injury** or **property damage** to those who have purchased the product. Many times when an accident with a product occurs, a recall of that product is close to follow. Strict liability will cover the bodily injury and property damage that occurs from the product. **It will not pay for the cost of a recall.** The business will be responsible for the cost of a recall.

Vicarious Liability

Vicarious liability means to be liable for another person's actions. This will be important for the **parent to child** relationship and the **employer to employee** relationship.

Joe has a tree trimming business. He has one employee, Bob. Joe sends Bob out to do a job. As a result of Bob's incompetence, the customer's automobile is damaged. The customer chooses to hold Joe responsible, not Bob, since Joe was responsible for the work being done.

Absolute Liability

Absolute liability arises when **dangerous operations, hazardous materials, or dangerous animals** cause damage to a third party. In these extremely dangerous situations, fault is not established but the party in charge of the dangerous operation, hazardous material, or dangerous animals will be held liable for the damage.

Martha has a demolition business. She demolishes buildings with the use of explosives. Since this is not a exposure that the city is normally exposed to, Martha will be responsible for any mishaps that occur in the course of her operation.

Care, Custody, and Control

Property that is owned by a third party but in the **care, custody, and control** of the insured will be **excluded from the liability** coverage if the said property is damaged. This damage will be excluded, whether it is personal lines or commercial lines. *Coverage* *for these items is provided in property insurance policies under the No Benefit to Bailee Clause.* This encourages the Bailee to use the property clause to get the property fixed quickly and avoid a lawsuit.

Damage to Rented Premises

Damage to Rented Premises pays when one **negligently causes fire damage to a dwelling or structure in his/her care, custody, and control**.

Normally, if property is in the care, custody, and control of the insured and it is owned by a third party, then it is excluded under liability policies and covered by property policies under the No Benefit to Bailee Clause. Negligent fire damage to a rented dwelling or structure is the exception to the No Benefit to Bailee Clause and will be covered under Damage to Rented Premises.

Example: In the HO-4, renter's policy, there is no available property damage for the dwelling of the structure since the insured, renter, has no insurable interest in the home. Therefore, No Benefit to Bailee cannot take precedence over liability coverage because there is not property coverage for the dwelling. Care, custody, and control is excluded under liability, therefore, Damage to Rented Premises had to be created to fill in the gap.

Note: Damage to Rented Premises used to be titled as Fire Legal Liability

Umbrella and Excess Liability Policies

In today's litigious society, does anyone really know if he/she has adequate insurance limits? Even if Joe maxes out his liability limits on his Auto or Homeowners Policy, he may find that these limits do not provide adequate coverage. The Umbrella and Excess Liability policies are designed to provide **high limits** for a **minimal premium**. These policies may be used for **personal lines** or **commercial lines**.

Umbrella Policies

The Umbrella Policy does two things,

- Provides coverage **over and above** underlying limits, and
- **Expands protection** for exposures not covered by the underlying policies.

Once the underlying policy has exhausted its limit, the Umbrella Policy kicks in to pay the claim. Some policies will have a retention limit that must be paid before the policy pays a benefit. The retention limit basically acts like a deductible.

The Umbrella Policy may also provide coverage that is not covered by the underlying policies. For example, the auto policy does not cover if driving in Mexico. The Umbrella Policy may pick up coverage if the insured is driving in Mexico after the retention limit is met.

Note: Underlying policies would be the policies that the company requires the insured to own in order to qualify for the Umbrella or Excess Liability Policy. These policies pay first, the Umbrella or Excess Liability kicks in only after coverage has been exhausted by the underlying policy.

Excess Liability Policies

The Excess Liability Policy is very similar to the Umbrella Policy. The major difference is that it only provides protection if the peril was covered first by the underlying policy. In other words, excess liability does not expand coverage. It only increases the amount of protection. If the underlying policy will not pay, neither will the Excess Liability. In the above example, if the insured drove in Mexico the Auto Policy would not provide protection and as a result the Excess Liability Policy would also deny coverage.

Terms to know

Liability/Casualty

3rd Party contract

Bodily injury

Property damage

Personal injury

Advertising injury

Tort law

Economic (special/specific) damages

Noneconomic (general) damages

Punitive damages

Aggregate limit

Occurrence limit

Negligence

Settlement/judgment

Legal duty

A breach of legal duty

Proximate cause

Damage

No fault benefits

Medical payments

Additional coverages/Supplementary payments

Legal defense

Assumption of risk

Intervening cause

Statute of limitations

Contributory negligence

Strict liability

Vicarious liability

Absolute liability

Care, custody, control

Fire legal liability

Umbrella

Excess liability

Acronyms to know

BI- Bodily injury

PD- Property damage

LAPD- establishing negligence (**L**egal duty owed, **A** breach of legal duty, **P**roximate cause, **D**amages)

Numbers to know

3 Party contracts

Medical payments- Personal 3 years/ Commercial 1 year

Contributory- insured 100% at fault

Practice Exam

1. All the following are necessary to establish negligence, except:
   a) Duty
   b) Proximate cause
   c) Not meeting the prudent person rule
   d) Punitive damages
2. A liability policy provides coverage for the ________ and pays a benefit to the __________.
   a) Insured, insured
   b) Injured 3rd party, insured
   c) Insured, injured 3rd party
   d) Insured, insurance company
3. Liability coverage includes protection for different types of damages. Which of the following is NOT covered by the liability policy?
   a) Punitive
   b) General
   c) Special
   d) Specific
4. Which of the following types of damage coverage pays for the pain and suffering of the injured 3rd party?
   a) Special
   b) Specific
   c) General
   d) Punitive
5. What element is NOT necessary to establish negligence?
   a) Intervening cause
   b) Damages
   c) Legal duty owed
   d) A breach of legal duty

6. Which of the following statements about Medical Payments is FALSE?
   a) Commercial claims must be filed within 1 year
   b) Personal claims must be filed within 3 years
   c) It guarantees that all charges against the insured will be dropped
   d) It is used as a preventive measure
7. Legal defense is an Additional Coverage on the liability policy. Which of the following statements is FALSE? Legal defense…
   a) Is free, automatic and pays over and above
   b) Will only pay if the insured is not at fault
   c) Will pay as long as the insurer has money at stake
   d) Is not a part of aggregate or occurrence limits
8. Which legal defense is used as a way to share the blame with both the insured and 3rd party share the fault?
   a) Assumption of risk
   b) Comparative fault
   c) Contributory negligence
   d) Intervening cause
9. Which defense is used to point the blame at someone other than the insured?
   a) Contributory negligence
   b) Comparative negligence
   c) Proximate cause
   d) Intervening cause
10. ______ is products liability and provides coverage for bodily injury and property damage, but does not pay for the recall itself.
   a) Strict liability
   b) Vicarious liability
   c) Absolute liability
   d) Intervening cause

11. If the city zoo brings in a tiger and it breaks out of the zoo and does property damage around the city, the zoo is responsible for the damages. This is called…

    a) Vicarious liability
    b) Strict liability
    c) Excess liability
    d) Absolute liability

12. When dealing with supplementary payments in a liability policy, what will the insurance company cover?

    a) Defense cost
    b) Medical payments
    c) Ordinance or law
    d) Economic or special damages

13. Which of the following is required to establish negligence?

    a) Intervening cause
    b) A breach of duty
    c) Intentional damage
    d) Absolute liability

14. Which type of policy pays over and above and expands protection?

    a) Umbrella
    b) Excess liability
    c) Strict liability
    d) Vicarious liability

15. Which of the following would be covered by the tenants "Damages to Rented Properties?"

    a) Personal property of a tenant
    b) Building damage resulting from negligence of a tenant
    c) Damage to personal property as a result of negligence
    d) Damage to someone else's personal property due to negligence of the tenant

Answer key: 1,d 2,c 3,a 4,c 5,a 6,c 7,b 8,b 9,d 10,a 11,d 12,a 13,b 14,a 15,b

Chapter

5

Homeowners and Dwelling Policies

The Homeowners Policy is a crucial form of Personal Lines insurance. With this multiline policy, the homeowner has property, theft, and liability coverage combined into one product. It stems from the Dwelling Policy, which solely gives Property coverage. Today, the Dwelling Policy is used commonly for landlords or a simple renter's form.

The Homeowners Program

A home is often a person's largest asset. It is essential to protect one's home from the many different exposures. As the homeowner chooses the necessary policy, he/she must consider the type of home in which he/she dwells. Many people live in a single family home, but there are also those who rent and others who may own a condo. Therefore, it is necessary to create insurance policies to meet all of these needs.

ISO, *Insurance Service Organization*, has provided six standard forms that homeowners may choose:

- HO-8 Modified Coverage Form (Replaced the HO-1)
- HO-2 Broad Form
- HO-3 Special Form
- HO-4 Tenant Form
- HO-5 Comprehensive Form
- HO-6 Condominium Unit Owners Form

Eligibility & Qualifications`

To be eligible for a Homeowners Policy, one must **own and live in the dwelling** that is insured. This is true for all Homeowners Policies, except the HO-4 Tenant Form. The H0-4 only requires residential use of the premises.

Owned dwellings with multiple units can also be insured under a Homeowners Policy, if eligible. To remain as a Personal Lines product, a **dwelling can have up to four units**. Units allow multiple families in one home, each having separate entrances and living quarters. This creates the option to cover dwellings like duplexes, triplexes, and other dwellings of a similar nature.

Incidental Businesses in Home

The Homeowners Policy is **primarily for residential use only**, however, some incidental business use in the home is allowable. The stipulations are that the dwelling must be the insured's primary place of residence and any other structure must be used primarily for personal use with any **business use as a secondary purpose** for the structure. If this is the case, then the policy will allow **property coverage** for those structures.

This allows for an office in the home or a tenant in an extra room. This will cover the main dwelling and the other structures on premises as long as the business use is incidental. This will not cover a garage on premises used by a mechanic as a shop to fix cars brought in by the public. In that case, the mechanic is using the garage primarily for business uses, not personal uses. If there is an extra parking spot in the insured's garage to store a friend's car for a small fee, then the garage is used as a private garage and would be covered as incidental business because the primary use was personal.

Note: Incidental business covers property damage, it does not cover the liability exposures of the business.

Who is Insured

The insured of a Homeowners Policy is anyone **named** on the Declarations page of the policy. By definition, insureds will also include the **family residing** in the household of the named insured and anyone **under the age of 21** in the care of the named insured.

For example, if Jonah is the named insured on the Declarations page then he is covered. His wife, Susie, may not be named on the policy but since she is family to the name insured and living in Jonah's household, then she is covered by definition. Together they have a son named Albert. While Albert is growing up in his parents' household, he is insured by definition. Albert will also be covered when he moves into his college dorm; but once he moves into his own home, he will no longer be covered by Jonah's insurance policy. However, if Albert is in a position where he moves back into his parents' home, he would again be covered by definition as family residing in the household. This will be true as long as it is for an indefinite period of time.

If Jonah and Susie had **foster** kids or **foreign exchange students** in their care, then the children would be covered, as long as they are under the age of 21. These children are insured by definition because they are in care of the insured and under the age of 21. That definition is not for slumber parties, birthday parties, or invited guests.

WHAT IS COVERED

Homeowners Policies are multiline policies, they provide coverage for property and liability. As such, the policy has two sections: **Section I**, property, and **Section II**, liability. In each Section, there are multiple types of coverage available to insure different risks the insured is exposed to when owning a home.

Under Section I and Section II, the policy will cover the insured location. The insured location is defined as the residence premises and any other structures on the premises used by the insured. Any property owned or rented to an insured is covered as the insured location. This could include vacant land, land in which a dwelling is being built as a residence for the insured, or even an individual or family cemetery plot.

Section I - Property & Theft

- Coverage A - Dwelling
- Coverage B - Other Structures
- Coverage C - Personal Property
- Coverage D - Loss of Use

Section II - Liability

- Coverage E - Liability
- Coverage F - Medical Payments

Section I – Property Coverage

Section I deals with the Property insurance of a Homeowners policy. Property insurance provides coverage for the insured **when he/she suffers a financial loss due to damaged or destroyed property.** This is a **two-party contract** between the insurance company (the insurer) and the owner of the policy (the insured). With this insurance, one's dwelling, other structures, and personal property are covered from certain risks detailed in the policy. It will also include coverage for loss of use, which is an indirect, financial loss to the insured.

Section I - Property & Theft

- Coverage A - Dwelling
- Coverage B - Other Structures
- Coverage C - Personal Property
- Coverage D - Loss of Use

COVERAGE A - DWELLING

Coverage

The main purpose of Coverage A is to insure the dwelling. This structure will be declared in the Declarations page. Looking further in the policy, **Coverage A will also insure structures attached to the dwelling, permanent fixtures, and construction material used to repair or alter the dwelling or other structures**. Land is not covered.

To expand further on the dwelling coverage, the dwelling is the living quarters of the insured. This does not cover the shed out back or any other structures on the premises not attached to the home. If another structure is attached to the dwelling, then coverage for such a structure will be covered in Coverage A. For example, a garage can be either attached or detached. *If the garage is attached, it will be covered under Coverage A. If the garage is detached, it will not be covered under Coverage A.* Permanent fixtures may include, but are not limited to: furnaces, sinks, cabinets, countertops, showers, tubs, toilets, and light fixtures. These are objects that are permanently installed in the dwelling. If it is a permanently installed fixture, then it will be covered under Coverage A. Coverage A will also include coverage for construction material, but the *construction material must have a designated purpose to either alter or repair the dwelling or another structure on premises.* Purchased deck boards to repair an already installed deck would be considered construction material that is covered in Coverage A.

Primary Coverage

As a homeowner, it would be devastating to have a total loss on the dwelling. This is the homeowner's residence and the homeowner has invested a great amount of money into the home. Losing the dwelling means the homeowner has a loss of financial interest, as well as the loss of living quarters. Since this is so crucial to the homeowner, Coverage A is the primary coverage for the *HO-1, HO-2, HO-3, HO-5, and HO-8.* **The primary coverage is typically the greatest insurable interest for the insured and the base for limits of liability on other areas of coverage in the policy**. A limit of liability is the amount of coverage provided by the policy. The insurer will not exceed the limit of liability. For a coverage that is primary, the insured will choose the limit of liability.

Notice that the HO-4 and the HO-6 were left out of the list above. Primary coverage shows the most important coverage to the insured and, for the HO-4 and HO-6 the dwelling is not the most important concern.

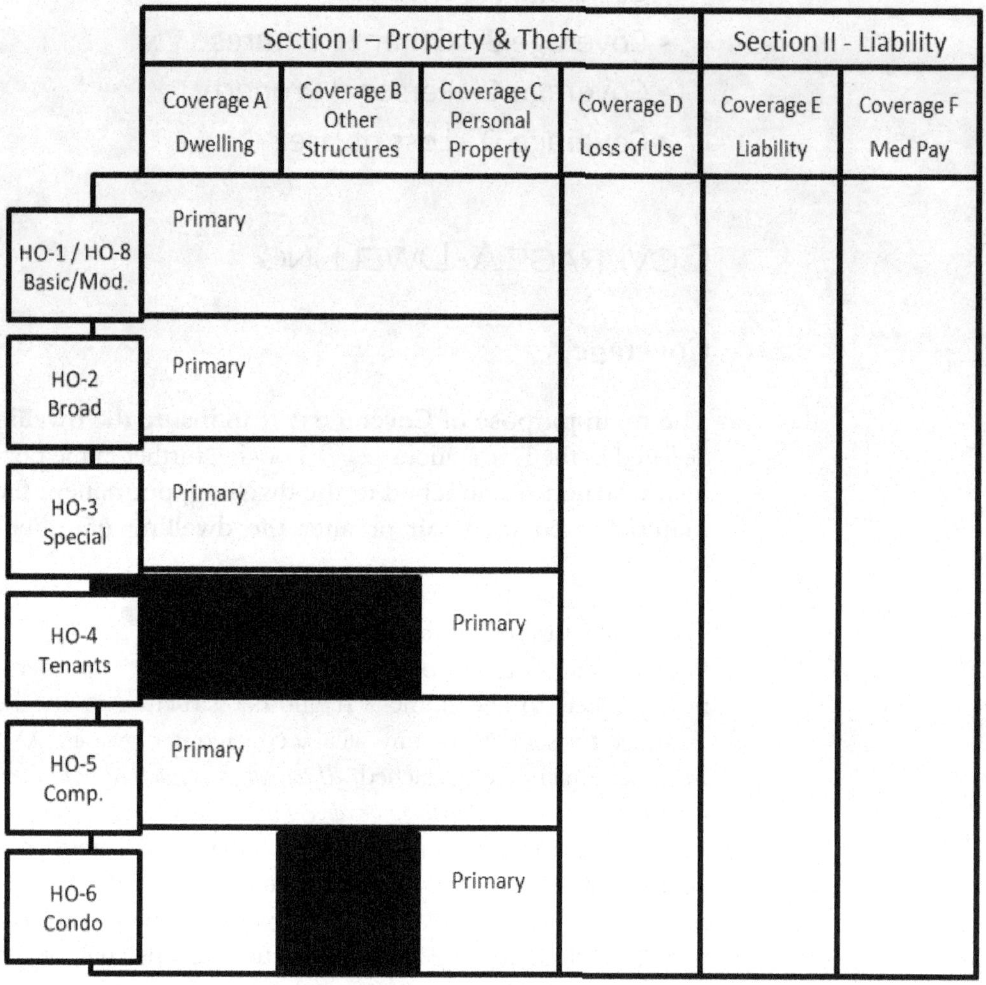

For the HO-4 Tenant's Form, the primary concern is not in the dwelling because there is no insurable interest in the dwelling for the insured; the dwelling is owned by another party (landlord). The insured of an HO-4 is a renter of the dwelling and therefore has no insurable interest, or financial interest in the dwelling. *In the case of an HO-4, the insured's main concern is the contents of the dwelling, not the dwelling itself.*

HO-6 policies are known as the Condominium Unit Owners Form. In this situation, the insured is not a renter; the insured is an owner of the condo unit. However, the condo unit owner does not own the entire condominium complex; they only own the individual unit. The condominium association owns the entire complex. *Therefore, in an HO-6 policy, the insured does not have an insurable interest for the entire dwelling, just the unit.* Coverage A will still be built into the HO-6, but the coverage will only be for what the condo owner contractually owns.

Note: The Condo Association will cover the building in Commercial Lines.

Coverage B – Other Structures (Appurtenant Structures)

Coverage

Though the dwelling is the main concern for most homeowners, **it is not the only concern of homeowners.** Many residence premises have more than just a home on the premises. This could include detached garages, sheds, pools, fences, and many other structures. **Coverage B, other structures, gives coverage for the structures on the residence premises that are set apart from the dwelling by clear space.** A structure cannot become attached by fence, utility lines, or things of similar nature. *Coverage B is for the HO-1, HO-2, HO-3, HO-5, and HO-8.* The HO-4 and HO-6 do not have insurable interest in other structures and does not use Coverage B.

Exclusions

Land is again excluded in Coverage B. Coverage B will also **exclude coverage for any other structure, if the structures primary use is to conduct any type of business.** If any other structure is being used for business, *the business must be incidental* to the structure. For example, if an insured, Cassidy, has a three car garage but owns only two vehicles, then there is an open parking spot in her garage. Cassidy's friend, Wendy, restores vintage vehicles and needs a place to store the car when not in use. Wendy asks to use Cassidy's extra parking spot in the garage and offers to pay $100 a month for the spot. If Cassidy accepts, the insured garage would still be covered under Coverage B. Other structures may be used as a private garage like in this example. However, if Cassidy converts her garage into an auto body repair shop and starts working on cars of the public for a fee, then the garage would not be covered under Coverage B.

Limit of Liability

The limit of liability is **the amount of insurance provided by the insurer.** If the loss is greater than the limit of liability, *the insurer will pay up to the limit but not exceed the limit.* The insured will be responsible for the excess amount. Therefore, it is important to know what the standard limit of liability is in Coverage B and if it needs to be increased.

Coverage B's limit of liability is automatically 10% of the primary coverage. Since this coverage is only used for the *HO-1, HO-2, HO-3, HO-5, and HO-8*, all primary coverage is Coverage A. Therefore, whatever limit is chosen for Coverage A; Coverage B automatically will have a limit of liability of 10%. If Joe has a $200,000 limit for Coverage A, he will also have $20,000 limit for Coverage B. Coverage B's limit is separate from Coverage A and will not take money from Coverage A's limit of liability. In this example $20,000, which is 10% of Coverage A, may or may not be enough coverage. This amount can be increased at an additional cost. Coverage B's 10% limit of liability is not dependent upon having other structures on premises. Even if the residence premise has only a dwelling and no other structures, Coverage B and the limit of liability are both still a part of the policy.

COVERAGE C – PERSONAL PROPERTY

Coverage

Personal Property is a much needed coverage in the Homeowners Policy. **In Coverage C, the insurer covers the personal property that is owned or used by an insured.** In other words, the coverage is for the homeowner's stuff. This provides coverage for tables, chairs, electronics, cookware, books, clothes, toiletries, toys, games and any other type of personal item one may have. Personal property that is insured under **Coverage C will be covered worldwide**, with a few exceptions.

Coverage C will cover personal property well, but one must know and understand how the coverage is described in the policy. For most of the plans Coverage C will provide an automatic limit of 50% of A, the primary limit. This is true for all forms except the HO-4 and HO-6. In these forms Coverage C is the primary limit and the amount will be chosen by the insured. This coverage will have many items covered fully, some may be covered to a limited amount, and other items may not be covered at all.

For instance, personal property owned by others may be covered after a loss, upon the insured's request, if the property is on the part of the residence premises occupied by an insured. This means if the insured's house is burned down in a fire, personal property of another person can be covered on the insured's Homeowners Policy. The other person may have his own coverage on the property lost, therefore if the insured wants to cover the property, it must be requested. Another example where property of others may be covered is if a guest or a residence employee's personal property is in any residence occupied by an insured. Again, it will be covered if requested by the insured after the loss.

Limit for Property at Other Locations

Other Residences

The insurer will cover personal property worldwide, but a limitation is added if personal property is **usually located at an insured's secondary residence that is not the covered** residence premises. A college dorm is an example of a secondary residence. An insured may live in a college dorm, which is not the covered residence premise. If there is a loss with the personal property usually kept in the college dorm, then the insured's Homeowners Policy will give either **10% of the limit of liability for Coverage C or $1,000, whichever is greater.**

This limitation **does not apply** if the personal property is at a secondary residence because the residence premises is not fit for living or the storing of personal property due to the covered residence premises being repaired, renovated or rebuilt. The limit will not apply 30 days after a new principal residence is acquired, giving coverage for an insured while in process of moving into a new home. In regards to these stipulations, coverage of personal property will not be limited to 10% of Coverage C or $1,000, whichever is greater, but will be restored to the original limit of liability for Coverage C.

Self-Storage Facilities

Stipulations have been made specifically for personal property stored in a self-storage facility because self-storage facilities have become more used by homeowners. When **personal property is usually stored in a self-storage facility, the 10% of Coverage C or $1,000, whichever is greater, limitation applies**. However, this limitation does not apply to personal property if it is being stored temporarily while the residence premises is being repaired, renovated, or rebuilt and the residence premises is not fit for living or the storing of personal property.

Special Limits of Liability

These special limits of liability are **stated limits** in the policy that will limit the amount of coverage for specific personal property based upon ISO's 2022 updates:

- $300 for money, bank notes, and medals
- $2,000:
  - securities, accounts, and deeds
  - watercraft of all types, including its trailer
  - trailers not used for watercrafts
  - portable electronic equipment that may operate in or separate from a motor vehicle
- Personal Property Used for Business:
  - $3,000 for property **on** the residence premises
  - $1,500 for property **off** the residence premises
- Due to Theft:
  - $2,000 for jewelry, watches, furs, and stones
  - $3,000 for firearms
  - $3,000 for silverware, gold ware, etc.

Personal Article Floater

To better cover personal property, an insured could attach a personal article floater to the policy. This will cover a specific item that may be hard to insure. Jewelry, firearms, 1st edition items, and collections are good examples of items that may use a personal article floater.

Personal Article Floaters have **no deductible**, they are **open peril/all risk**, and set at **agreed value**. Agreed value allows the insurer to cover the item for the agreed appraisal price instead of actual cash value or replacement cost. The idea of this policy being a *floater* policy is that the insurance follows the item. Coverage applies to the item wherever it is, whether it is on the residence premises or not

Note: Another way to insure items like this would be through a scheduling endorsement. Scheduling is a very similar process, but added to the Homeowners Policy as an endorsement. The Personal Article Floater is a separate policy altogether.

Exclusions

- Items covered elsewhere
- Animal, birds, or fish
- Motor vehicles unless…
    - Used solely to service the residence
    - Designed to assist the handicapped
- Aircrafts and hovercrafts
- Property of tenants
- Business data
- Water or steam

COVERAGE D – LOSS OF USE

Loss of use coverage is an **indirect loss**. This means that it is a **financial loss**, not physical. In Coverage A, B, and C, the losses are direct losses which are physical. Coverage D will cover the insured for a financial loss resulting from, or as a consequence of, a direct loss. For example, if a house burns down, the insured suffers a direct loss; the insured may need to live in a hotel during the time of repairs. The extra cost of living in a hotel for an extended period of time would be covered under Coverage D, since it is an indirect loss due to the fire.

There are three covered areas under Coverage D:

- **Additional Living Expense**

  The insurer will cover any necessary **increased** living expense due to a covered direct loss to **the residence premises, if it is not fit for living**

Payment will last through the repairs, unless the insured relocates

If an insured normally does laundry at home but no longer can due to a fire, then additional living expense will pay for the above and beyond cost of doing laundry at a laundry mat. The money to do each load would be covered since it is an **extra expense**. The detergent and dryer sheets are not covered because it is not an added expense; this is an expense the insured has even when doing laundry at home.

- **Fair Rental Value**

  The insurer will cover any **loss of rent** if the rented portion of the residence premises is not fit for living due to a covered direct loss

  Payment will last through repairs and cover the loss of rent

  If there was no tenant at the time of the loss, loss of rent will not be paid

- **Civil Authority Prohibits Use**

  The insurer will cover the additional living expense and fair rental value of one's home if **civil authority prohibits** the insured from living in the residence premises as a result from direct damage to neighboring premises

ADDITIONAL COVERAGES

What are Additional Coverages?

Additional Coverages are built into all Homeowners Policies. When looking in a Homeowners insurance policy, the additional coverages will be shown after Coverage A, B, C, and D. There is no extra cost to have the additional coverages, **they are free**. No one has to request the additional coverages to be put into the policy, **it is automatic**. More coverage is provided because of the additional coverages, **they are paid over and above** Coverage A, B, C, and D.

Additional Coverages Provided

- **Debris Removal** – will pay to remove the debris of a covered structure, if the structure is damaged by a covered peril. The coverage is built into the limit of liability of said structure, but if the cost exceeds the limit of liability an additional 5% will become available for use.

  Also, debris removal will pay up to $1,500 for trees if the tree damages a covered structure or blocks a driveway or entryway due to **wind, weight, or hail**. Debris removal may also pay if a neighbor's tree falls onto the covered property and blocks an entryway or driveway. This additional coverage will pay no more than $500 for any one item.

- **Reasonable Repairs** – will reimburse the insured for the reasonable costs incurred to protect the covered property from further damage after a loss.

- **Trees, Shrubs and Other Plants** – will pay up to 5% of the limit of liability that applies to the dwelling to cover the loss of trees, shrubs, plants or lawns of the residence premises if the loss is due to a covered peril. Wind, weight, and hail are not covered perils since they are used for debris removal. This is so the insured cannot double collect on a claim. The additional coverage will pay no more than $1,500 for any one item.

- **Fire Department Service Charge** – will pay up to $500 for any liability assumed by the insured to pay the fire department if a covered peril damages the insured property. No deductible applies to this coverage.

- **Property Removed** – covered property removed from a premises endangered by a covered peril will be insured against direct loss from any cause for 30 days.

- **Loss Assessment** – will pay up to $2,000 for any loss assessment due to a covered peril charged against the insured by a corporation or association of property owners.

- **Landlord's Furnishings** – will pay up to $3,000 for appliances, carpeting and other household furnishings in each unit on the residence premises held for rent to others by the insured due to a covered loss.

- **Ordinance or Law** – will pay up to 10% of Coverage A for any increased cost on construction due to any ordinance, law, or code being enforced.

- **Grave Markers** – will pay up to $5,000 for grave markers on or away for the residence premises due to a covered peril.

- **Collapse** – will cover abrupt collapse which is sudden, unexpected and unusable, or collapse due to a covered peril, decay, insects and vermin, weight of property or people, or weight of rain.

PERILS INSURED AGAINST

Named Perils

Named perils are **listed in the insuring clause**. Whatever is listed as a peril in the insuring clause will be covered by the policy. If the peril is not listed in the insuring clause, it is not covered. There are **two different named peril forms** to choose from, the basic form and the broad form.

The Basic Form – Perils Listed

- Fire & Lightning
- Extended Coverages
  - Riot
  - Explosion
  - Vehicles
  - Civil Commotion
  - Smoke
  - Hail
  - Aircraft
  - Windstorm
  - Volcano
- Vandalism and Malicious Mischief
- Theft

The Broad Form – Perils Listed

- Fire & Lightning
- Extended Coverages
  - Riot
  - Explosion
  - Vehicles
  - Civil Commotion
  - Smoke
  - Hail
  - Aircraft
  - Windstorm
  - Volcano
- Vandalism and Malicious Mischief
- Theft
- W. I. F.
  - Weight of Ice, Snow or Sleet
  - Intentional Water
  - Falling Objects

Note: Collapse is an additional coverage that enhances other perils on the Broad Form. It is not available on the Basic Form

Open Perils/All Risk

Open perils *are not* listed in the insuring clause. To find out what is covered under open perils, one must look on the **exclusions page**. The open perils will cover everything except what is specifically excluded. This means that **the insurer must make a special effort to list everything that is not covered in the exclusions page.** Otherwise, the policy will cover it.

The Special Form

Everything Except what is Excluded

- Includes Open Perils/All Risk within the policy
- Coverage will include everything listed in the Basic Form and Broad Form

VALUATION

The valuation of a Homeowners Policy tells the insured how the insurer will pay out the claim, in the event of a loss. Most policies will have the **Replacement Cost valuation for Coverage A and B.** The exception to this is the HO-8, which will use the Fair Market Value valuation. All Homeowners Policies use the **Actual Cash Value** valuation initially for **Coverage C.**

When Replacement Cost is given for Coverage A and Coverage B, an **80% coinsurance or insurance to value** clause will apply. In this case it will be an insurance to value clause. Payments will be completed once repairs or replacement of the residence premises is finished. The exception to this is if the loss is **less than 5% of Coverage A or less than $2,500**. Then the payments of Replacement Cost will be paid before restoration is complete.

<table>
<tr><th></th><th colspan="4">Section I – Property & Theft</th><th colspan="2">Section II - Liability</th></tr>
<tr><th></th><th>Coverage A
Dwelling</th><th>Coverage B
Other Structures</th><th>Coverage C
Personal Property</th><th>Coverage D
Loss of Use</th><th>Coverage E
Liability</th><th>Coverage F
Med Pay</th></tr>
<tr><td>HO-1 / HO-8
Basic/Mod.</td><td>Primary
Market</td><td>Market</td><td>ACV</td><td rowspan="6">Indirect

Financial in nature

Triggered by a covered peril

1. Add. Living Expense

2. Fair Rental

3. Civil Authority</td><td rowspan="6"></td><td rowspan="6"></td></tr>
<tr><td>HO-2
Broad</td><td>Primary
Rep.</td><td>Rep.</td><td>ACV</td></tr>
<tr><td>HO-3
Special</td><td>Primary
Rep.</td><td>Rep.</td><td>ACV</td></tr>
<tr><td>HO-4
Tenants</td><td>■</td><td>■</td><td>Primary
ACV</td></tr>
<tr><td>HO-5
Comp.</td><td>Primary
Rep.</td><td>Rep</td><td>ACV</td></tr>
<tr><td>HO-6
Condo</td><td>Rep.</td><td>■</td><td>Primary
ACV</td></tr>
</table>

POLICY FORMS

HO-1 Basic/HO-8 Modified

Originally, there was the HO-1 Basic but it has been updated and replaced by the HO-8 Modified. Both the HO-1 Basic and the HO-8 Modified cover the residence premises with the **basic perils**; fire and lightning, extended coverages, vandalism and malicious mischief, and theft. The basic perils are used in all of Section I of this policy, which is Coverage A, B, C, D, and the Additional Coverages.

Note: The difference in the HO-1 and HO-8 was made to prevent financial gain for a homeowner who has a loss of an old house that has a high replacement cost but a low market value.

The difference in the HO-1 Basic and the HO-8 Modified is in the valuation of the policy. The HO-1 used the Replacement Cost valuation for Coverage A and B, whereas the **HO-8 uses the Fair Market Value valuation for Coverage A and B total losses.** If there is a partial loss to Coverage A or B, then Actual Cash Value will be used. Both policies use the Actual Cash Value valuation for Coverage C.

HO-2 Broad

The HO-2 Broad policy covers the residence premises with the **broad perils**; fire & lightning, extended coverages, vandalism and malicious mischief, theft, and W.I.F. These perils will be used for all of Section I of the policy, which is Coverage A, B, C, D, and the Additional Coverages.

The HO-2 Broad uses the **Replacement Cost valuation for Coverage A and B. Actual Cash Value valuation is used for Coverage C.**

Note: Collapse is added to the Broad Form under the Additional Coverages

HO-3 Special

The HO-3 Special policy is unique. **Coverage A and Coverage B uses the Open Peril/All Risk** idea for perils covered. That means everything is covered except what is excluded for Coverage A and Coverage B. However, Coverage C does not use the Open Peril/All Risk idea. **Coverage C uses the Broad Perils** to cover the personal property.

The HO-3 Special uses the **Replacement Cost valuation for Coverage A and B. Actual Cash Value valuation is used for Coverage C.**

Note: Endorsement HO-15 bumps Coverage C from Broad Perils to Open Peril/All Risk. This makes the policy look very similar to the HO-5.

HO-4 Tenant

The HO-4 Tenant policy is designed for the renter. Coverage A and Coverage B is not given to the renter because the renter does not have insurable interest in the dwelling or other structures. The most important coverage for the renter is Coverage C. **Broad perils** will be used for Coverage C, D and the Additional Coverages.

The HO-4 Tenant uses the **Actual Cash Value valuation for Coverage C**. There is no valuation for dwelling or other structures since those are not covered.

HO-5 Comprehensive

The HO-5 Comprehensive policy covers the residence premises with the **Open Peril/All Risk idea throughout Section I**. That means that Coverage A, B, C, D, and the Additional Coverages cover everything except what is excluded.

By adding open peril coverage to Coverage C, one of the changes that will occur is that theft will be expanded to include mysterious disappearance.

The HO-5 Comprehensive uses the **Replacement Cost valuation for Coverage A and B. Actual Cash Value valuation is used for Coverage C.**

HO-6 Condo

The HO-6 Condo policy covers what the condo unit owner is contractually responsible for. The HO-6 uses the **Broad Perils** for Coverage A, C, D, and the Additional Coverages. There is no Coverage B in the HO-6 Condo.

The HO-6 Condo uses the **Replacement Cost valuation for Coverage A**. There is a limit of **$1,000 for Coverage A, but this limit can be raised**. The limit is because Coverage A does not cover the entire Condo building, just what the unit owner is contractually obligated for. What the limit is intended to be used for is property upgrades like flooring, cabinets, countertops, fixtures and other items the insured has made a part of the dwelling. **Actual Cash Value valuation is used for Coverage C**

Note: *. Coverage is provided from the "dry-wall in" because this is the unit owned by the policy holder, thus this is where the insurable interest is. However, there can be more if the owner is contractually obligated to cover more. Some condos have plumbing or electricity in the contract, which would be outside the dry-wall. If it is in the contract, the HO-6 can provide coverage.*

	Section I – Property & Theft				Section II - Liability	
	Coverage A Dwelling	Coverage B Other Structures	Coverage C Personal Property	Coverage D Loss of Use	Coverage E Liability	Coverage F Med Pay
HO-1 / HO-8 Basic/Mod.	Primary Basic *Market*	Basic *Market*	Basic *ACV*	Indirect Financial in nature Triggered by a covered peril 1. Add. Living Expense 2. Fair Rental 3. Civil Authority		
HO-2 Broad	Primary Broad *Rep.*	Broad *Rep.*	Broad *ACV*			
HO-3 Special	Primary All Risk *Rep.*	All Risk *Rep.*	Broad *ACV*			
HO-4 Tenants			Primary Broad *ACV*			
HO-5 Comp.	Primary All Risk *Rep.*	All Risk *Rep*	All Risk *ACV*			
HO-6 Condo	Broad *Rep.*		Primary Broad *ACV*			

Exclusions

Standard Exclusions

The exclusions listed in this section are seen on all Homeowner policies:

- Ordinance or law
- Pollutants
- Earth movement
- Earthquake
- Flood
- Sewer back up
- Sump pump discharge or overflow
- Freezing of plumbing – Covered if heat is maintained or pipes properly drained
- Off premises power failure
- Neglect
- Intentional loss
- War
- Nuclear hazard
- Vandalism, glass breakage, and water damage to a home vacant over 60 days

Open Peril/All Risk Exclusions

The exclusions listed in this section are seen on Homeowner policies with Open Peril/All Risk:

- Freezing of patios, decks, or fencing
- Theft to a dwelling under construction
- Mold, fungus or wet rot

- Wear and tear
- Mechanical breakdown, defect, or inherent vice
- Pollutants
- Settling of patios, pavements, foundations, or structures
- Birds, rodents or insects
- Animals owned by the insured, pets

Concurrent Causation is normally excluded. This is when an excluded event occurs and leads to a covered peril. For example, an earthquake occurs and leads to a fire. In that instance, the earthquake and fire both will be excluded.

Conditions

- **Deductible** – The minimum deductible of any Homeowners Policy is $250
- **Duties After Loss** – The insured must give prompt notice, notify police if necessary, and protect the property from further damage.
- **Loss to a Pair or Set** – The insurer will either repair/replace the damaged piece of the set or pay the value of the set before the loss minus the value of the set after the loss. If Jill had two ear rings worth $1,000 prior to the fire and was only able to salvage one from the fire, what was the value of Jill's loss? Since the individual pieces of a set are worth less than the full value of the set, Jill may find that the remaining ear ring is only worth $300 on its own. In this case, Jill lost $700.
- **No Benefit to Bailee** – The Bailee will receive coverage for the property in his/her care, custody, and control but the payment will go to the Bailor.
- **Recovered Property** – If any property is found after a claim has been filed for the loss, the other party must be notified and the claim amount will be adjusted. If Jill later found the second ear ring and discovered that it had not been damaged in the fire, she would be expected to notify the company. The insurer would either salvage the piece or adjust the claim.
- **Volcanic Eruption Period** – Any volcanic eruptions occurring within a 72-hour period will be considered as one volcanic eruption. This only covers eruptions above ground. Earthquakes and land shocks will be excluded.
- **Concealment or Fraud** – Any intentionally concealed, misrepresented, or fraudulent conduct concerning a claim will prevent coverage for the insured.

- **Cancellation** – Cancellation made by the insured will be given in a short rate manner, cancellation made by the insurer will be given in a pro rata manner.
- **Subrogation** – The insured waives the right of recovery against any person before a loss.

Section II – Liability Coverage

Section II of the Homeowners policy deals with **liability** insurance. Liability insurance is defined as the **financial loss of the insured when the insured damages someone or someone else's property**. This is a **third-party contract.** The three parties consist of the insurer, insured, and the third party which has had either bodily injury or property damage. When the insured is obligated to pay due to damages toward another party, the liability insurance will pay. It is designed to help the insured when faced with a lawsuit or the potential of a lawsuit.

Liability Coverage E and Coverage F is the same in all Homeowners policies.

Section II - Liability

- Coverage E - Liability
- Coverage F - Medical Payments

Coverage E – Personal Liability

Personal liability will cover claims if an agreement is made by settling outside of court or if a lawsuit is brought against the insured and the insured is found to be at fault. Compensatory damages caused by **bodily injury** or **property damages** will be covered by the insurer, up to the limit of liability. The insurer will pay and provide a defense for the insured when a lawsuit is brought against the insured, even if the lawsuit is groundless, false, or fraudulent.

Coverage E, Personal Liability, is third-party insurance. It will pay for bodily injury and property damage if the insured is at fault or negligent for the damage done to the third party. All Homeowners Policies will allow a **$100,000 occurrence limit**. This limit can be raised, if the insured needs more coverage. Coverage E will cover the liability resulting from damage caused by insureds, pets, covered property, and resident employees. Examples would include a dog that bites a neighbor, a tree that falls on the neighbors garage, or the gardener throws a rock and hits a neighbor while mowing your lawn.

The insureds are the ones covered by the policy. They could be the **named insured**, a **relative residing** in the household of the named insured, or one who is a dependent of the named insured but not family and **under the age of 21**. Any of the insureds could cause damage and be liable for the damage. The **pets** of the named insured or the property itself could also cause damage to a third party. This would be like a dog biting a guest or a friend falling down the stairs. A **resident employee** is one the insured has hired to work on the covered property, such as a lawn care company. Since the insured brought the resident employee to the covered property, the insured may be held liable to some degree if the resident employee causes damage.

	Section I – Property & Theft				Section II - Liability	
	Coverage A Dwelling	Coverage B Other Structures	Coverage C Personal Property	Coverage D Loss of Use	Coverage E Liability	Coverage F Med Pay
HO-1 / HO-8 Basic/Mod.	Primary Basic *Market*	Basic *Market*	Basic *ACV*	Indirect Financial in nature Triggered by a covered peril 1. Add. Living Expense 2. Fair Rental 3. Civil Authority	3rd Party Negligent Fault BI & PD $100,000 Results from Insureds, Pets, or Covered Property	
HO-2 Broad	Primary Broad *Rep.*	Broad *Rep.*	Broad *ACV*			
HO-3 Special	Primary All Risk *Rep.*	All Risk *Rep.*	Broad *ACV*			
HO-4 Tenants			Primary Broad *ACV*			
HO-5 Comp.	Primary All Risk *Rep.*	All Risk *Rep*	All Risk *ACV*			
HO-6 Condo	Broad *Rep.*		Primary Broad *ACV*			

COVERAGE F – MEDICAL PAYMENTS

Medical Payments will be paid to the injured third party when bodily injury occurs, **whether or not negligence is established**, and if an insured, pet, covered property or resident employee caused the damage. This is a preventive measure intended to avoid a lawsuit. However, if the Medical Payments does not fully compensate the third party, the third party could sue for further compensation if they choose. In that case, Coverage E will pay minus what has already been paid out by Medical Payments.

For the third party to collect Medical Payments, Medical Payments claims must be filed within 3 years. Medical Payments cannot be given out to trespassers. A trespasser is someone who is on the property uninvited. The reason for this is simple. More than likely the trespasser will be at fault for their own injuries, not the insured, if they come onto the insured's property uninvited and get hurt. Therefore, the insurer does not want to be preventive if, more than likely, there will not be anything to prevent.

Note: If a trespasser does sue the insured and win the case Coverage E – Personal Liability will pay the claim.

<table>
<tr><th></th><th colspan="4">Section I – Property & Theft</th><th colspan="2">Section II - Liability</th></tr>
<tr><th></th><th>Coverage A
Dwelling</th><th>Coverage B
Other Structures</th><th>Coverage C
Personal Property</th><th>Coverage D
Loss of Use</th><th>Coverage E
Liability</th><th>Coverage F
Med Pay</th></tr>
<tr><td>HO-1 / HO-8
Basic/Mod.</td><td>Primary
Basic
Market</td><td>Basic
Market</td><td>Basic
ACV</td><td rowspan="6">Indirect

Financial in nature

Triggered by a covered peril

1. Add. Living Expense

2. Fair Rental

3. Civil Authority</td><td rowspan="6">3rd Party

Negligent

Fault

BI & PD

$100,000

Results from Insureds, Pets, or Covered Property</td><td rowspan="6">3rd Party

No Fault

Proactive

Preventive

$1,000

3 years

No trespasser

Results from Insureds, Pets, or Covered Property</td></tr>
<tr><td>HO-2
Broad</td><td>Primary
Broad
Rep.</td><td>Broad
Rep.</td><td>Broad
ACV</td></tr>
<tr><td>HO-3
Special</td><td>Primary
All Risk
Rep.</td><td>All Risk
Rep.</td><td>Broad
ACV</td></tr>
<tr><td>HO-4
Tenants</td><td></td><td></td><td>Primary
Broad
ACV</td></tr>
<tr><td>HO-5
Comp.</td><td>Primary
All Risk
Rep.</td><td>All Risk
Rep</td><td>All Risk
ACV</td></tr>
<tr><td>HO-6
Condo</td><td>Broad
Rep.</td><td></td><td>Primary
Broad
ACV</td></tr>
</table>

DAMAGE TO RENTED PREMISES COVERAGE

Fire Legal Liability pays when one **negligently causes fire damage to a dwelling or structure in their care, custody, and control**.

Normally, if personal property is in the care, custody, and control of the insured and owned by a third party, then it is excluded under liability policies and covered by property policies under Coverage C. Negligent fire damage to a **rented dwelling or structure** is treated differently because the structure does not fit under Coverage C. Fire Legal Liability would take precedence if it was a rented home, apartment, hotel room or other structures in the insured's care, custody, and control.

Note: In the HO-4, renter's policy, there is no available property damage for the dwelling of the structure since the insured (renter) has no insurable interest in the home. Therefore, Section I cannot take precedence over liability coverage because there is no property coverage for the dwelling. Care, custody, and control are excluded under liability; therefore, Fire Legal Liability had to be created to fill in the gap.

Exclusions for Section II

- Motor Vehicles – *unless* they are in storage on the insured location, solely used to service the residence, designed to assist the handicapped, or for recreational use off public roads.
- Watercrafts –under 26 feet in length, or 25 horsepower or less. Over 26 feet or 25 horsepower if rented or borrowed
- Intentional Acts – ***unless*** committed by an insured under the **age of accountability.**
- Aircrafts/Hovercrafts
- Professional Liability
- Business Pursuits
- Insured's Own Property or Bodily Injury
- War
- Workers Compensation Loses
- Drones (Remote Controlled Aircraft)

Note: The insured's own property damage and bodily injury are not covered under liability because it is 3rd party insurance. The insured's property damage will be covered under Section I – Property and the insured's bodily injury can be covered by his/her health insurance..

Additional Coverages (Supplementary Coverages)

No matter which line of insurance is being looked at, **all additional coverages are free, automatic, over and above**. For Section II – Liability of Homeowners policies claim expenses, legal defenses, first aid expenses, damage to property of others, and loss assessments are in the policy as additional coverages for the insured.

Claim Expenses/Legal Defense

The insurer will pay for the legal defense and fees, regardless if the insured is at fault or not. Since the defense will be paid regardless of fault, this is a no fault benefit.

When the insurer pays for legal defense and fees, they will provide a defense for the insured. Below are some of the defenses used in a liability policy:

- Comparative Fault
- Assumption of Risk
- Intervening Cause
- Statute of Limitations
- Contributory Negligence

Note: The five listed legal defenses are defined in more depth in Chapter 4, Basics of Third Party Coverage.

Due to a loss of earnings, the insurer will pay the insured up to **$250 per day** for assisting in the investigation or defense.

First Aid

Expenses incurred for first aid given to the injured third party will be covered, if the injury occurred due to the insured or insured's property. First aid will not be covered if it is the insured who received the care.

Damage to Property of Others

$5,000 may be used as a preventive measure in attempts to keep the third party from seeking further compensation through a lawsuit. This is very similar to Coverage F – Medical Payments. **The difference is that Damage to Property of Others will pay for damaged property, whereas Medical Payments will pay for bodily injury**.

Homeowners Policy Endorsements

- Incidental Occupancies – Liability coverage for a business you **own**. This may be an in home dance studio, hair station, or office if owned by the insured.
- Business Pursuits – Liability coverage for a business you **do not own**. This may be a salesperson, collector, or other occupation if the insured is an employee working from home and does not have ownership.
- Home Day Care – Liability coverage for a day care. Premiums are based on caring for three children that are not your own. The endorsement can cover more children, but the premiums will increase if there are more than three.

- Personal Injury – Liability coverage due to the insured's defamation and slander of a third party.

- Drone (Remote Controlled Aircraft)

- Earthquake – Extension of Coverages A, B, and C for property damage resulting from earthquakes and land shocks. A single occurrence includes all quakes within a **72 hour** timeframe. This is a separate deductible that is based off a percentage of the primary coverage.

- Water Back Up and Sump Discharge or Overflow – Adds property coverage back into the policy to cover the back up of sewers, drains or sump pump overflow. If damage was caused due to the insured's negligence, coverage will not apply.

- Personal Property Replacement Cost – Upgrade of Coverage C- Personal Property, from actual cash value to replacement cost.

- Scheduled Personal Property – Allows an item to be covered at agreed value with no deductible and covered on an all risk basis.

- Watercraft – Boatowners Policies may be bundled to the Homeowners Policy instead of a separate policy.

- Inflation Guard – Replacement cost increases over time as the cost of construction increases.

- Mobile Homes – Mobile homes may be covered if fixed to a foundation or tied down. The coverage for the dwelling will be given as **actual cash value**, not replacement cost.

The Dwelling Policy

Dwelling Policy	Homeowners Policy
• Property only • Own it • Ideal for landlords	• Property, Theft, Liability • Own it, Live in it • Ideal for family home

The Dwelling Policy is a simplistic and smaller policy compared to the Homeowners Policy. It is only meant to give coverage for **property insurance**. Therefore, the

Dwelling Policy **does not have liability** coverage automatically built into it. This makes the Dwelling Policy very similar to just Section I – Property of the Homeowners Policy. However, the Dwelling Policy **does not automatically include the theft peril** like the Homeowners Policy.

To have a Dwelling Policy, it is not required for the insured to live in the home. They must have insurable interest in the home, so they must own the home. The only exception is the Dwelling Policy for renters. If a renter purchases a Dwelling Policy, they must have insurable interest in their personal property, but not the home. Since it is not required to live in the home to obtain a Dwelling Policy, it is a very good policy for landlords.

Note: Liability and theft can be added by endorsement.

Policy Forms

DP – 1 (Basic Form)

Fire, Lightning & Explosion

DP – 2 (Broad Form)

Fire & Lightning

Extended Coverages

- Riot
- Explosion
- Vehicles
- Civil Commotion
- Smoke
- Hail
- Aircraft
- Windstorm
- Volcano

Vandalism and Malicious Mischief

W. I. F.

- Weight of Ice, Snow or Sleet
- Intentional Water
- Falling Objects

DP – 3 (Special Form)

Perils follow the HO-3

- Open Peril/All Risk for the dwelling and other structures
- Broad Coverage for Personal Property

DP – 4 (Tenant's Form)

Primary Coverage is on Personal Property

- No coverage will be given for the dwelling since the tenant has no insurable interest in the dwelling

Coverages

Coverage A - Dwelling

Coverage B - Other Stuctures

Coverage C - Personal Property

Coverage D - Fair Rental Value

Coverage E - Additional Living Expense

- Only Available for the DP-2 and the DP-3

Terms to know

HO- 1 Basic Form

HO-2 Broad Form

HO-3 Special Form

HO-4 Tenant Form

HO-5 Comprehensive Form

HO-6 Condominium Unit Owner Form

HO-8 Modified Coverage Form

Incidental business

Section I- Property

Coverage A- Dwelling

Primary coverage

Coverage B- Other Structures

Coverage C- Personal Property

Personal articles floater

Coverage D- Loss of use

Reasonable repairs

Property removed

Loss assessment

Ordinance or law

Collapse

Basic Form Perils

Broad Form Perils

Special- Open Peril/ All Risk

Inherent vice

Loss to a Pair or Set

No Benefit to the Bailee

Section II- Liability

Coverage E- Personal Liability

Resident employee

Coverage F- Medical Payments

Damage to Rented Premises Liability

Damage to Property of Others

Business pursuits

Home day care

Personal injury

Earthquake

Water Back Up/ Sump Pump Discharge

Personal Property Replacement Cost

Scheduled Personal Property

Inflation guard

The Dwelling Policy

DP- 1 Basic

DP-2 Broad

DP-3 Special

DP4- Tenant's form

Numbers to know

Homeowners Chart

HO- 1 Basic Form

HO-2 Broad Form

HO-3 Special Form

HO-4 Tenant Form

HO-5 Comprehensive Form

HO-6 Condominium Unit Owner Form

HO-8 Modified Coverage Form

4 units

Insured- under 21 years old

Section I- Property

Section II- Liability

Coverage B- Limit is 10% of A

Property off premises - 10% of Coverage C or $1,000, whichever is greater

Ordinance or law- 10% of A

80% Co-insurance

HO-6- Replacement cost $1,000 for Coverage A

Exclusion- Vandalism, glass breakage, water damage- if vacant over 60 days

Minimum deductible - $250

Volcanic eruption- 72 hours

Covearge E- Personal Liability $100,000 occurrence

Coverage F- Medical Payments $1,000, 3 years

Watercraft- included if under 26 feet, or 25hp or less

Age of accountability- 13 years old

Earthquake- 72 hours

DP 1- Basic

DP-2 Broad

DP-3 Special

DP-4 Tenant's form

Practice Exam

1. Jim rents a two bedroom apartment. Which type of form does Jim need since he is a renter?
   a) HO-3
   b) HO-4
   c) HO-5
   d) HO-6
2. Sue owns her own condo. Which type of form fits Sue's needs as a condo unit owner?
   a) HO-3
   b) HO-4
   c) HO-5
   d) HO-6
3. A dwelling can have up to ___ units and still qualify as a personal policy.
   a) 2
   b) 4
   c) 6
   d) 8
4. Who is NOT an insured?
   a. Joe's daughter who lives in a college dorm
   b. Joe's father-in-law who lives in Joe's basement
   c. A 20 year old college student staying for the summer
   d. A 2 year old foster child that Joe has had for one month
5. On the Homeowners policy, Section I is __________ and Section II is ________.
   a) Property, Liability
   b) Property, Personal
   c) Personal, Casualty
   d) Personal, Commercial

6. Under Section I, Coverage A provides coverage for the dwelling. Which of the following statements is FALSE about Coverage A?
   a) An attached garage is covered
   b) Permanently installed fixtures are covered
   c) Land is covered
   d) Covers structures attached to the dwelling
7. Coverage B provides protection for Other Structures. Which of the following statements is FALSE about Coverage B?
   a) The limit is automatically 10% of Coverage A
   b) Land is excluded
   c) Coverage is provided for a detached garage
   d) Includes coverage for a structure being used for business purposes
8. Coverage C provides coverage for:
   a) Medical payments
   b) Other structures
   c) Personal property
   d) Loss of use
9. Which of the following statements is FALSE about Coverage C? Coverage C provides coverage for……
   a) Personal property worldwide
   b) Watercraft over 26 feet
   c) Theft protection
   d) Business personal property used on residence premises
10. The Personal Articles Floater is a separate policy. Which of the following characteristics is FALSE?
    a) There is no deductible
    b) Agreed value is used
    c) Open peril coverage
    d) Provides blanket coverage
11. The limit of liability on Coverage B is automatically:
    a) 10% of A
    b) 10% of C
    c) $1,000
    d) 20% of A

12. Coverage D is Loss of Use. Which of the following characteristics describes Coverage D?

    a) Direct loss
    b) Physical loss
    c) Indirect loss
    d) Coverage D is only available to condo owners

13. The additional coverages under Section I of the policy include:

    a) Sump pump discharge
    b) Off premises power failure
    c) Defense
    d) Fire department service

14. Which of the following is excluded under the Homeowners forms:

    a) Glass breakage if vacant over 60 days
    b) Watercraft liability
    c) Property off premises
    d) Landlord furnishings

15. Which form is unique in that it uses Open Peril coverage only on Coverage A and B?

    a) HO-2
    b) HO-3
    c) HO-5
    d) HO-8

16. The HO-2 Broad Form uses _______ for Coverage A and B and __________ for Coverage C.

    a) Replacement Cost, Actual Cash Value
    b) Actual Cash Value, Replacement Cost
    c) Fair Market Value, Actual Cash Value
    d) Fair Market Value, Replacement Cost

17. Volcanic eruption within __ hours is considered one volcanic eruption.

    a) 148
    b) 72
    c) 75
    d) 48

18. Which of the following perils is not a part of Extended Coverages?

    a) Volcano
    b) Vandalism
    c) Wind
    d) Vehicles

19. Which of the following perils is only included on the Broad Form?

    a) Falling objects
    b) Theft
    c) Fire
    d) Volcano

20. Which of the following covers the residence with the Basic Form?

    a) HO-3
    b) HO-5
    c) HO-6
    d) HO1/HO8

21. Gina has an HO-4. What type of coverage is used on Coverage C and D for the HO-4?

    a) Basic
    b) Broad
    c) Special
    d) Coverage C and D is excluded on HO-4

22. Which of the following uses Open Peril for Coverages A, B, C, and D?

    a) HO-3
    b) HO-4
    c) HO-5
    d) HO-6

23. The HO- 6 form uses ______ form for Coverages A, C, and D and uses ________ for Coverage A.

    a) Broad, ACV
    b) All Risk, Replacement Cost
    c) Broad, Replacement Cost
    d) All Risk, ACV

24. The HO- 6 provides _______ valuation for Coverage C.

   a) ACV
   b) Replacement Cost
   c) Fair market value
   d) Agreed value

25. Under Section II, Coverage E is _______ and Coverage F is ________.

   a) Personal, Commercial
   b) Personal Liability, Medical Payments
   c) Personal Property, Medical Payments
   d) Medical Payments, Personal Liability

26. Which of the following about Coverage E is FALSE?

   a) Pets are excluded
   b) BI and PD are covered
   c) $100,000 limit, but it can be raised
   d) Resident employees are included

27. Coverage F provides protection for?

   a) Umbrella
   b) Dwelling
   c) Personal Property
   d) Medical Payments

28. Which of the following is NOT TRUE concerning Coverage F?

   a) Negligence must be established
   b) Must be within 3 years
   c) Limit is $1,000
   d) Excludes trespassers

29. What is the age of accountability?

   a) 13
   b) 15
   c) 16
   d) 18

30. The Homeowners policy contains Additional Coverages. Which of the following is FALSE about these Additional Coverages?

    a) For loss of earnings, the insurer pays up to $250
    b) Pays above the limit of liability
    c) Free and automatic
    d) Pays legal defense only if the insured is at fault

31. Jay has an endorsement on his policy that allows Replacement Cost to increase over time as the cost of construction increases. What is this endorsement called?

    a) Incidental Occupancies
    b) Personal Injury
    c) Inflation guard
    d) Personal Property Replacement Cost

32. Which two policies do not have coverage for Coverage A and B?

    a) HO-3 and HO-5
    b) HO-4 and HO-6
    c) HO-4 and HO-5
    d) HO-5 and HO-6

33. Joe owns his own condo. Which of the following statements is FALSE?

    a) The condo association owns the complex
    b) Joe only has insurable interest in his unit
    c) Joe is not a renter
    d) The condo association owns Joe's unit

34. If Joe has a $300,000 limit for Coverage A, how much coverage is available for Coverage B?

    a) $30,000
    b) $1,000
    c) $10,000
    d) $300,000

35. If Joe's son Alec lives in a college dorm, Alec's personal property is covered under the other residences section of which coverage?

    a) Coverage A
    b) Coverage B
    c) Coverage C
    d) Coverage D

36. Watercraft is covered if::

    a) Over 26 feet and owned
    b) Over 26 feet or 25 horsepower
    c) Under 26 feet or 50 horsepower
    d) Under 26 feet or 25 horsepower

37. Julie's home is broken into and several items have been stolen. Which areas have limited theft coverage?

    a) Personal property
    b) Jewelry, firearms and silverware
    c) Collectables jewelry
    d) Theft is covered the same as other perils

38. If Julie wanted to properly insure her diamond and ruby necklace, it could be covered by:

    a) Blanket coverage
    b) Personal Articles Floater
    c) Coverage D
    d) Jewelry endorsement

39. The Dwelling Policy gives coverage for:

    a) Only property insurance
    b) Basic perils
    c) Property and casualty
    d) Liability only

40. The DP is similar to Section I of the Homeowners policy, however one difference is the _____ peril is not automatically included on the DP.

    a) Earthquake
    b) Fire
    c) Theft
    d) Vandalism

Answer key: 1,b 2,d 3,b 4,c 5,a 6,c 7,d 8,c 9,b 10,d 11,a 12,c 13,d 14,a 15,b 16,a 17,b 18,b 19,a 20,d 21,b 22,c 23,c 24,a 25,b 26,a 27,d 28,a 29,a 30,d 31,c 32,b 33,d 34,a 35,c 36,d 37,b 38,b 39,a 40,c

Chapter

6

Personal Auto Policy

Of all the products provided by the insurance industry, the personal auto policy (PAP) is the most used product that is purchased. Auto accidents are not unusual and the automobile itself has the potential to do devastating damage. Today's driver assumes much responsibility when he/she drives on the road. The personal auto policy is designed to meet the many needs of the road.

Who and What Can be Insured?

The Personal Auto Policy is designed to meet the needs of most everyday drivers. The policy can be written to cover a multiple of private passenger automobiles. The Personal Auto Policy can be used to cover:

- **Cars with at least 4 wheels** - A vehicle with **less than 4 wheels would not be automatically covered** by the Personal Auto Policy. Motorcycles and 3 wheeled vehicles can be covered by endorsement. Also keep in mind that this is a Personal Auto Policy, with emphasis on the word personal. An auto that is used as a public or livery conveyance (taxicabs or limousines) would not be eligible for coverage.

- **Pickup trucks and vans** – The vehicle is covered on the PAP as long as the vehicle has a gross vehicle weight of **10,000 pounds or less** and it is not being used for delivery or transportation of goods for a business. An exception to the delivery and transportation limitation would be if it is incidental to farming, ranching or used in the named insured's business of installing, maintaining or repairing.

- **Trailers** used with the private passenger auto, pickup or van – Liability coverage on a trailer used with the covered vehicle is automatically included

Note: ***Miscellaneous Type Vehicle Endorsement*** *can be added to cover vehicles with less than 4 wheels (motorcycles) or vehicles with GVW of over 10,000 pounds (motor home).*

The Declaration Page

The declaration page includes the detailed information concerning the policy purchased. It includes the "who, what, where and how much." In particular, it will include:

- A description of the vehicle including the year, make, model and serial number of the car.
- Garaging territory – A description of where the car is kept or where it will be parked.
- Classification code – This is based upon the age, gender and marital status of the automobile's operator.
- Limits and the coverages included – Liability coverage is usually required by law to maintain financial responsibility. Other coverages are optional and may or may not be included.
- Policy period and applicable premium

Definitions

The following are some of the definitions within the Personal Auto Policy:

Named Insured – The insured that is specifically named on the declaration page. Typically, the named insured is the head of the household. The spouse may be listed. If not, the spouse and children could still have coverage provided by definition.

Family Members - Includes a person related to the named insured by blood, marriage or adoption and at the same time is a **resident** of the insured's household. This could include the named insured's spouse, children, mother and father- in- law. It also includes a **ward** or **foster** child. But do not forget, **not only must they be a family member to be insured, they must also reside in the household**. If Jane's mother- in-law sells her house and moves into Jane's house to stay, she is now a family member by definition. If Jane's son moves out into his own home, he is no longer family according to this definition.

Occupying – According to the auto policy, occupying includes someone in, upon, getting in, getting on, getting out or getting off of the covered auto. An insured is covered while occupying the covered auto.

Covered Auto – This is an important term in the policy; this term determines if coverage will exist or not in a given situation. Covered auto means:

- Any vehicle listed in the **Declarations**
- A newly **acquired auto**, this could include either an:
    - **Additional auto** – For all coverage except physical damage, coverage will be provided as long as it is requested within 14 days after becoming the owner. Physical damage (collision or other than collision) will apply if coverage is applied to at least one other auto. Physical damage must also be requested by the insured in order for coverage to apply. If the coverage did not exist on the other existing autos, then 4 days of coverage will apply with a $500 deductible.
    - **Replacement auto** – Liability will be automatic, without having to ask for it. Physical damage (collision or other than collision) will apply if coverage applied to at least one other auto. Physical damage must also be requested for coverage to apply. If coverage did not exist on the other autos, then 4 days of coverage will apply with a $500 deductible.
- **Trailer** – A trailer is defined as a vehicle designed to be pulled by a private passenger auto, pickup or van.
- **Temporary substitute** – This is a vehicle or trailer that is being used because the insured's vehicle is out of normal use due to:

Note: *Temporary substitute does not apply to coverage for physical damage.*

- Breakdown;
- Repair;
- Servicing;
- Loss; or
- Destruction.

Non-owned Auto – A non-owned auto is a vehicle that belongs to another. An example might be a company car or you might be driving the neighbors' car.

Hired Auto – One that you have paid for to drive, a leased or rented auto.

Contents of the Personal Auto Policy

The PAP consists of the following sections:

Part A – Liability

Part B - Medical Payments

Part C – Uninsured Motorists Coverage

Part D – Coverage for Damage to Your Auto (physical damage)

Part E – Duties after an Accident or Loss

Part F – General Provisions

Coverage A – Liability

When driving on today's roads, each driver has much responsibility to the other drivers, pedestrians and their property. The liability coverage of the PAP is designed to provide third party coverage to help meet this responsibility.

Financial Responsibility

States require drivers to show that they can meet minimum financial responsibility to other drivers in order to be licensed to drive on the roads. The most common way that a driver can show that this responsibility is being met is with insurance. In some states, the only way to meet this requirement is with insurance.

Split Limits

A split limit policy is one that uses three different numbers to represent three separate limits. For example, Indiana and Kentucky have a state minimum for split limit plans set at 25/50/25. Each state has a legal requirement for drivers to hold auto insurance, but each state sets their own minimum limit and may vary from state to state. Look in the state law manual to verify what the state minimum limit is for other states. The purpose of this section is to determine what each number represents and how the work together.

The **first number (25)** represents the limit in the thousands for **bodily injury per person**. If Mary had an at-fault accident and did $30,000 worth of bodily injury to the other driver, this policy would only pay up to $25,000 for the other driver's bodily injury. Anything over this amount, Mary will be responsible for. In this example, we can see that Mary did not have adequate insurance limits. She is responsible for $5,000 of the damages.

The **second number (50)** represents the limit in the thousands for **bodily injury per accident.** If Mary hit the other car and it had multiple passengers, then this number would come into play. Let's say that the above driver had two other passengers riding in their car at the time of the accident. Total bodily injury is:

- $30,000 for the driver
- $15,000 for the first passenger
- $5,000 for the second passenger

Mary's policy would first pay based upon the first number (25). The policy will pay up to $25,000 in bodily injury per person. That would be:

- $25,000 for the driver ($30,000)
- $15,000 for the first passenger ($15,000)
- $5,000 for the second ($5,000)

When we add the bodily injury damages together, it totals $45,000. The second number in Mary's policy now comes into play. For all bodily injury in the accident, the policy will pay no more than $50,000. Since Mary is within the $50,000 limit, all passengers should be covered.

Note: Watch out always look at the first number first. If you move to the second without considering the first, you will miss the answer. Notice that even though there is a total of $50,000 worth of damage, the policy is not paying $50,000.

The **third number (25)** represents the limit for **property damage** in the thousands. Mary not only injured three people, she is also responsible for the physical damage done to the other car. The total damage done was $15,000. Since Mary's limit is $25,000 the policy will fully cover this damage. If property damage had exceeded $25,000, then Mary's policy would only pay up to its limit.

Remember, 25/50/25 is just an example. Limits could be 100/300/100 or 200/500/200. Our example uses a common limit that several states use as a minimum requirement. Just because an insured meets minimal limits does not mean that he/she is adequately insured.

SINGLE LIMITS

Some insurance companies use a single limit instead of a split limit in their policies. A single limit policy will use only **one limit for all bodily injury and property damage**. All damages come from this one limit. If Mary carried a single limit policy of $75,000, how would her policy have paid? In the above example, the insurer would have added the damages together ($30,000 BI + $15,000 BI + $5,000 BI + $15,000 PD = $65,000 total liability). Since the single limit is $75,000, $65,000 will be paid. The split limit would have only paid $60,000 in total ($5,000 of the driver's bodily injury would not be paid by the policy and is Mary's responsibility).

COMPARABLE POLICIES

If a client carried a split limit policy of 100/300/100 and wanted to switch to a comparable single limit policy, how much should the agent recommend? Since the most that the 100/300/100 policy could pay in a single accident is $300,000 in BI and $100,000 in property damage, a comparable single limit policy would be $400,000. There is no way to accurately compare them. It is like comparing apples with oranges. This is considered to be the most practical way to compare the two.

EXTRA EXAMPLE

If Joe carried 100/300/100 and was responsible for an accident resulting in the following damages:

- $50,000 in BI to the other driver
- $110,000 in BI to a passenger
- $40,000 in property damage

How much would the policy pay?

The policy would pay a total of $190,000. Remember, no more than $100,000 in bodily injury per person. What if the test question added that Joe's accident also created another $40,000 in legal expenses? **Legal expenses will be paid over and above the limits of the policy.** If we add in legal expenses, the total payout would be $230,000.

OUT OF STATE COVERAGE

If Joe has met the financial responsibility requirements in his home state or the state in which the vehicle is garaged, then coverage will be provided in each state. That means that if Joe meets the requirements for Indiana (25/50/25), when he travels to Maine, he will also meet their minimum required limits (50/100/25). It also means that if he travels to a state that has a no fault requirement, his policy will comply with that state's requirements.

Defense

Defense is always one of the most important coverages under liability. Defense is covered as long as there is a possibility of coverage under the policy. If it is determined that the damage will not be covered by the policy, then defense ends if a suit has already begun or it may never begin. When defense is paid, it is paid in addition to the liability limits of the policy.

Since the insurer is responsible for the defense expense, then they get to settle or defend as they consider appropriate. Defense also ends when limits of liability has been exhausted. It will be the responsibility of the insurer to defend to the best of their ability and in a fair and proper manner.

Who is Insured?

Under the liability section of the policy, the insured is defined to include:

- **You** or any **family member** for the ownership, maintenance or use of **any auto or trailer.**

- Any person **using your covered auto**

- Any person or organization using your covered auto, but only with respect to legal responsibility for acts of a person for whom coverage is afforded under this part of the policy.

Notice in the above definition, there could be the possibility of double coverage. For example, Matt loans his car to Mark and Mark has an accident in which he is at fault. Matt carries insurance that says that it covers "any person using his covered auto." Mark also carries his own auto insurance. His policy says that it will cover him for the "use of any auto." Thus both policies could provide coverage in this situation.

In this scenario. the policy will pay on a **primary/secondary or primary/excess** basis. This means that one policy will pay as if it were the only coverage available. If after it pays, there are still some uncovered expenses, then the second policy will pay up to its limits. Which policy pays first? Insurance is said to go with the auto. Since Matt put Mark on the road, Matt's insurance (the owner of the vehicle) will be primary and pay first.

Supplementary Payments

Supplementary payments are paid in addition to the liability limits. They include:

- Up to $250 for the cost of bail bonds required because of an accident, including related traffic law violations. The accident must result in BI or PD covered under this policy.

- Premiums on appeal bonds and bonds to release attachments in any suit the insurer defends.

- Interest accruing after a judgment is entered in any suit the insurer defends.

- Up to $200 per day for loss of earnings because of attendance at hearings or trials at the insurer's request.

- Other reasonable expenses incurred at the insurance company's request.

Liability Exclusions

- Intentional damage

- Property owned or transported by the insured

- Property rented, used by or in the care of the insured. This does not apply to damage to a residence or private garage.

- If it is business related, it will likely be excluded

    - Employees during the course of employment

    - Ownership or operation of a vehicle while being used as a public or livery conveyance. This does not apply to carpooling.

    - In the business of selling, repairing, storing or parking

- Using a vehicle without reasonable belief that the insured is entitled to do so. This does not apply to a family member using a covered auto.

- Any vehicle:

    - Less than 4 wheels

    - Designed to be used off public roads, except non owned golf carts

- Available for regular use and not a covered auto
- Used for racing

Part B – Medical Payments Coverage

The policy will pay reasonable expenses incurred for necessary medical and funeral services due to bodily injury. These expenses will be paid as long as they are rendered within **3 years** from the date of the accident.

The limit chosen here are per person per occurrence.

Who is Insured?

Since Medical Payments coverage is separate from liability, it is not limited to third party. Coverage under Part B applies to:

- **The insured or any family member** while occupying or **as a pedestrian** in an auto accident, and/or
- Passengers or any other person occupying the insured's covered auto.

This benefit will not pay in addition to anything paid in the liability section of the policy. A passenger is injured and receives $5,000 from medical payments. Later the passenger sues the driver/owner of the vehicle and wins a judgment of $20,000. $5,000 will be deducted from the judgment owed.

Part B, Exclusions

The exclusions are similar to those found in the liability section:

- Intentional damage
- If it is business related, it will likely be excluded
  - Employees during the course of employment
  - Ownership or operation of a vehicle while being used as a public or livery conveyance.
  - In the business of selling, repairing, storing or parking

- Using a vehicle without reasonable belief that the insured is entitled to do so.
- Any vehicle:
    - Less than 4 wheels
    - Available for regular use and not a covered auto
    - Used for racing

Part C – Uninsured/Underinsured Motorists

Anywhere from 10 – 20% of drivers in a given state may be driving without insurance. Even though the law requires financial responsibility, there are many who have found ways around the law. So what is the insured to do if he/she is hit by one of these drivers? Collecting from them personally may be impossible. Part C of the PAP is designed to pay the insured if they are damaged by an "at fault" uninsured driver.

Defining Uninsured

The PAP will define uninsured as any vehicle or trailer of any type:

- To which **no BI liability bond or policy applies** at the time of the accident.
- Which carries a limit **less than the financial responsibility** law of the state in which your covered auto is garaged.
- Which is **hit and run**. Most states allow coverage for **BI only for a hit and run**. Property damage may not be covered here because it could encourage fraud. If Matt and Mark are both wanting new vehicles, they could hit each other with their trucks and then file a claim under their own policies for a hit and run. This is fraud.
- Whose insurer **denies coverage or becomes insolvent**.

Uninsured **does not include any vehicle or equipment**:

- Owned or furnished for regular use of you or a family member.
- That meets self-insurance financial responsibility requirements.
- Owned or operated by any governmental agency.

- Operated on rails or crawler treads.
- Designed for public roads while not on public roads.
- While located for use as a residence or premises.

Uninsured Limits

Limits will be equal to the Part A – Liability limits. Part C will not duplicate any benefits paid under Part A or Part B of the policy. It also will not duplicate any underinsured benefits.

Underinsured Coverage

An underinsured driver is someone who has purchased enough auto liability insurance to meet state minimum limits, but it is not enough coverage to pay for the total damage that they are responsible for. **The driver is legal, but does not carry adequate coverage.**

Joe carries a split limit of 100/300/100. He is hit by another driver, Bob, and sustains $150,000 worth of BI. Bob only carries a limit of 25/50/25. Since Bob is the at-fault driver, his policy will pay first. There is only $25,000 BI available under his policy. **He is underinsured.** Joe will then file a claim under his policy. Since his limit is $100,000 for BI, he will only be able to collect up to this amount. Bob's company has paid $25,000, Joe's policy will pay another $75,000. Notice that Joe does not get $100,000. His coverage is brought up to the $100,000 amount.

Since the limit deducts the at-fault drivers limit, in a state with a minimum financial responsibility law of 25/50/25, the minimum amount for underinsured would be $50,000 for bodily injury. In order to collect something from your insurance, the limit must be higher than the minimum required under financial responsibility laws. Otherwise there would be nothing left to pay. Property damage may be offered or required at the discretion of the state or insurer.

Part D – Coverage for Damage to Your Auto (Physical Damage)

Part D is designed to pay for damage to the insured's auto when there is no one else to blame. It may be that the insured is responsible for the accident, fell asleep at the wheel or the car was damaged in a wind storm. Coverage is available for both "**collision**" and "**other than collision**." Physical Damage is not always included in a policy. If the coverage is chosen, the insured could include both collision and other than collision or one or the other. To have the coverage included in the policy, it must be listed on the Declaration Page.

Covered Auto

Part D is designed to provide protection for two different types of autos. Protection is provided for the "**covered auto,**" which was defined earlier in the unit. It also provides protection for the "**non-owned auto.**"

Non-Owned Auto means:

- Any private passenger auto, pickup, van or trailer not owned by or furnished or available for the regular use of insured or family members.

- Any auto or trailer you do not own while used as a temporary substitute.

Collision

Collision is defined as the **upset** of the covered auto or a non-owned auto. It also includes **impact** with another vehicle or object. Examples could include hitting a tree, running into another vehicle or falling asleep and overturning your car.

A **deductible** will apply before any payments are made under collision.

Other than Collision

Other than collision includes a variety of issues. It is an **all risk** type of coverage. **It would not cover anything considered under collision.** Whereas collision occurs while the car is moving and then strikes something, other than Collision may occur while the car is moving or sitting still. The car is under attack. Examples of other than collision include:

- Missiles or falling objects;

- Fire;

- **Theft** or larceny;

- Explosion or earthquake;

- Windstorm;

- Hail, water or **flood**;
- Malicious mischief or vandalism;
- Riot or civil commotion;
- **Contact with bird or animal**; or
- **Breakage of glass**.

Glass breakage is something that could happen as a result of a collision or as a result of Other than Collision. If it is caused by collision, the insured may elect to have it considered as a loss caused by collision. This would avoid paying two deductibles.

Note: Contact with bird or animal is always covered under Other than Collision. It may seem that you hit the deer, but always view it as the deer jumping out and catching you by surprise as it attacks your car.

A **deductible** will apply before any payments are made under Other than Collision.

Transportation Expense

Without the application of a deductible, the policy will provide up to **$600** for temporary transportation in the event of a loss to the covered auto. The policy will pay up to **$20** per day. This is an important coverage for Joe to have if he is involved in an accident that leaves his car unable to drive. The transportation expense coverage allows Joe to drive a rental while his car is being repaired.

Coverage begins after **24** hours. If the loss is due to theft, coverage will not begin until after **48** hours. Payment is then limited to the period of time reasonably required to repair or replace the vehicle.

Part D, Exclusions

Some of the more common exclusions include:

- Breakdown, road damage to tires, **wear and tear**;
- **Electronic equipment** that is not permanently installed;
- Tapes, records disks or other similar media;
- Customized equipment;

- Business issues like being used as a livery or selling, servicing and parking;
- Used without reasonable belief that the insured is entitled to do so.

Limit of Liability

Physical Damage will cover the vehicle on an actual cash value basis or the cost to repair/replace, whichever is less.

Part E Duties after an Accident or Loss

Part E is very similar to the other policies that we will discuss. It is the customer's responsibility to use reasonable means to protect the property from further damage and to work with the insurer during the processing of the claim. Duties include:

- Proper notification to the insurance company
- Cooperation with the investigation and defense;
- Promptly send copies of notices or legal papers connected with the claim;
- Submit to physicals and examination under oath if needed;
- Notify the police when appropriate (hit and run or theft)
- Protect the property from further harm;
- Allow the insurer to inspect and appraise the damaged property.

Part F Provisions

Many of the provisions under Part F have been discussed in earlier units. Provisions listed under Part F include:

- Bankruptcy – It does not resolve the company of responsibility
- Changes to the policy – Must be done properly through the insurance company
- Fraud

- Legal Action Against the Insurer
- The Insurer's Right to Recover Payment – Subrogation rights
- Policy Period and Territory – United States, its territories, Puerto Rico and Canada
- Termination and Nonrenewal – Establishes the days of notice required prior to termination
- Appraisal and Arbitration
- Other Insurances

Transportation Network Company Drivers

Definition

Transportation network company (TNC) is an entity that uses a digital network to connect individual riders to TNC drivers for compensation. TNC drivers then use their personal vehicles to provide prearranged rides. It does not include:

- A shared expense carpool or vanpool arrangement
- Use of a taxicab, limousine, or other for hire vehicle
- A regional transportation authority

The TNC driver is an independent contractor. The driver is not:

- A common carrier
- A contract carrier
- A motor carrier

Financial Responsibility and Other Driver Requirements

To be a TNC driver, certain guidelines and requirements must be met. In addition to a valid driver's license and a registered personal vehicle, applications must include the following:

- Proof of financial responsibility
- Criminal background check
- A search of the national sex offender registry
- Driving record

The financial responsibility requirement for the TNC driver differs depending on whether the driver is hauling a passenger or using the vehicle for their own personal use. *While driving for their own personal use the driver is required to carry a minimum of* **50/100/25**. *When using the vehicle to provide for compensated prearranged rides the driver must carry liability limits of at least one million dollars* (**$1,000,000**). This coverage can be provided by the TNC, the TNC driver or a combination of the two.

Proof of coverage must be maintained with the vehicle and available upon request by the interested parties, in the event of an accident. If an accident occurs the TNC shall provide upon request, the precise times that the driver has logged on and off. This must be provided for the twelve hours prior to the accident and 12 hours afterwards.

Since the TNC arrangement is basically a commercial scenario, an insurance company providing personal auto coverage, may exclude coverage under a TNC arrangement. Insurance that does cover the TNC driver must specifically state that the TNC arrangement is covered.

Driver Expectations and Responsibilities

It is the responsibility of the TNC to provide a safe and secure service for the passengers. As a result, the TNC must establish and enforce the following guidelines for their drivers:

- A zero-tolerance policy for drug and alcohol use

- Compliance with applicable vehicle requirements
- Motor vehicle insurance requirements
- Privacy policy
- Nondiscrimination policies
- Record maintenance guidelines

At the time that the rider arranges their ride, the TNC is required to display a photograph of the driver and the license plate number of the personal vehicle used. A TNC may not knowingly allow an individual to act as a TNC driver on their network, under any of the following conditions:

- Judgements for more than three moving violations or on violation involving reckless driving in the preceding three years
- Conviction of a felony or a misdemeanor involving:
    - Resisting law enforcement
    - Dishonesty
    - Injury to a person
    - Operating while intoxicated
    - Operating a vehicle in a manner that endangers a person
    - Operating a vehicle with a suspended or revoked license
    - Damage to the property of another person

In the preceding seven years:

- A match on the national sex offender registry
- Less than nineteen years of age

TNC Fare Requirements

Guidelines have been established concerning the fare charged the passenger. These guidelines are designed to protect the passenger and create secure procedures. Fares must be disclosed on the TNC digital network and publicized to the rider at the time of service. Estimates must be made available before the rider enters a personal vehicle.

TNC drivers may not solicit or accept cash payment from their passengers. Payments may only be made by electronic means using the TNC's digital network.

Auto Endorsements

An endorsement or rider is a change or addition to the original contract. The PAP has several endorsements available to the insured, some of them include:

TNC Drivers Endorsement

Provides legal limits for the driver of a transportation network company. When driving with a passenger for a fee the TNC driver must have at least $1,000,000 single limit. If driving on personal time, the TNC driver must have at least 50/100/25.

Extended Nonowner Coverage for Named Individuals

This endorsement gives permission for a named person to drive a nonowned auto. Joe drives a company car. Joe would like for his wife to be able to drive the car also. Since Joe does not own the vehicle, he does not have the authority to give his wife permission to drive the company car. The Extended Nonowner Coverage for Named Individuals endorsement could allow her to drive the car.

Miscellaneous Type Vehicle

The PAP excludes coverage on a vehicle with less than 4 wheels or over 10,000 pounds GVW. The Miscellaneous Type Vehicle endorsement provides coverage on these types of vehicles. . Motorcycles, 3 wheelers, and motorhomes are all provided coverage with this endorsement.

Towing and Labor

When an insured's vehicle is disabled and needs to be towed, jumpstarted, or otherwise serviced on the road, this endorsement pays for service. The base amount paid is $25 per disablement.

Rental Reimbursement

Reimburses the cost of using a rental vehicle while the declared auto is in the repair shop for a covered claim.

Terms to know

Who is an insured?

Family members

Occupying

Covered auto

Acquired auto

Additional auto

Replacement auto

Trailer

Temporary substitute

Split limits

Single limit

Out of state coverage

Uninsured motorist

Underinsured motorist

Part D Coverage for Damage to the Auto

Collision

Other than Collision

Non-owned auto

Extended Nonowner Coverage for Named Individual

Miscellaneous Type Vehicle

Transportation Network Companies

Towing and Labor

Numbers to know

Covered auto- 4 wheels/less than 10,000 lbs

Newly acquired- 4/14 days, $500 deductible

25/50/25 split limit

$75,000 single limit

Medical payments- 3 years

Transportation expenses- $600/ $20 per day

24 hours/ 48 hours for theft

Acronyms to know

PAP- Personal Auto Policy

BI- Bodily injury

PD- Property damage

GVW- Gross vehicle weight

DAARTT- Declarations, Acquired auto, Additional auto, Replacement auto, Trailer, Temporary substitute

UM- Uninsured

UIM- Underinsured

Practice Exam

1. Which of the following would be considered a hired auto:
   a) A leased vehicle
   b) A borrowed vehicle
   c) A temporary substitute
   d) A company car
2. Which of the following would not be an insured under Medical Payments?
   a) Insured as a pedestrian
   b) Passenger in the other vehicle
   c) Insured occupying another vehicle
   d) Passengers in a covered auto
3. Joe's truck is in the shop and is driving another vehicle while his truck is being repaired. This vehicle is called a:
   a) Temporary substitute
   b) Acquired auto
   c) Replacement auto
   d) Additional auto
4. Which of the following is Part A?
   a) Physical damage
   b) Uninsured
   c) Medical payments
   d) Liability
5. Which of the following provides coverage for collision and other than collision?
   a) Part A
   b) Part B
   c) Part C
   d) Part D
6. In a split limit, the second number is:
   a) The total BI and PD for the accident
   b) Property damage
   c) BI per accident
   d) BI per person

Use the following information for 7 -10

Joe carries: 25/50/25 and has an at fault accident with the following damages:

Driver BI= $10,000

1st Passenger BI= $30,000

2nd Passenger BI= $40,000

PD= $30,000

Legal defenses=$50,000

7. What is the most that Joe's policy could pay for the 2nd passenger's BI?
   a) $50,000
   b) $30,000
   c) $40,000
   d) $25,000
8. How much will Joe's policy pay for the total BI?
   a) $80,000
   b) $50,000
   c) $25,000
   d) $30,000
9. How much will the policy pay for legal defense?
   a) $50,000
   b) $30,000
   c) $25,000
   d) $40,000
10. How much will the policy pay for property damage?
    a) $30,000
    b) $10,000
    c) $25,000
    d) $20,000
11. A comparable single limit policy for a split limit of 250/500/200 is:
    a) $500,000
    b) $700,000
    c) $250,000
    d) $600,000

12. Who is NOT an insured?

    a) Joe's wife Laura
    b) Joe's son who is away at college
    c) Joe's mother staying with Laura during maternity leave
    d) Joe's foster son

13. Supplementary payments will pay up to ___ a day for loss of earnings

    a) $200
    b) $250
    c) $500
    d) $100

14. In order for a medical payments claim to be paid, it must be filed within __ year(s) of the accident.

    a) 1
    b) 2
    c) 3
    d) 4

15. Which is NOT a definition of uninsured?

    a) No insurance
    b) Insurer denies coverage
    c) Insurer becomes insolvent
    d) Legal limits, but not enough coverage for this accident

16. Under Part D, collision and other than collision definitions provide coverage for different perils. Which of the following is covered under collision?

    a) Theft
    b) Flood
    c) Car overturns
    d) Contact with an animal

17. Which of the following would qualify as a newly acquired auto?

    a) Trailer
    b) Replacement Auto
    c) Any vehicle listed in the Declarations
    d) Temporary substitute

18. If the insured's vehicle is stolen, the PAP will provide coverage for temporary transportation within __ hours.

    a) 48
    b) 24
    c) 40
    d) 22

19. Which endorsement provides coverage for a vehicle over 10,000 pounds?

    a) Towing and Labor
    b) Trailer and Camper
    c) Extended Nonowned Coverage
    d) Miscellaneous Type Vehicle

20. Joe is injured in an auto accident that is the fault of a driver. He has over $60,000 worth of medical bills. Which would be considered underinsured:

    a) The other driver carries 20/40/10
    b) The other driver has no insurance
    c) The other drivers insurance company has filed bankruptcy
    d) The other driver carries 50/100/25

21. A TNC driver will be required to carry:

    a) 25/50/25 personally and $1,000,000 with a passenger
    b) 50/100/25 personally and $1,000,000 with a passenger
    c) 25/50/25 personally and $5,000,000 with a passenger
    d) 50/100/25 personally and $5,000,000 with a passenger

22. A company providing personal auto insurance will:

    a) Be required to include coverage limits to a TNC driver
    b) Be required to add a TNC Drivers Endorsement to the PAP
    c) Be allowed to reject coverage under a TNC arrangement
    d) Be allowed to limit coverage under a TNC arrangement

Answer key: 1,a 2,b 3,a 4,d 5,d 6,c 7,d 8,b 9,a 10,c 11,b 12,c 13,a 14,c 15,d 16,c 17,b 18,a 19,d 20,d 21,b 22,c

Chapter

7

Miscellaneous Personal Policies

The homeowners and auto policies are two of the most commonly used and sold policies in our industry. The following policies in this chapter may not be as common, but they may be as important for those who have the need for these protections. This chapter will look at a few miscellaneous policies that are commonly needed in the personal market place.

Flood Insurance

Why Flood Insurance?

When our country was first settled, people crossed our country and began to establish cities. One of the primary means of transportation and moving goods at that time was through the waterways. Water is necessary to sustain life. At the time that our country was being established, it made sense to settle as close to the waterways as possible. Of course, this meant people were establishing in low lying areas. Today, most cities are next to waterways and in low lying areas, which are prone to flooding.

The insurance industry assumes risk for the insured. We defined risk as the chance of a loss. Cities built in low lying areas **will experience flood; it is not an uncertainty**. Insurance also is designed to spread risk. It is the many that pay for the few. Since the only people that would be interested in flood insurance are those living in flood zones, when a flood occurs, it affects large numbers of people and becomes a catastrophic event. As a result of this **adverse selection** and the catastrophic nature of the risk, flood is uninsurable for the insurance industry.

This creates a problem for the general public. There is a need for protection against flood, but the insurance industry cannot provide protection for flood because of the high risk. When a catastrophic event occurs, it is the government that the people turn to. In 1968, Congress created the **National Flood Insurance Program (NFIP)** managed through the **Federal Management Agency (FEMA).** The flood program has two primary focuses:

1. **Provide protection** for the people that have homes and property in low lying area.

2. To **reduce future flood damage** through floodplain management.

Delivery System

Providing flood protection is an important objective of the **Federal Government**, but they do not have a proper means of getting the product into the hands of those who need the coverage. The insurance industry is the delivery system for the program. Flood insurance can only be purchased through an insurance agent. **The agent sells the policy, but the government assumes the risk.** Agents selling flood insurance must first take a **3 hour flood class in order to be certified to sell flood policies**.

In 1983, the Federal Government created the **Write Your Own (WYO)** program. The WYO program allows participating property and casualty insurance companies to write and service flood policies in their own names. The companies receive an expense allowance for policies written and claims processed, while the Federal Government retains responsibility for underwriting losses. Under the WYO, the government still assumes the risk on the flood policy.

Defining Flood

The most important definition of the policy will be the definition of flood. Flood is defined as a general and temporary condition of partial or complete inundation of **2 or more acres** of normally dry land area or of **2 or more properties** from:

- **Overflow** of inland or tidal waters;

- Unusual and **rapid accumulation or runoff** of surface waters from any source; or

- **Mudflow**; or

Collapse or subsidence of land along the shore of a lake or similar body of water as a **result of erosion** or undermining caused by waves or currents of water exceeding anticipated cyclical levels that result in a flood as defined above.

Who is Eligible for Flood Insurance?

In order for an individual to be able to purchase a flood policy, the community that the property is located in must first participate in the NFIP. Communities must agree to a review of the area and may be required to establish some flood prevention and management procedures in order for FEMA to offer flood insurance in the area. These will typically include building code requirements, drainage rules, upgrade of sewer systems or perhaps the building of a levee. In addition, a Base Flood Elevation is established and added to the Flood Insurance Rate Map.

Once a community has shown an interest in participating, the community will be placed into the **emergency program.** This is the initial phase of a community's involvement. Insurance will be available in limited amounts during this phase.

When the community agrees to the recommended changes from FEMA, the community can then participate in the final phase of the program. This phase is referred to as the **regular program.** Property owners will be allowed to purchase the full amount of coverage available under the program.

	Emergency Program	***Regular Program***		
Building Coverage		Basic Limit	Additional Available	Total Available
1 – 4 Family Units	$35,000	$50,000	$200,000	$250,000
Other Residential	$100,000	$150,000	$100,000	$250,000
Non Residential	$100,000	$150,000	$350,000	$500,000
Contents				
Residential	$10,000	$20,000	$80,000	$100,000
Non Residential	$100,000	$130,000	$370,000	$500,000

Buildings with mortgages from federally regulated or insured lenders in high risk flood areas are required to have flood insurance. **Buildings do not have to be in the flood zone to be eligible for flood insurance.** In fact, buildings outside the flood zone may qualify for a preferred policy with preferred rates.

Effective Date

The **agent does not have binding authority** with the flood policy. Coverage typically has a **30 day waiting period** from the date of purchase. The effective date on a new policy will be 12:01 a.m. local time on the 30th calendar day after the application date. Exceptions are made if the community is new to the program or a home is being newly financed.

Deductibles

The standard deductible on the flood policy is $1,000 for the emergency program and $500 for the regular program. Deductibles are separately applied to buildings and contents. Higher deductibles are available for a lower premium.

Valuation

If an 80% co-insurance requirement is met, valuation will be replacement cost for a single family building. Contents will be covered on an actual cash value basis.

Watercraft

There are three different policies that are designed to cover watercraft. One of them has already been discussed, the Homeowners Policy. The other two policies that are made to cover personal watercraft are the Boat Owners Policy and the Yacht Policy.

Homeowners

The Homeowners Policy is designed to cover small boats that may be in a backyard lake or perhaps a boat that is being temporarily used. Property coverage is limited to $2,000. Liability coverage is only provided on very small boats or sometimes not owned or rented boats. If the boat is of any size, a separate coverage needs to apply. Coverage available under the Homeowners Policy includes:

- $2,000 property coverage
- No liability unless:

- It is under 26 feet or less than 25 horsepower motor whether owned, rented or borrowed
- Over 26 feet sailboat or more the 25 horsepower motor if rented or borrowed

Boatowners

A Boatowners policy is designed to cover a more substantial vessel than what the Homeowners is designed to cover. This is a boat that is **up to 26 feet** in length and can be hauled to and from the water. This policy will work much like an auto policy. The boat owner will need liability protection for boating accidents, as well as physical damage. The policy can also include medical payments and uninsured boaters.

Yacht Policy

The main difference between a boat and a yacht is the size. Where a boat is up to 26 feet, a yacht is **over 26 feet**. Yachts are not easily taken home. This means that yachts are typically left on the water and this creates a different risk. Also, yachts have the potential to travel beyond territorial waters and possibly around the world. Because of these differences, yachts have a different risk factor than boats.

In order to cover a yacht, an insurer might require certain issues be **warranted (condition of coverage)**. The method of storage, being limited to territorial waters, or perhaps a specific trip outside of territorial waters could require a warranty. If the warranty is not maintained, coverage would be in jeopardy.

The yacht coverage is similar to the Boat Owners policy. It is designed to cover the hull, machinery, equipment, furnishings, sails and fittings on a **valued basis**. Policies are generally written on an **all risk** basis for the hull. Named peril policies may be available.

One other difference with a yacht is that, the yacht could have employees working onboard. Based upon the Jones Act, Workers Compensation does not automatically cover those working around boats. **The Yacht Policy will include coverage for work related injuries.**

Personal Inland Marine Policies

An Inland Marine policy is designed to provide coverage on property, wherever the property is. The protection moves with the property. An Inland "Marine" Policy has nothing to do with water. Later we will describe the Ocean Marine Policy, which is all about coverage on the waterways. Inland Marine extended coverage beyond the waterways and is now designed to cover items "inland." There are three types of Inland Marine Policies:

Note: Marine policies are sometimes referred to as "floaters.

Personal Articles – This works much **like scheduling** a specific article. Coverage is provided on an all risk basis. An appraisal may be required to establish the value of the item. Valuation is based on a stated amount. It is used to insure those difficult to value items.

Personal Property – Covers your **personal property on a blanket basis**. It would be similar to purchasing Coverage C of the Homeowners Policy independently. Coverage is on an all risk basis. A renter who does not have a renter's policy could insure his personal property with this policy.

Personal Effects – This provides **short term** coverage of personal property. This might be useful for someone that needs coverage on personal property for a specific trip.

FAIR Plan

The FAIR Plan is a **high risk property** insurance that is available for both **personal and commercial** needs. FAIR is an acronym that stands for **Fair Access to Insurance Requirement**. It is sold on a pool basis. The pool concept requires participation from admitted companies. Together the companies share the risk and responsibility of the plan. Insurer participation is a requirement in order to be admitted into the state.

The FAIR Plan provides insurance **for those who have tried to get insurance through the normal market, but have been denied due to their risk category**. The FAIR Plan will not deny coverage based upon location or the surrounding neighborhood, but may deny coverage if the property owner has not maintained the property. For example, if the property owner does not have a handrail for the steps in the front of the home, the insurance company can deny the application. This home is not safe without a handrail at its entrance.

Umbrella and Excess Liability Policies

In today's litigious society, who really knows if they have adequate insurance limits? Even if Joe maxes out his liability limits on his Auto or Homeowners Policy, he may find that these limits do not provide adequate coverage. The Umbrella and Excess Liability policies are designed to provide high limits for a minimal premium.

Umbrella Policy

The Umbrella Policy does two things,

- Provides coverage **over and above** underlying limits, and
- **Expands** protection for exposures not covered by the underlying policies.

Once the underlying policies have exhausted their limits, the Umbrella Policy kicks in. Some policies will have a **retention limit** that must be paid before the policy pays a benefit. The retention limit basically acts like a deductible.

The Umbrella Policy may also **provide coverage that is not covered by the underlying policies.** For example, the auto policy does not provide coverage if the insured drives in Mexico. The Umbrella Policy may pick up coverage if the insured is driving in Mexico, after the retention limit is met.

Excess Liability Policy

The Excess Liability Policy is very similar to the Umbrella Policy. The major difference is that the Excess Liability Policy only provides protection if the peril was covered first by the underlying policy. In other words, the Excess Liability Policy does not expand coverage like the Umbrella Policy. Excess Liability only increases the amount of protection. If the underlying policy will not pay, neither will the Excess Liability. In the above example, if the insured drove in Mexico the Auto Policy would not provide protection, so as a result the Excess Liability Policy would also deny coverage.

Windstorm

Some areas are more likely to experience severe wind damage. Areas that experience extreme windstorms like hurricanes may exclude wind on the base policy and allow customers to pay extra to have it covered.

Earthquake Policies

An earthquake policy is specifically designed to cover ground movement. This is normally excluded on most all other property policies. The deductible on this policy may be a percentage of the policy limit.

Terms to know

Flood

NFIP

FEMA

Emergency Program

Regular Program

Boat Owners

Yacht

Warranted

Personal Inland Marine

Personal Articles

Personal Property

Personal Effects

FAIR plan

Umbrella

Windstorm

Excess Liability

Numbers to know

3 hour class- for an agent to sell flood

Flood- cover 2 acres

30 day waiting period

Effective date- 12:01 am on 30th calendar day

Deductible- $500 Emergency program $1,000 Regular program

Boat- up to 26 feet

Yacht- over 26 feet

Acronyms to know

NFIP- National Flood Insurance Program

FEMA- Federal Management Agency

WYO- Write Your Own

Practice Exam

1. In order for an insurance agent to sell a flood policy, how many credit hours are required?

    a) 3 hours

    b) 8 hours

    c) 2 hours

    d) 6 hours

2. Which of the following is NOT a part of the definition of flood?

    a) Mudslide

    b) Landslide

    c) Collapse

    d) Overflow of tidal waters

3. Concerning the Flood Policy, which of the following is FALSE?

    a) The agent sells the policy, but the government assumes the risk

    b) A building does not have to be in a flood zone to be eligible to purchase a flood policy

    c) The agent does not have binding authority

    d) The deductible on the emergency program is $500 and the deductible on the regular program is $1,000

4. On the Homeowners policy, coverage for property for watercraft is a stated value. How much coverage is provided?

    a) No coverage is available on the Homeowners policy

    b) Unlimited coverage is available

    c) Limited coverage is available

    d) Coverage is limited to the Part C limit

5. If a boat is over 26 feet in length, which type of policy provides coverage?

   a) Boat Owners

   b) Homeowners

   c) Yacht

   d) Warranty

6. Which of the following statements is FALSE?

   a) Yachts have the same risk as boats under 26 feet

   b) The yacht policy includes coverage for work related injuries

   c) The yacht policy is written on an All Risk basis for hull

   d) The insurer may require a warrant on the policy

7. Which Personal Inland Marine Policy schedules a specific item?

   a) FAIR Plan

   b) Personal effects

   c) Personal articles

   d) Personal property

8. In regards to the FAIR Plan, which of the following statements is FALSE?

   a) Insurer participation is voluntary

   b) It is a high risk program for personal and commercial property

   c) The FAIR Plan is for those who have been denied a homeowners policy due to risk

   d) The insurer cannot deny coverage due to location or neighborhood

9. Which type of policy only pays over and above the limit on the underlying policy?

   a) Umbrella

   b) Excess liability

   c) Personal articles

   d) Personal effects

10. Which of the following statements is FALSE?

    a) Excess liability and Umbrella policies may require a retention limit

    b) The umbrella policy pays over and above underlying limits

    c) The excess liability policy kicks in only after coverage has been exhausted by the underlying policy

    d) The excess liability policy expands protections and covers exposures not covered by underlying policies

Answer key: 1,a 2,b 3,d 4,c 5,c 6,a 7,c 8,a 9,b 10,d

Chapter

8

The Commercial Package Policy

Every business is unique. Some businesses use automobiles and trucks in their everyday business operations. Some businesses own buildings, while others build buildings. A bank may be interested in protecting money against theft. A grocer is concerned with his/her freezers and the perishables that they protect. Because of the unique risk that each business experiences, one prepackaged policy will not work for every business. Commercial policies have to be designed to meet the individual needs of each business. The Commercial Package Policy is a policy that allows the agent to create a plan that addresses the different needs of different businesses.

Concept of the CPP

The Commercial Package Policy (CPP) is a **cafeteria policy** that allows the insured to choose the areas of coverage that best addresses the needs of their individual business. Business owner Holly Brown is in the market to buy a CPP. Let's compare the CPP to a cafeteria line. At the beginning of the line, Holly is supplied with a tray, silverware and glass. These are the elements needed to create the meal that best meets her needs and desires. These elements alone provide no sustenance; however, when Holly proceeds down the line she comes to a section that allows her to make a choice. Let's say that the first section that Holly comes to is the salad section, she may decide to pass this section all together but other insureds will pause and make a choice based on their business needs. Within the salad section there will be multiple choices. Holly may reach for the tossed salad, cottage cheese or an attractive tomato topped with tuna salad. **Each insured makes a choice and moves on to the next section.**

As Holly proceeds through the line, she will come to the drinks, meats, vegetables, breads and of course the best section, the desserts. Each section will have multiple choices and every insured will have the same options. But at the end of the line, when Holly compares her meal with other business customers, each will end up with a unique meal that will satisfy their own individual needs and desires.

This is how the CPP works. It starts out with just the shell. The client will then proceed through each section. Choices will be made based upon the needs of the business. **At the end of the presentation, each client will end up with a unique policy with coverage designed to meet their individual business needs.**

The CPP Structure

To create a Commercial Package Policy, it will need to have certain elements included. We will first start at the beginning of the line with our basic elements: Common Declarations and the Common Conditions.

Common Declarations

We learned earlier that the Declaration page listed the specifics and details unique to the insured. It was described as the "**fill in the blank**" section. It consisted of the "**who, what, when, where and how much**" that applied to the insured. The "common declarations" are the details that apply to all modules of the CPP. We will see later that there are seven areas of coverage that the insured may choose from. The different areas of coverage are referred to as modules. Some information will be specific to each module and will need to be listed as the declarations to that specific module, but some of the declarations will apply to every module. These declarations are called the "common declarations." Since they are consistent, there is no need to duplicate them. These declarations will be listed once and only on the Common Declaration page. The following are examples of what would be considered common:

- **Who** is the name of the business we are insuring? Who is the insurance company?

- **What** type of business is insured? Which modules did this business choose to purchase? **All seven modules will be listed and the declaration page will designate which modules were chosen.**

- **When** does the policy go into effect? What is the policy period?

- **Where** is the mailing address or home office of the business? Who is the **first named insured**?

- **How much** is the overall premium of the policy?

Examples of declarations that would not be common are a description of the auto that is insured or the specific location of a building that may not be located at the home office. These are specific to their modules and do not apply to the other modules of the policy.

Common Conditions

The "common conditions" are conditions that would be common to all the modules chosen by the insured. We have described the condition section of the policy as the part that describes the **rights, rules, duties, obligations and provisions** of the policy. Some of the conditions listed in this section include:

- **Cancellation Condition** – This condition states the rules of cancellation. Cancellation will only be processed through the **"first named insured" listed on the policy.** A business may have multiple insureds and multiple locations. The first named insured is the individual listed on the declaration page. This is the company's "contact person."

- **Changes Condition** – This provision states that any changes must be done by contacting the first named insured. The first named insured may request the change, but all changes to the policy will be made by an executive officer of the insurance company.

- **Examination of Books and Records** – This allows the insurer to examine books and records up to **three years** after the end of the policy. Examinations may be done to establish the amount of a claim owed, amount of coverage needed or to investigate fraud concerns.

- **Inspections and Surveys** – Insurance companies may want to inspect the property or business that they are insuring. This condition gives them the right to inspect at any time.

- **Premiums** – The first named insured will be responsible for meeting premium obligations.

- **Transfer of Rights and Duties** – When a business is sold, the new owner may want to take over the existing insurance as is. The transfer of rights and duties condition states that rights cannot be transferred to another without consent from the insurance company first. In the event of death, rights will be transferred automatically to the insured's legal representative.

The Seven CPP Modules

There are seven areas of coverage provided by the Commercial Package Policy. Each module will have options within that specific area. The seven modules are:

Any one of these modules can be sold alone. If it is sold on its own, it will still need the Common Declaration and Common Condition section because it includes information essential to the contract. Also, if it is sold on its own, it is not referred to as a "Package" policy. **A "Package" policy requires at least two modules**. Remember, the word "package" implies bringing more than one together. When sold on its own, the policy will be referred to as a **mono-line** policy. When sold with more than one module, it is a package policy or a multi-line policy.

If asked, what makes up a Commercial Package Policy? The answer is:

- The Common Declaration page
- The Common Conditions

- Two or more modules or coverage parts

Interline Endorsements are riders that are added to the policy to make changes in more than one of the modules or lines of insurance. Perhaps a rider is issued to change the first named insured. This type of change is considered an interline endorsement since it applies to the entire policy.

Terms to know

Commercial Package Policy (CPP)

Cafeteria Policy

Common Declarations

Common Conditions

First Named Insured

7 Modules (Commercial Property, Commercial General Liability, Crime, Commercial Auto, Equipment Breakdown (Boiler and Machinery), Inland Marine, Farm)

Package Policy

Mono-line Policy

Interline Endorsements

Numbers to know

7 Modules of CPP

3 years- Examination of Books and Records

2 modules- Minimum to be a package policy

1 module- mono-line policy

Practice Exam

1. Which part of the policy contains "all of the details?"

   a) Common conditions

   b) Insuring clause

   c) Exclusions

   d) Common declarations page

2. Which of the following is NOT a Common Condition?

   a) Cancellation

   b) Examination of First Named Insured

   c) Inspections and Surveys

   d) Changes

3. Which is NOT a module of the CPP?

   a) Personal Auto

   b) Farm

   c) Commercial General Liability

   d) Equipment Breakdown

4. Which components make up a CPP?

   a) Common Declarations Page, Common Conditions, 2 or more modules.

   b) Common Declarations Page, Common Conditions, Interline Endorsements

   c) Cafeteria policy, Common Conditions, 2 or more modules

   d) Farm, Crime, Inland Marine, Commercial Auto

5. Choose the FALSE statement from the following:

   a) Each business can build its own policy to meet its individual needs

   b) Any one module can be sold on its own

   c) A mono-line policy requires one policy

   d) A package policy requires at minimum 3 modules

Answer key: 1,d 2,b 3,a 4,a 5,d

Chapter

9

Commercial Property Policy

If the Commercial Package Policy is a cafeteria line, then the Property module is the vegetable section of the line. Most businesses will have some type of property exposure, therefore the Property module of the CPP is one of the staples of the policy. Just like the vegetable section of the cafeteria line, there are many different choices in this area. There are a wide variety of property needs for a business. Some businesses will want to insure a building and its contents, while others will need to insure the building being built during the construction process. We also have condominiums and business interruption insurance. The Commercial Package Policy is designed to meet these different exposures and help agents meet the needs of their commercial clients.

The Commercial Property Policy Structure

If Holly chooses to add this module or line of coverage to her Commercial Package Policy, several parts must be included. There will be declarations and conditions that apply specifically to the Commercial Property module only. Holly will also need to specify which "cause of loss" form she would like to include, and on what property (basic, broad or special). Most importantly, Holly will need to designate the type of property insured by choosing the Property Coverage Forms needed.

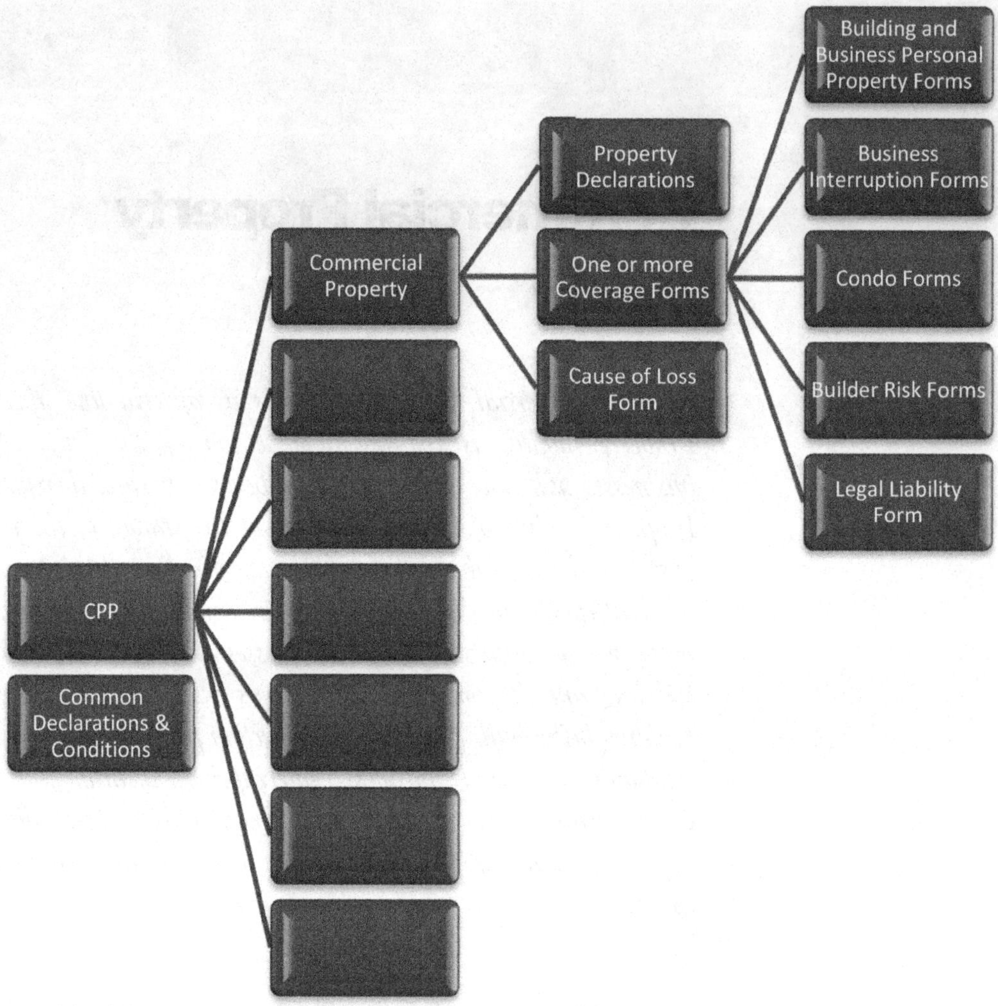

Property Declarations

These declarations will be specific to the property insured. A business may have multiple buildings at multiple locations. Addresses of these multiple locations may need to be included. Different buildings will need different limits on them.

Property Conditions

As stated before, these are the rules, rights, duties, obligations and provisions of the coverage. In this case, the conditions are specific to the property listed in the declarations. Some of the conditions that would be listed include:

- **Concealment, Misrepresentation or Fraud** – If the insured is guilty of concealment, misrepresentation or fraud, the policy can be voided.

- **Subrogation** – This gives the insurer the right to proceed against another party for **recovery of a claim**. When the insurer pays a claim and it is determined that another party was at fault, this allows the insurer to recover its losses.

- **Insurance Under Two or More Coverages** – This condition is designed to deal with the over insured issue. When the insured has too much insurance, **the insurer will not over indemnify**. The insured can collect no more than the amount of the loss or his/her insurable interest.

- **Liberalization** – This condition allows the insurer to broaden coverage on current policies, typically due to legislation changes. This can be done as long as no extra premium is being charged. Insurance companies will always be allowed to broaden coverage, especially if no extra premium is being charged. This helps keep policies current without issuing riders on every single policy when state laws are updated

- **No Benefit to Bailee** – A bailee is defined as someone who has another person's property in his/her **care, custody or control**. If the insurer pays a claim on property in the insured's control, payment will go to the owner of the property, not the bailee.

- **Other Insurance** – This condition describes how the insurer will respond when there is more than one coverage available to the claim. If the policies are concurrent (same type), then the two policies will pay on a pro-rata basis. Each will pay based upon its limit in proportion to the total limit of insurance between the two policies. If the policies are non-concurrent, then the Commercial Property Policy will respond on an excess basis.

- **Policy Period and Coverage Territory** – The policy period is based upon the effective date. Protection begins on the effective date and coverage is in effect throughout the policy period. The coverage territory includes the United States and its territories, Puerto Rico and Canada. The policy does not provide protection in any other territories.

The Commercial Property Forms

There are several forms available under the Commercial Property Policy. These forms are designed to meet the property needs of most businesses. Forms include:

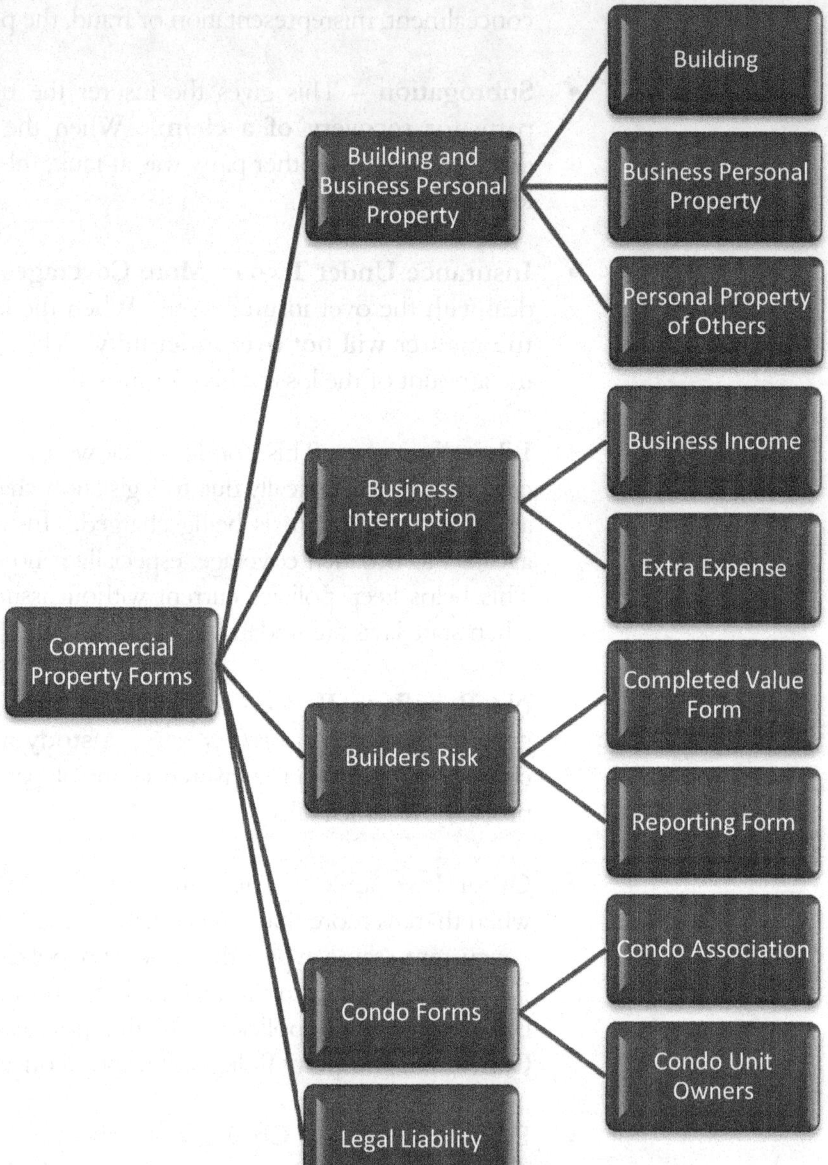

Building and Business Property Coverage Form

One of the most popular forms on the CPP is the Building and Business Personal Property Coverage Form. Most businesses will have some form of property exposure. Holly's business may own a building, or the items in the building or the business may be responsible for the property of its customers. This form is designed to cover all three of these areas or just the areas that apply to the business. The key to understanding what is covered is to understand the definitions of this form.

Coverages

When chosen on the Declaration page, the policy will pay for damages resulting from any Covered Cause of Loss to:

Commercial Building

This definition includes the building described in the Declarations, including:

- Completed additions;

- Fixtures, including outdoor fixtures; Examples include sinks, lights and other items that are assumed to be a part of the building. Signs that are attached to the building are also covered, but only up to **$1,000**.

- Permanently installed machines and equipment; Examples include items like furnaces and air-conditioning units. The key to this one is that the equipment is permanently installed and is part of the building.

- Personal property owned by the insured that is used to maintain or service the building and premises; one such item would be a **fire extinguisher**. Extinguishers are required to be mounted based upon the layout of the building and are expected to stay with the building. Maintaining the property is in the insurer's best interest as well as the building's owner. The insurance company wants to encourage maintenance to protect both the insurer and insured's interest.

- Additions under construction and alterations to the building;

- Materials, equipment, supplies and temporary structures within **100 feet** of the premises used for alterations or repairs to the structure;

Business Personal Property

Business Personal Property includes that which is located in the building described or within 100 feet of the described premises. Within 100 feet includes property in the open or within a vehicle. Property also includes:

- Furniture and fixtures; this includes items like desks, chairs, and tables
- Machinery and equipment; (copy machines and computers)
- Stock and inventory
- Personal property owned by the insured and used for business purposes;
- **Labor** performed on personal property owned by others; Labor is considered to be earned. Once the property of others has been destroyed, collecting for labor performed will not be possible.
- **Tenant improvements** and betterments made to part of the building the insured occupies, but does not own; when renting commercial property it is common for tenants to invest their own money into final improvements in the space to meet the needs of their specific business. In this case, the tenant has insurable interest in the improvements.
- **Leased personal property** that the business has a contractual responsibility to insure. This could include copy machines, computers, and snack machines.

Personal Property of Others

Personal Property of others includes property in the insured's **care, custody or control** located in the building or within **100 feet** of the described premises. Payment for loss or damage to personal property of others will only be paid to the owner of the property.

Note: that coverage in all three areas is limited to property within 100 feet of the described premises. This could include a wide variety of items including items as large as bulldozers or forklifts. Some of these items may also need to be covered outside of 100 feet. Later we will discuss the Inland Marine Form. This is another commercial property form. The difference between these two forms is where we need to insure the property, on premises only or wherever we may end up taking the property

PROPERTY NOT COVERED

The exclusions section is sometimes the most important part of the policy. The following is a list of items **not covered** by the Commercial Property Form:

- Accounts, bills, currency, and **money**; A business may need to have money covered, but this is something that is better covered separately. There are other concerns with money, such as theft or crime. These will be excluded here, but covered later as needed under the Crime Form.

- Animals, unless owned by others and boarded by the insured; If owned by the business, it must be stock and inside a building. (Veterinarians, pet store and boarding would be covered by this definition)

- Automobiles held for sale. Vehicles licensed for use on public roads; Autos licensed for the road and held for sale can be better covered elsewhere. We will see that these will be covered later under Commercial Auto. Remember this exclusion is very specific. **Vehicles not licensed for the road, but used on the premises would be covered.** This would not exclude forklifts, mowers, golf carts, and backhoes.

- As a general rule, things that are "**ground level or below**" will likely be excluded also. Bridges, roadways, walks, patios, foundations of buildings, land, growing crops, bulkheads, pilings, piers, wharves, docks, retaining walls, underground pipes, flues or drains;

- Property covered under another coverage form;

- The cost to replace or restore information

ADDITIONAL COVERAGES

The Additional Coverages section allows the company to add coverage back in that may have been previously excluded. This allows the insurer to add these additional coverages with separate limitations and explanations. Some of these coverages are added in because the company knows that the insured will have a need for these coverages and also expect these items to be covered. Additional coverages do not have to be paid for separately and they do not have to be requested from the insured. They are built into the policy and they will come with their own limits.

Debris Removal – The debris removal coverage pays for cleanup of the property after a covered loss has occurred. The limit of this coverage is up to **25% of the covered loss**, not to exceed an extra 10% over the total limit of coverage on the property.

Preservation of Property – The policy will pay for any reason, if covered property is damaged because it is being moved or has been moved to protect it from a covered loss. Coverage applies for up to 30 days after the property is first moved. Afterwards, coverage reverts back to the original terms. This is similar to the Homeowners Policy.

Fire Department Service Charge – The policy will pay up to **$1,000** for liability for fire department service charges.

Pollutant Clean Up and Removal – If caused by a covered loss, the insurer will pay up to **$10,000** for clean-up and removal.

Increased Cost of Construction – If replacement cost is chosen, the insurer will pay up to **$10,000** or 5% of the covered claim, whichever is less, for increased cost of construction. This might be due to building codes and city ordinances.

Electronic Data – This coverage pays the cost to replace or restore electronic data, up to $2,500 due to a covered loss.

Coverage Extensions

Coverage Extensions appear to be similar to the Additional Coverages, but there is a significant difference to note. Both are free and come with separate limits, but **extensions have to be qualified for**, they are not automatic. To qualify for these extensions, the business must meet an **80% co-insurance** requirement. Earlier we used the co-insurance requirement to encourage customers to insure their properties up to an adequate amount. If they did, they received full replacement cost coverage for partial losses. The problem we have here is that under the cafeteria approach, the insurance company is not giving the insureds replacement cost, unless they choose it. We will see that the valuation on all property, buildings included, will begin as Actual Cash Value.

Because Holly may not have replacement cost on her buildings, the insurer cannot give her the incentive of replacement cost coverage on partial losses. The incentive is lost. The Coverage Extensions become the new incentive designed to encourage Holly to carry adequate (80% or more) limits.

The following are the extensions that Holly qualifies for after meeting the 80% Co-insurance Clause:

Newly Acquired or Constructed Property – The policy will increase limits up to **$250,000** worth of additional coverage for newly acquired or constructed property. Coverage is available for **30** days after purchase or construction begins.

The Insured's Business Personal Property – This provides an additional $100,000 worth of business personal property coverage, assuming that Business Personal Property has been previously chosen. Coverage is available for 30 days after purchase or construction begins.

Personal Effects and Property of Others – This extension adds **$2,500** worth of coverage on items in the insured's care, custody and control. It includes property belonging to clients of the business, as well as the employees at the business.

Valuable Papers and Records (Other than Electronic Data) – This covers valuable papers and records that have been destroyed due to a covered loss. It will pay up to **$2,500** at each described premises.

Property off Premises – The property off premises coverage provides **$10,000** of Inland Marine Insurance. Coverage now applies to property off premises, such as in storage, at fairs, tradeshows or at premises the insured does not own or lease. It does not cover property while in or on a vehicle.

Outdoor Property – Extends coverage to provide protection for fences, radio towers, antennas, signs, trees, shrubs and plants. Plants will be limited to **$250** per plant. The most that will be paid for any one occurrence is **$1,000**.

Non-Owned Detached Trailers – Covers the trailers up to $5,000. If any other coverage applies, this will act as excess.

Policy Deductible

The deductible is the amount of risk the insured assumes. It is the amount that Holly will pay before the policy benefits are provided. The standard deductible for the Commercial Property Form is **$500**. Deductibles can be increased at the request of the insured. An increase in deductible lowers the premium, but also increases the risk that the insured assumes.

Loss Conditions

The Conditions section of the policy lists the rules, regulations, and obligations of both the insured and insurer. The following are the conditions listed in the Commercial Property Policy form:

Abandonment – This condition states there will be no abandonment of any property to the insurance company.

Appraisal – If the insured and insurer disagree on the value of the property or the amount of loss, either party may request the appraisal process in order to settle the loss. Each party selects an appraiser. If both appraisers cannot come to agreement, then the appraisers will choose a third, called an umpire. Agreement by two out of three will be binding. Each party will be responsible for one half of the cost of the umpire's appraisal

Duties in the Event of Loss or Damage – In the event of a loss, the insured must:

- Notify police when appropriate
- Provide prompt notice and submit a signed proof of loss within 60 days

- Provide necessary descriptions and inventories
- Protect property
- Allow the insurer to inspect property or records
- Cooperate with the insurer in the investigation or settlement of claim

Loss Payment – In the event of a covered loss, the insurer has the option and right to:

- Pay the value of the lost or damaged property
- Pay the cost to repair or replace
- Take all or any part of the property at an agreed or appraised value, or
- Repair, rebuild or replace the property with other property of like kind and quality.

Recovered Property- If property is recovered after a loss has been settled, the insurer has the right to salvage at the insured's option: the amount paid or the property provided.

Vacancy Provision – If loss occurs to a building after it has been vacant for more than **60** consecutive days:

- The insurer will **not pay** for any loss caused by:
    - Vandalism
    - Sprinkler leakage or water damage
    - Glass breakage
    - Theft or attempted theft
- The insurer will reduce payment on any other covered losses by **15%**

Valuation – The standard valuation of the Commercial Property Policy is **actual cash value**. Since this is a cafeteria approach, the insurer will allow Holly to choose to better her valuation with an endorsement, if she so chooses. The business may want ACV on some property and may want to enhance protection on other properties.

If the claim is less than $2,500, the insurer will pay the cost to repair or replace. Small claims are not worth the effort of depreciating.

Co-Insurance – The co-insurance clause requires Holly to maintain an adequate amount of insurance coverage. If she does not meet the co-insurance percentage, then she will be penalized upon payment of the claim. The penalty would be:

The standard co insurance percentage is 80%. If it is met, the penalty will not apply. The new incentive is the Coverage Extensions.

Example:

Property value	$200,000
Co-insurance %	80%
Loss	$40,000
Deductible	$500
Customer carried	$120,000
Should carry	$200,000 X 80% = $160,000
Did/Should X Loss	$120,000/$160,000 X $40,000 = $30,000
Amount Paid	$30,000 - $500 = $29,500

Mortgage holders – If the mortgage holders are listed in the Declaration page, then they have certain rights:

- The right to receive payment for losses up to their insurable interest in the property.
- If Holly is denied coverage due to her acts or failure to submit a claim, the mortgage holders have the right to file their own claim and pay any premiums due.
- Mortgage holders will receive notices of renewal, nonrenewal or cancellation
  - 10 days notice is required for nonpayment
  - 30 days notice is required for any other reason

Optional Coverages

If shown on the Declaration page, the following optional coverages may also be added:

Agreed Value – This allows the insured to schedule hard to value property at a predetermined value.

Inflation Guard – Limits will increase based upon the percentage listed on the Declaration page in an attempt to keep pace with inflation.

Reporting Forms – A Reporting Form allows the insured to more adequately insure fluctuating inventory values by reporting expected future needs on a regular basis.

> Peak Season reporting form – allows the business to set different limits for on and off season.
>
> Value Reporting form – limits are changed as needs change

Replacement Cost – This allows the insured to replace the valuation of ACV with replacement cost.

Business Interruption Insurance Forms

Earlier we learned that an indirect loss was a loss that was the result of a direct loss. It is also sometimes referred to as a consequential loss. These losses are typically a financial loss that is a result of a covered physical loss. For example, a business experiences a small fire and has to close its doors for two weeks in order to make repairs. During the two week shutdown, the business loses out on income; this is an indirect loss. In Business, indirect losses could be covered under a Business Interruption Form. There are two such forms that we will look at. The first one is the Business Income form and the second is the Extra Expense form. These forms can be sold separately or could be sold together in one policy.

Business Income Coverage Form

The Business Income Coverage Form provides an indirect coverage designed to replace the lost income of a business after suffering a covered direct loss. This form is perfect for bowling alleys, restaurants, grocery stores or manufacturers that have lost their building(s) due to a fire, tornado or other covered peril. These are examples of **businesses that are dependent upon their physical building in order to run a successful business**. If the building is destroyed, then the business loses the opportunity to generate business income; they are out of business until their building is rebuilt. This could take months or years and can be devastating to the future of the business.

Period of Restoration

The policy will pay for the actual loss of Business Income sustained by the insured due to the necessary "suspension" of operations during the "Period of Restoration."

The Period of Restoration begins 72 hours after the time of direct physical loss. It **ends on the date that the property should be repaired, within a reasonable period of time**. It would also end if the business relocated to a new, permanent location. The word reasonable may seem vague, but keep in mind there are numerous issues that could delay a building project that may be out of the control of the insured. At the same time, the use of the word allows the insurer to challenge whether or not the delay is reasonable. The use of the word also allows for flexibility on behalf of the insured with some control for the insurer.

Business Income

Business Income is what this coverage is going to replace. That means the definition of Business Income is important. The policy defines it as:

- **Net Income** that would have been earned; and
- Continuing normal **operating expenses** incurred, including **payroll**.

This coverage is designed to replace the net income that would have been earned (or lost) at the end of the year. In addition, it is designed to cover the insured's ongoing expenses that will be incurred, regardless of income. It is also designed to replace payroll. Imagine a French restaurant that is out of business for nine months due to a fire. If the authentic French Chef is not paid during this time, the insured may not have a business to return to after nine months.

This policy can be sold with a Co-insurance as low as 50%. If the restaurant above did burn down, the insured may not want to replace all payroll or expenses. The restaurant owner could find busboys and dishwashers when the restaurant re-opens.

This coverage can be limited to a period of time, a monthly limit or based upon a valued amount. Remember, any limitations would also have an impact on the premium obligation.

Extra Expense Coverage Form

The Extra Expense Form is designed to **keep a business open** after it has experienced a covered loss. A service business like an insurance agency, a contractor, or real estate agency is not dependent upon its building to pursue income. These businesses could continue to operate even if they lost their building; but, they would have extra expenses over and above their normal operating expenses in order to conduct business at a new location. They may need a temporary office space to set up or telephones and computers installed that would allow them to continue conducting business.

Extra Expense

Extra Expense means necessary expenses during the "period of restoration" that would never have been incurred without the loss. These expenses are necessary in order to keep the business open and operating.

Period of Restoration

The policy will pay for the Extra Expenses sustained by the insured in order to keep the business operational during the "Period of Restoration."

The Period of Restoration begins at the time of direct physical loss and **ends the date the property should be repaired, within a reasonable period of time**. It would also end if the business relocated to a new permanent location.

Condominium Coverage Forms

Condominium Association Coverage Form

This form is purchased by the **Association** to cover their insurable interest in the property. The primary coverage under this form is the building itself. It would also cover their interest in other structures and office equipment owned by the association.

Condominium Unit Owners Coverage Form

The **Unit Owners** Form is designed to cover the insurable interest of the commercial unit owner and their insurable interest. Like the HO-6, this form is designed to cover the unit and the improvements made by the owner. The difference is, this is a commercial inhabitant, not a personal one.

Builders Risk Coverages

When a building is under construction and in the process of **being built**, it has a unique exposure and need for coverage. The risk literally changes every day as more materials are added to the building. Limits may change as the project progresses and, ultimately it is a very limited need and exposure. Once the building project is completed and put to use, the insurance needs of the building will change. The Builders Risk Form is designed for the specific needs of a building project and the building industry.

Coverage Forms

Depending on the needs of the insured, there are two ways in which the Builders Risk Form can be written.

Anticipated Completed Value Form

The (Anticipated) Completed Value Coverage Form establishes a limit of coverage based upon the anticipated completed value of the project. Many construction projects will be completed within a very short period of time. Because of this, the exposure will also be limited. It makes more sense to all parties involved to establish an anticipated completed value of the property, set the limit based upon this amount and determine the value of the loss, if and when a loss occurs. Contractors keep record of all costs and expenses. If a loss occurs, determining its value would be relatively simple.

Reporting Form

With a larger construction project, the exposure may be for much more and for much longer than a typical construction project. If the project that is being insured is a stadium or high rise, the risk is much different than if it were a home. Because of this difference, it may make more sense to both parties to keep a more accurate track of the exposure that is being insured. The Reporting Form allows the insurer to "report" on a regular basis the progress of the project. As the project increases in value and need, then the limits will be adjusted accordingly. This means that the customer is covered as needed without over insuring them in the process. It also means that the insurer is aware of what they are insuring and the risk they are assuming as the project proceeds.

When Does Coverage Begin and End?

Coverage starts when there is something to insure. It begins at the time of construction. Coverage ends when one of the following occurs:

- Policy expiration or cancellation;

- Property has been accepted by a purchaser;

- The insured has no further interest in the property;

- Construction has been abandoned with no intent to complete it;

- Unless specified otherwise:
    - 90 days after completion of construction; or

    - 60 days after building is occupied or put to use

Legal Liability Coverage Form

This coverage is designed to cover property of others in the insured's care, custody or control, which the insured becomes legally obligated to pay as a result of damages arising from any covered cause of loss.

Cyber First-Party Coverage

First-party cyber coverage protects businesses from the financial losses they directly incur due to cyber incidents like data breaches and attacks, covering costs like business interruption, data recovery, and incident response.

Commercial Property Cause of Loss Forms

When Commercial Property is chosen on the Commercial Package Policy, then a Cause of Loss form must be chosen to determine how the property will be covered. Since we are using the "cafeteria" approach, a different Cause of Loss form can be chosen for different property forms. The Cause of Loss forms are the:

- Basic – Fire, lightening, riot, explosion, vehicles, civil commotion, smoke, hail, aircraft, windstorm, volcanic action, **sprinkler leakage** and **sinkhole collapse**

- Broad - Fire, lightening, riot, explosion, vehicles, civil commotion, smoke, hail, aircraft, windstorm, volcanic action, weight of ice and snow, intentional water, falling objects, **sprinkler leakage** and **sinkhole collapse**

- Special – all risk/open peril

The Perils listed are very similar to what we learned in the personal products. The exception is that two new perils are added, sprinkler leakage and sinkhole collapse.

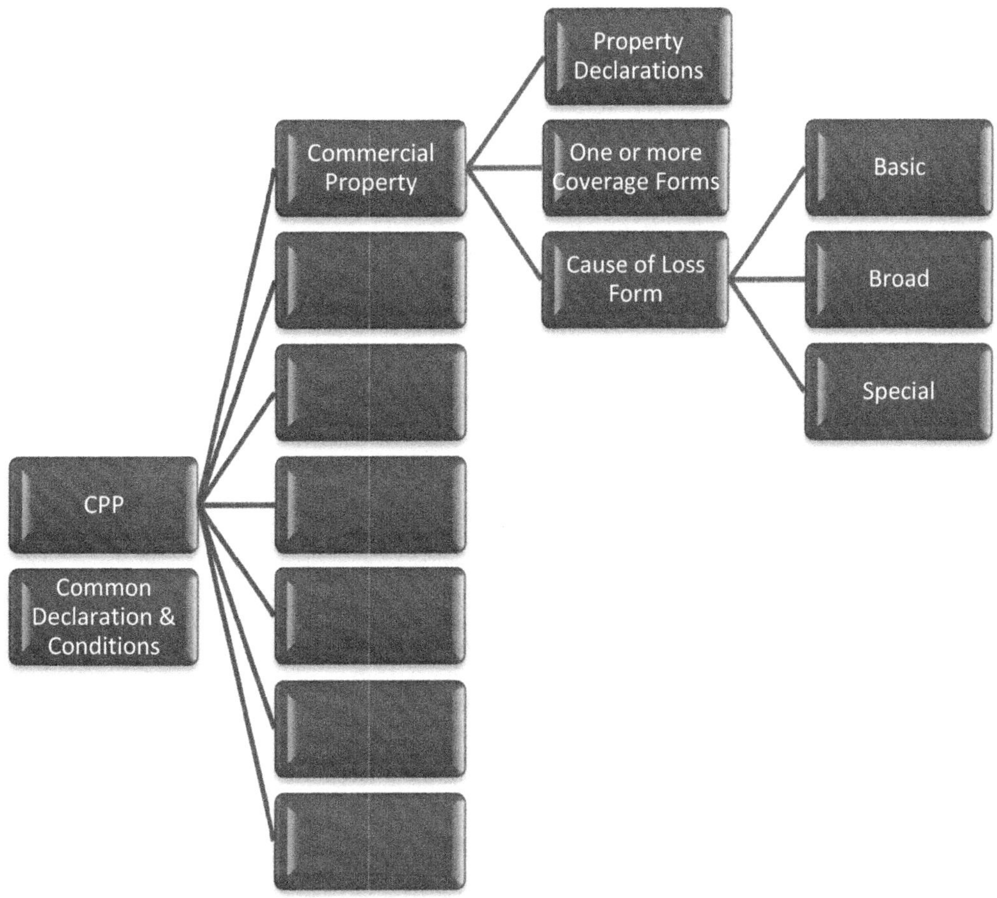

Volcanic Action includes damage from **above ground effects only**. All volcanic eruptions that occur within any **168 hour** period will constitute a single occurrence.

Exclusions Common to All Cause of Loss Forms

Every policy will have a list of things excluded and the Commercial Property Policy will be no exception to that rule. The following are exclusions common to all forms on the Commercial Property Policy:

- Ordinance or Law
- Earth movement or Earthquake
- Government Action
- Nuclear Hazard
- Utility Services
- War and Military Action
- Flood
- Leakage or Seepage
- Fungus or Wet Rot
- Damage caused by or resulting from:
    - Artificially Generated Electrical Current
    - Leakage or Discharge that occurs over a period of time of over 14 days
    - Explosion of pressure vessels
    - Mechanical Breakdown
    - Neglect

Exclusions Unique to the Special Cause of Loss Form

The Special all risk form has a few extra exclusions within it. Here are some of the exclusions that are added to the Special Cause of Loss form:

- Delay, loss of use or loss of market
- Wear and Tear
- Rust, corrosion and decay
- Smog

- Settling, cracking and shrinking
- Nesting or infestation or release of waste products by birds, rodents or other animals
- Dishonest or criminal acts
- Voluntarily parting with property
- Rain, snow, ice or sleet to property left in the open
- Discharge of pollutants
- Neglect of an insured, or failure to act
- Faulty planning, design, materials or maintenance

Endorsements

An endorsement is a change in the policy. There are numerous endorsements available with the Commercial Property Policy. The business can choose the endorsements based upon their business' needs. Here are three of the most common endorsements:

Earthquake

The Earthquake endorsement adds coverage back in for damage done by an earthquake or ground movement. Like Volcanic Action, **168 hours** between events will constitute a new event.

Inflation Guard

This coverage is designed to keep the policy limits up to date and current. Limits will be increased on an annual basis based upon the percentage chosen and specified in the policy.

Replacement Cost

Under the cafeteria approach, we took nothing for granted. We started with the minimum and added to it, to meet the business' individual needs. The valuation of the policy begins ACV or Actual Cash Value. If the insured wants to enhance this coverage, the Replacement Cost Endorsement could be added. This would change valuation from ACV to Replacement Cost.

Terms to Know

Building and Business Property Coverage Form

Commercial Building

Business Personal Property

Personal Property of Others

Coverage Extensions

Business Interruption Coverage Form

Business Income Coverage Form

Period of restoration

Business income

Extra Expense Form

Condominium Coverage Forms

Condominium Association Coverage Form

Condominium Unit Owners Coverage Form

Builders Risk Form

Anticipated Completed Value Form

Reporting Form

Legal Liability Coverage Form

Numbers to Know

$1,000- Coverage for attached signs

100 feet Business Personal Property and Personal Property of Others

$1,000- Fire Department Service Charge

$10,000- Pollutant Clean Up and Removal

80% Co-insurance Clause

$250,000- Newly Acquired/Construction Property

$100,000/ 30 Days- Business Personal Property

$500- Deductible Commercial Property Form

60 Days/ 15% of loss- Vacancy

Mortgage Holders Notices 10 days nonpayment/ 30 days any other reason

50% Co Insurance Business Income

Reporting Form Coverage ends 90 days after construction completion, 60 days after occupied

168 hours- Volcanic Eruption/Earthquake Single Occurrence

Practice Exam

1. There are some exclusions on the Commercial Property Form. Of the following, which is NOT an exclusion?

    a) Animals boarded by the insured

    b) Money

    c) Things ground level or below

    d) Autos for sale

2. Which of the following would be considered part of the commercial building?

    a) Tenant improvements in the building

    b) Permanently installed machines and equipment

    c) Leased personal property

    d) Personal property of others

3. Often, commercial buildings are left vacant. Certain losses are not covered if a building is vacant for more than ___ days.

    a) 90

    b) 50

    c) 30

    d) 60

4. Which form is used to provide coverage to a building during the construction process?

    a) Extra Expense Coverage Form

    b) Builders Risk Form

    c) Legal Liability Coverage Form

    d) Condo Coverage Form

5. Which of the following would be considered as Business Personal Property?

    a) Property in the businesses care, custody and control

    b) Betterments made to the building by a tenant

    c) Supplies, within 100 feet of the premises used for alterations or repairs to the structure

    d) Attached signs

6. The standard valuation of the Commercial Property Policy is:.

    a) Actual Cash Value

    b) Replacement Cost

    c) Stated Value

    d) Market Value

7. If vacant for more than 60 days, the insurer will not pay for certain losses. All of the following are excluded EXCEPT for:

    a) Fire

    b) Vandalism

    c) Theft

    d) Water damage

8. Which form is designed to keep a business open after a loss?

    a) Period of restoration

    b) Business income

    c) Builders risk

    d) Extra expense

9. All of the following are rights of a mortgage holder except:

   a) The right to recover property after a loss has been settled

   b) The right to receive payment for their losses up to their insurable interest

   c) The right to file their own claim

   d) The right to pay a premium if not paid by the insured

10. What is the standard co insurance percentage?

    a) 100%

    b) 90%

    c) 75%

    d) 80%

11. The purpose of a Reporting Form is to:

    a) Allows the insured to more adequately price fluctuating coverage

    b) Allow the insured to more adequately insure fluctuating values

    c) Provide continual information concerning an ongoing claim

    d) Provide fluctuating values during the claim process

12. Volcanic eruptions occurring within a(n) ___ hour period constitutes as a single occurrence.

    a) 132

    b) 90

    c) 168

    d) 60

13. Which of the following businesses would Business Income work best for:

    a) A restaurant

    b) A plumber

    c) An insurance agency

    d) An internet influencer

14. When does the period of restoration end on a Business Interruption Form?:

    a) After 90 days

    b) After 120 daiys

    c) After completion of repairs

    d) Within a reasonable period of time

15. Which of the following would you recommend Extra Expense coverage to?

    a) Retail store

    b) Bowling alley

    c) Real estate agency

    d) Manufacturer

16. How does the period of restoration differ between Business Income and the Extra Expense Forms?

    a) Under Business Income it starts after 72 hours

    b) Under Extra Expense it starts after 72 hours

    c) Extra Expense includes payroll

    d) Business Income ends within a reasonable time period

17. In the event of a loss, the insured has duties. Which of the following is NOT a duty of the insured?

    a) Notify police when appropriate

    b) Cooperate with the insurer

    c) Allow the insurer to inspect the property

    d) Abandon the property

18. In regards to Loss Conditions, which of the following statements is FALSE?

    a) In the event of loss, the insured must contact the insurer

    b) The fee of an umpire's appraisal is paid in full by the insurer

    c) If the property has been recovered after a loss, the insurer has the right to salvage the property at the insured's option: amount paid or property

    d) After a loss, the insurer has the right to pay the cost to repair or replace

19. Which term includes both of these definitions: Net income that would have been earned and continuing normal operating expenses including payroll?

    a) Extra expense

    b) Period of restoration

    c) Business income

    d) Inflation guard

20. In the construction of a building, coverage begins when there is something to insure, while coverage ends when all of the following occur EXCEPT:

    a) Policy expiration or cancellation

    b) The insured no longer has interest in the property

    c) After 30 days

    d) The property has been accepted by a purchaser

21. How does the commercial property cause of loss form differ from the personal forms?

    a) They add sprinkler leakage and sinkhole collapse to the named perils

    b) They exclude volcanic action in commercial

    c) They include flood coverage in the named perils

    d) Loss to money is covered by the commercial forms

22. Which of the following would be used to cover the building that the condominium units are in?

    a) Building and Business Personal Property Form

    b) Builders Risk Anticipated Completed Value Form

    c) Condominium Unit Owners Form

    d) Condominium Association Form

23. First-party coverage that protects businesses from the financial losses they directly incur like data breaches and attacks, covering costs like business interruption, data recovery, and incident response, is called:

    a) Employment practices liability

    b) Cyber first party coverage

    c) Computer fraud

    d) Extortion party coverage

24. Under Builders Risk which form is typically used on smaller short-term projects?

    a) Reporting Form

    b) Anticipated Completed Value Form

    c) Period of Restoration Form

    d) Legal Liability Form

Answer key: 1,a 2,b 3,d 4,b 5,b 6,a 7,a 8,d 9,a 10,d 11,b 12,c 13,a 14,d 15,c 16,a 17,d 18,b 19,c 20,c 21,a 22,d 23,b 24,b

Chapter

10

Commercial General Liability (CGL)

By definition, having a business includes working with others within our society. Anytime you work with others, there is a liability exposure. If you make a product, it could be defective and cause others harm. If you own your own store and have customers on your property, you have a responsibility to keep them safe while they are on your property. The CGL policy is one of the most important policies for any type of business. If the property coverage is the vegetable, then the liability is the meat of the meal. This policy is designed to protect the business against its negligence to clients and other businesses that it may be liable to.

The Commercial General Liability Form is a **liability** policy that is designed to protect the business. It is designed to protect the insured against **negligence** on the insured's part. The policy never pays a benefit to the insured. It is **third party** insurance and is designed to protect the insured by paying the benefit directly to the third party.

The CGL is the second choice available in our Commercial Package Policy. It is the next option in the cafeteria line.

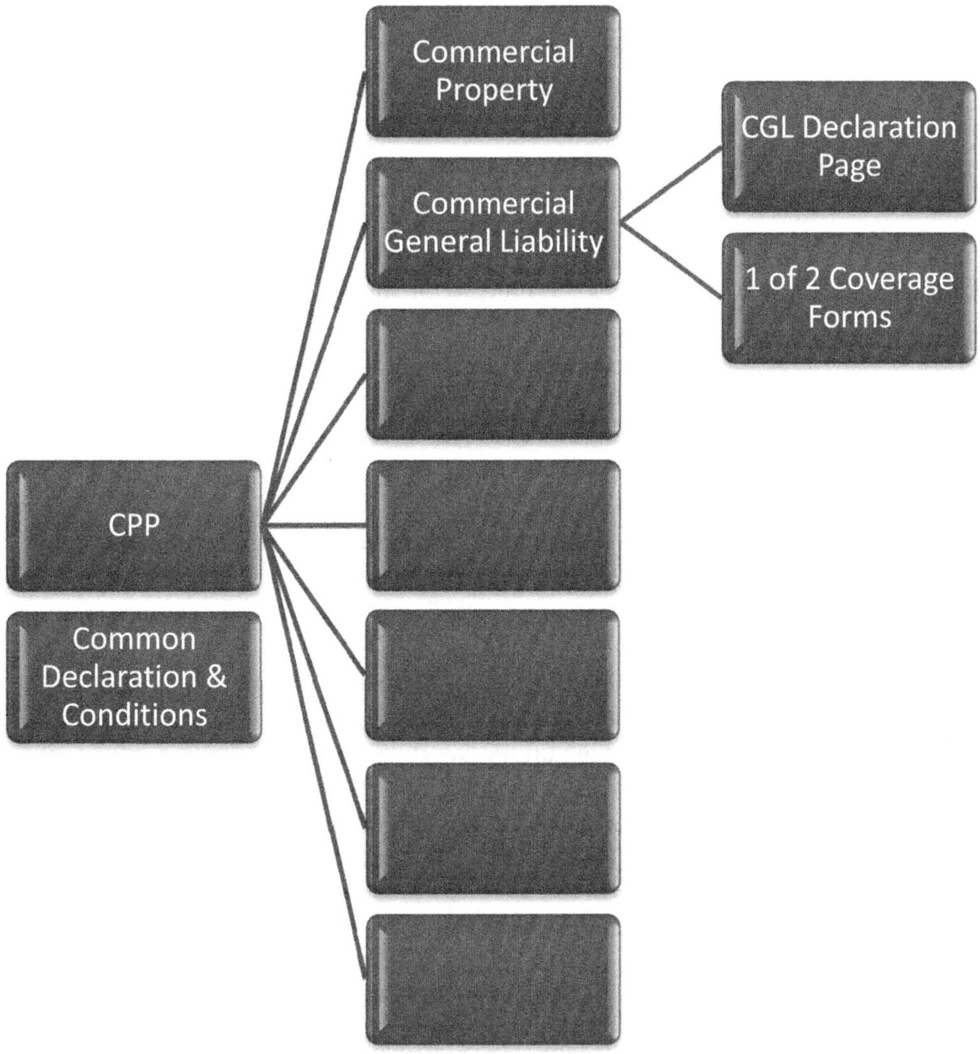

Coverages

The Commercial General Liability form is designed to cover most liability exposures that a business might be concerned about. There are nine exposures that the policy is designed to protect against. The first seven are covered under Coverage A: Bodily Injury and Property Damage Liability. The last two are covered under Coverage B: Personal and Advertising Injury.

Coverage A: Bodily Injury and Property Damage Liability

These coverages are all **physical** in nature. It is, as the title implies, physical damage that the insured is liable for to other people or to their property.

Premises Liability – In this scenario, the insured is liable or responsible to a third party for damage due to the premises itself. For example, a grocery store employee negligently leaves some water on the floor while mopping and a customer steps in the water, falls, and becomes injured. Or at an office, a customer trips over an extension cord. In both cases, the business was negligent and is responsible for damages.

Operations Liability – The insured becomes liable to a third party while performing a business operation. For example, a tree trimmer drops a limb on a car or the bucket operator of a back hoe swings the bucket around and strikes a bystander. The bystander now has medical bills and the insured is responsible for those bills.

Products –Products liability may be one of the biggest exposures of a business. It is when the business is liable to the public due to a faulty product. Examples include: toys that are unsafe, food products that are bad or any other type product that ends up doing damage to the public. If a business chose not to have coverage in this area and a faulty product was distributed, the damages owed to the public could easily bankrupt the business.

Completed Operations – This is an exposure that occurs after the fact. The job is completed, but damage occurs some time later because it was not finished properly. Perhaps a bridge collapses due to faulty workmanship. This coverage would protect the contractors who built the bridge.

Note: Products and Completed Operations typically will have a higher potential exposure than the others. For this reason, we will see that these two will be singled out later so that the insurer can apply a separate limit according to the need.

Independent Contractors – The insured becomes liable because an independent contractor working on behalf of the insured has done damage to a third party. Perhaps Doug hired a tree trimmer to trim the trees in his parking lot. But, Doug forgot to warn his customers to move their vehicles and damage was caused by falling branches. If the independent contractor was sued, he would be covered under his CGL (operations). If the owner of the building (Doug) was sued, he would be covered by his CGL (independent contractors).

Contractual Liability – This covers liability assumed by contract. This coverage will first be excluded in the policy, and then it can be added back in under the definition of "insured contract." There are five areas of contractual liability:

- **L**ease agreements
- **E**asements
- **A**greement to indemnify a municipality
- **S**idetrack agreements
- **E**levator maintenance agreements

Juan is building a two story department store. He has asked "We Lift Em" elevator service to install an elevator in the store. "We Lift Em" will be responsible for the product during the installation and up till it has passed inspection. Afterwards, Juan has signed an agreement to assume responsibility for the upkeep and maintenance of the elevator. After the insurance company is made aware of this agreement, they will then add coverage back into Juan's CGL policy. It is now an "insured contract."

Damage to Rented Premises – This coverage protects the insured against legal liability incurred for negligent acts resulting in fire damage to a premises rented to the insured. Normally a liability policy will exclude items in the insured's care, custody and control because these are usually covered on a property module. A tenant has the building in his care, custody and control. This adds coverage for this situation back into the tenants policy. Coverage would be provided if a tenant becomes liable for negligently starting a fire and damaging the property that he/she is currently leasing.

Coverage B: Personal and Advertising Injury

The last two exposures are covered under Coverage B of the Commercial General Liability policy. These exposures are separated because unlike the other seven, these are not physical in nature. These two exposures are very similar in nature and will be listed together in the policy. To distinguish the two, review the definitions:

Personal Injury – Is a negligent act that is done to a third party that does harm to their reputation or image. This could be done publically in an interview or on Facebook.

Advertising Injury – Is similar to Personal Injury. The main difference is how it is done. Advertising Injury is done through the advertising media such as radio ads, magazine or newspaper articles, or social media

Both include injury, including consequential bodily injury, arising out of one or more of the following:

- False arrest, detention or imprisonment
- Malicious prosecution
- Wrongful eviction or entry
- Oral or written publication that slanders or libels a person, organization, their products or services
- The use of another's advertising idea
- Infringing upon another's copyright, trademark or slogan in your advertisement.

Coverage C: Medical Payments

As we have seen previously, Medical Payments is a **no fault, pro-active and preventive** coverage. **Medical Payments will only be available under Premises and Operations for two reasons.** First, Medical Payments is limited to bodily injury. Secondly, it only covers something that occurred directly by the business or its property. It does not provide payments for any of the other exposures.

If a consumer purchased a microwave oven, took it home, turned it on, and it then exploded, Medical Payments would pay nothing. Liability would have to be established and the policy would then pay under Coverage A. But, fault and negligence would first have to be established.

If a consumer came onto the insured's premises to purchase a microwave and tripped over some cardboard left in the aisles of the store, Medical Payments would offer coverage. Fault would not have to be established, the policy would be proactive and pay in hopes of preventing a larger payout in court.

Medical Payment expenses must be reported within **one year** of the date of the accident in order to be covered.

Medical Expenses includes:

- Payment for first aid administered at the time of an accident;
- Necessary medical, surgical, x-ray and dental services, including prosthetic devices; and
- Necessary ambulance, hospital, professional nursing and funeral services.

Supplementary Payments – Coverages A and B

Supplementary Payments are extra payments included in the policy that protect both parties. This coverage is built into the policy at no extra cost. The primary benefit in this section is defense. The insurer prefers to have the option to provide **defense**, since it is their money at stake. Supplementary Payments includes:

- Up to $250 for cost of bail bonds required because of accidents or traffic law violations

- The cost of bonds to release attachments

- All reasonable expenses incurred by the insured at the insurer's request to assist them in the investigation or defense of the claim, including actual loss of **earnings up to $250 a day** because of time off work. If the insured is being sued, he will have to miss work in order to be present in court. This coverage helps replace the insured's lost wages.

- All court costs taxed against the insured in the suit

- Prejudgment interest awarded against the insured

- All interest on the full amount of any judgment that accrues after entry of the judgment

This coverage is provided in addition to the limits for Coverage A and B and **will not reduce the amount available for payment**, if the insured is found liable. The insurer's obligation to defend ends when they have used up the applicable limit of insurance in the payment of judgments or settlements. In other words, as long as there is money to defend in the policy, the insurer will defend it.

Exclusions

As usual, every policy comes with exclusions. This policy is no exception. Each of the coverages will have a list of exclusions.

Coverage A: Bodily Injury and Property Damage Exclusions

Coverage A does not apply to:

- Expected or Intended Injury – This is viewed from the insured's perspective. Intentional acts are excluded; however reasonable force to protect persons or property will not be excluded.

- Contractual Liability – Assumed liability is excluded. It will be added back in if it falls under the definition of "insured contract;"

- Liquor Liability – This exclusion only applies if you are in the business of manufacturing, distributing, selling, serving or furnishing alcoholic beverages. Liability realized as a result of serving liquor at an office holiday party would also be covered.

Note: Businesses that sell liquor will obviously need liability protection as well. These businesses have a unique risk and will be able to purchase their coverage through endorsement for an extra premium.

- Workers Compensation

- Employer's Liability – Discriminatory issues, hiring, firing, and harassment.

- Pollution – Catastrophic in nature

- Aircraft, Auto or Watercraft – These are better covered elsewhere. The policy will provide coverage for watercraft less than 26 feet in length on the insured's premises or non-owned and not being used to carry persons or property for a fee. It also covers machinery attached to mobile equipment.

- Transportation of Mobile Equipment by "auto" – Mobile equipment is covered while it is being used, on or off site. It is not covered while being transported. This should be provided under Commercial Auto.

- War

- Damage to Property Owned or in the Insured's Care, Custody or Control

- Damage to the Insured's Product

- Damage to the Insured's Work

- Damage to Impaired Property or Property Not Physically Injured
- Recall of Products, Work or Impaired Property
- Personal and Advertising Injury – This is excluded here under Coverage A, but is covered under Coverage B.
- Electronic Data
- Distribution of Material in Violation of Statutes

Coverage B: Personal and Advertising Injury Exclusions

Coverage does not apply to:

- Knowing Violation of Rights of Another
- Material Published with Knowledge of Falsity
- Material Published Prior to Policy Period
- Criminal Acts
- Contractual Liability
- Breach of Contract
- Quality or Performance of Goods – Failure to Conform to Statements
- Wrong Description of Prices
- Infringement of Copyright, Patent, Trademark or Trade Secret
- Insureds in Media and Internet Type Businesses – This is personal and advertising injury committed by an insured whose business is:
    - Advertising, broadcasting, publishing or telecasting;
    - Designing websites
    - Internet or service provider

Note: Obviously these businesses need this coverage more than most. But, for them it is their profession and they will be held to a higher degree of accountability. They will protect themselves by purchasing Professional Liability for their industry. This is a separate policy.

- Electronic Chat Rooms or Bulletin Boards
- Unauthorized Use of Another's Name or Product
- Pollution
- War
- Distribution of Material in Violation of Statutes

Coverage C: Medical Payments Exclusions

Medical Payments will not pay for bodily injury to:

- Any Insured
- Hired Person
- Injury on normally Occupied Premises – Rented property
- Workers Compensation and Similar Laws
- Athletics Activities
- Products-Completed Operations Hazard

Who is Insured?

The CGL is designed to meet various business structures and needs. An insured includes any party who is designated in the Declarations as:

- A **sole proprietor-** it would cover Holly and her spouse, with respect to conduct as owners
- In a **partnership**; Holly, her members, partners and their spouses

- If the business is a **limited liability company** it insures Holly, members and managers, but only with respect to their duties as managers

- A **corporation** would insure Holly, her executive officers and directors, based upon their duties as officers and directors. It would also cover stockholders, but only with respect to their liability as stockholders.

Employees and volunteer workers could also be covered, but only within the scope of their employment. Remember, this is liability coverage. There will be no protection against injury to a partner, owner, co-employee, and their family members or for property damage that is not third party.

Limits of Insurance

The Commercial General Liability Policy has several limits to consider within the policy. The limits fix how much will be paid regardless of the number of insured's, claims or persons bringing suit.

General Aggregate Limit

An **Aggregate Limit is the most the policy will pay within a fixed period of time**. The CGL has two different Aggregate Limits. The first limit is referred to as the General Aggregate Limit. The General Aggregate Limit is the most the policy will pay per year for all combined claims from Coverage A, B and C. It considers **everything except Products and Completed Operations.**

Products and Completed Operations Aggregate Limit

The second limit is called Products and Completed Operations, which has a separate Aggregate Limit that will not affect or reduce the amount of the General Aggregate Limit. These exposures are more extreme than most of the others. There may be a need to have a much higher amount of coverage on products than something like premises. Premises are limited by physical size and the amount of third party individuals that can be exposed throughout the year. Products may have been distributed worldwide over years of sales.

Note: If asked, which exposures would not reduce or which exposures are not included in the General Aggregate Limit, the answer would be Products and Completed Operations

Aggregate example: If a policy had an annual Aggregate Limit of $1 million and one claim of $300,000, the insured would have $700,000 worth of protection for the rest of the year. At the end of the year, the limit would return to $1 million.

Per Occurrence Limits

In addition to limiting coverage over the course of a year, there may also be a per occurrence limit. This creates a limit for each claim. The General Aggregate Limit may be $10 million, but the Medical Payments limit may be $20,000 per occurrence.

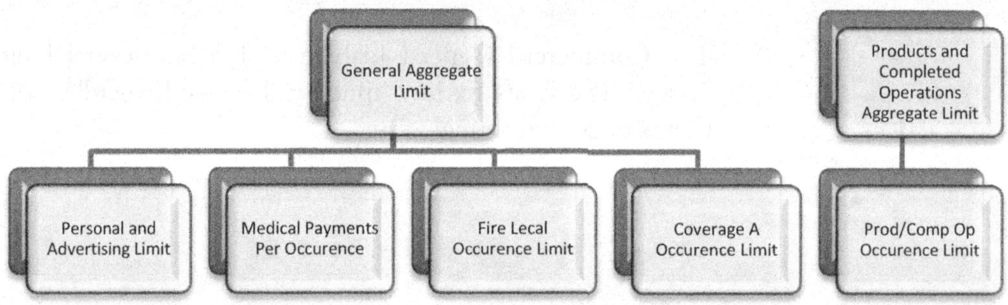

Commercial General Liability Conditions

Many of the Conditions should be familiar to you by now. The following is a list of the conditions listed in the CGL policy.

- Bankruptcy
- Duties in the Event of Occurrence, Offense, Claim or Suit
    - Notify the insured as soon as practicable. Include:
        - How, when and where the occurrence took place
        - Names and addresses of injured persons and witnesses

- If a suit is brought against the insured
    - Record the specifics and date received
    - Notify the insured
- The insured must also
    - Send the insurer copies of demands, notices, summons or any relevant legal papers
    - Authorize the insurer to obtain information
    - Cooperate with the insurer in the investigation or settlement
    - Assist the insurer in the enforcement of any right against any person which may be liable to the insured
- Do not volunteer payment or assume any liability without the insurer's consent

- Legal Action against Us
- Other Insurance
- Premium Audit – Premiums paid are advance deposits. Audits will be done at the end of the term to determine the actual premium for the past year. At this time, the insured will pay the remaining obligation or the insurer will refund any over payment to the First Named insured For example, last year Holly's premium was $250 each quarter. At the end of the year, she paid a total of $1,000 in premium. After the premium audit, it was determined she only needed to pay $750, so she was refunded $250. This year, she continued to pay $250 each quarter for her premium; however, her exposure was different this year. After the premium audit, it was determined that she needed to pay $1,200 for her annual coverage; Holly now owes $200 in premium.
- Representations – Statements made in the application were true to the best of the insured's knowledge
- Separation of Insureds – Insurance applies separately to each insured
- Transfer of Rights of Recovery against Others to Us – Subrogation clause

Policy Triggers

There are two ways in which the CGL policy can be written. It is the trigger (the event that triggers the claim), which determines the difference. The two triggers are "Occurrence" or "Claims Made."

Note: Trigger is the event that sets the policy off

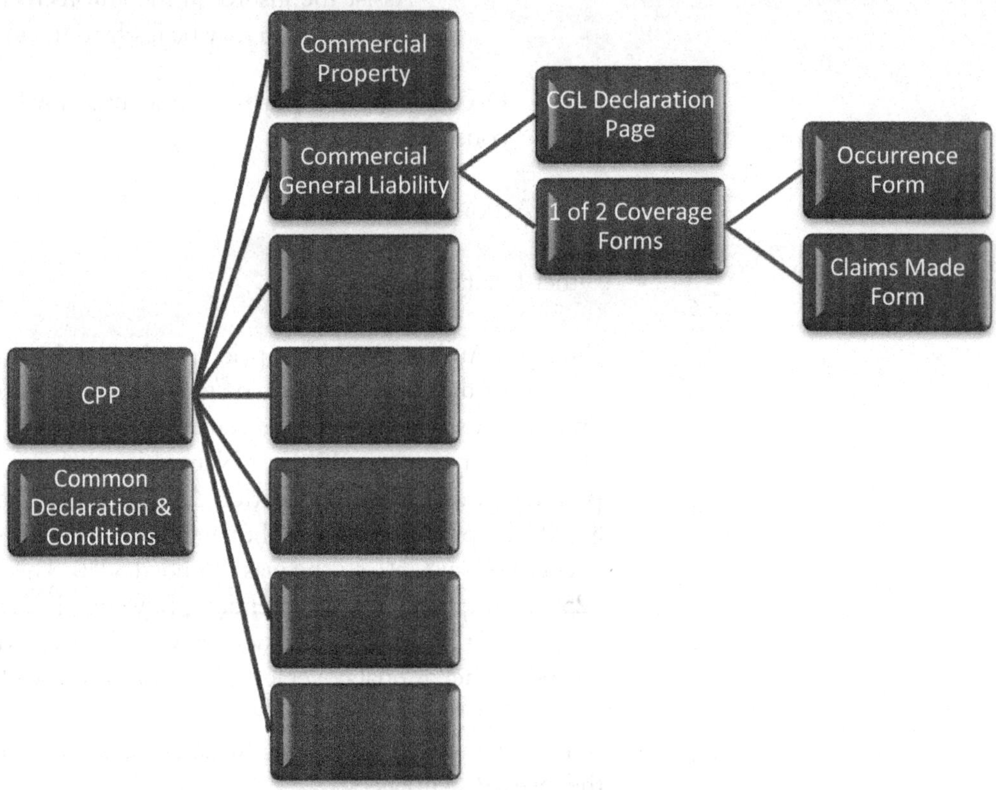

Occurrence Form

Under the Occurrence Form, the trigger is when the issue occurs. As long as the issue which leads to the liability claim **occurs while the policy is in force (during the policy period)**, then that is the policy that would provide protection. It does not matter when the claim is filed or the suit is brought. It may not become an issue until after the policy is dropped. The policy in force at the time of the occurrence is the policy that will pay the claim.

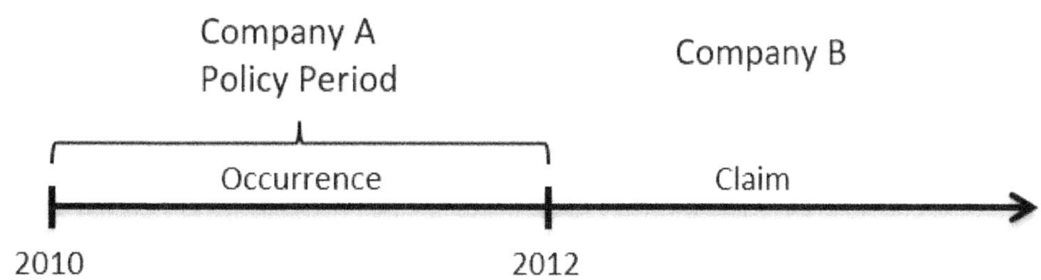

Joe owns a landscaping business and uses various chemicals, fertilizers and insecticides in his business. There is an accident in his store in 2011. A shelving unit collapses and some of the chemicals and insecticides burst open and spilled in his store. Customers were exposed to the fumes. Joe immediately cleaned up the mess and thought nothing more about it. In 2012, Joe decides to switch his policy over to Company B.

In 2013, one of the customers present in the store that day goes to the doctor with breathing problems. After a biopsy, it is discovered that his lungs have been chemically burned. It is determined that he was exposed in 2011 in Joe's store. A lawsuit ensues.

Which company will cover Joe's liability? Company A that Joe owned between 2010 and 2012 or Company B that Joe currently carries?

If it is an Occurrence Form, then the policy in effect at the time of the occurrence will cover Joe (Company A). Even though Joe dropped Company A, a few years ago, it was the policy in effect at the time of the occurrence.

Three issues arose with the Occurrence Form:

- No end to the liability of the insurance company
- Filing claims with companies which are no longer current
- Out of date policy limits

As a result of these concerns, a second form was created.

Claims Made Form

The focus of the Claims Made Form is the **time of the claim**, not the occurrence. As long as the policy is in force at the time of the claim, that is the policy that covers the insured.

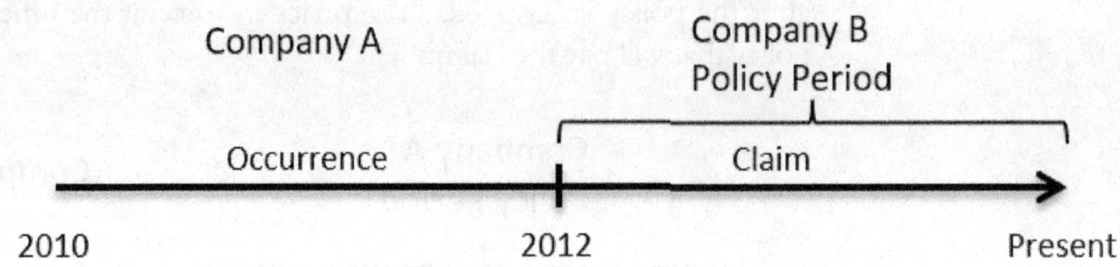

Let's look at our example again. If the policies that Joe carried had been Claims Made, then the responsibility would have changed. Now Company B will be responsible for the coverage. Since the claim is initiated during the policy period of Company B, then B is responsible.

The advantage is that it is today's policy covering Joe. That means that Joe will have the most current limits and coverage. When Joe drops the policy and switches to another company, then Company B's responsibility ends and the new company will assume future responsibility.

Retroactive Dates

So how far back will Joe's insurance company go back to cover claims? Ideally it will cover Joe from the inception of his business, but this could be quite a long period of time. **A Retroactive Date limits how far back a policy will go and still maintain coverage.**

Let's say that Joe started his business in 2008. When he purchased his policy, the Retroactive Date was set at January 1, 2010. Joe will still be covered in the previous example, since the occurrence was after the retroactive date and the claim is in the policy period of Company B.

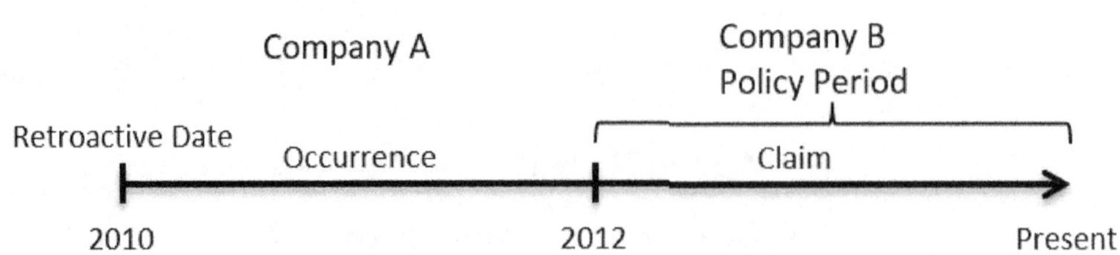

If a claim is filed based upon an event that occurred prior to the Retroactive Date, coverage will not be provided.

Typically when an insured switches insurance companies, retroactive dates are matched in order to provide continuous coverage. If an insured goes without coverage for a period of time and then requests a company to cover them retroactively, a company would deny the request and set a new Retroactive Date. As long as coverage is maintained with one company or another, coverage should be seamless. A gap in coverage is when an insured could be left without protection.

But, what if Joe is ready to retire? He could still be liable to the public, even after retirement. Joe cannot afford to go without coverage, but yet he may not want to continue making premium payments for something that he no longer does. An ERP will help cover Joe in this situation.

EXTENDED REPORTING PERIODS (ERP'S)

The Extended Reporting Periods go into effect in two events. The first event covers the insured if he is retiring, closing business, or getting out of business for any other reason. The second event covers, the insured if he is changing from a Claims Made form to an Occurrence form.

If Joe retires, he has no interest in continuing his business expenses. Yet, it is still possible that he may be liable today for something that occurred yesterday. Joe needs to know that he is still protected, even if something comes up after his retirement. The ERP's are designed to assist with this situation.

There are three types of ERP's. Two Basic ERP's and one Supplemental ERP.

- **Basic (Mini) ERP** – This ERP is typically **60 days long**. It is **free**. It goes into effect **automatically** upon retirement or situations as described previously. If a claim occurs during this time period, as long as the occurrence happened after the retroactive date and before retirement, coverage will apply. It basically extends the time to file a claim to 60 days, after the insured has left the business.

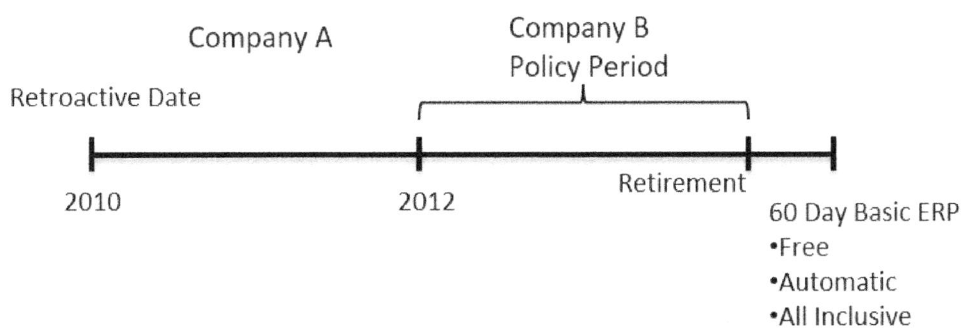

- **Basic (Midi) ERP** – This ERP is for a longer period of time. It is typically **3 to 5 years.** This ERP is also **free.** The main difference between this ERP and the 60 day mini ERP is that the 60 day covers anything that would have been covered under the original coverage. The 5 year midi ERP only covers that which has been **reported** previously. The more the insured reports, the more coverage is provided. **The policy will even give the insured the time during the mini ERP to report instances of concern.**

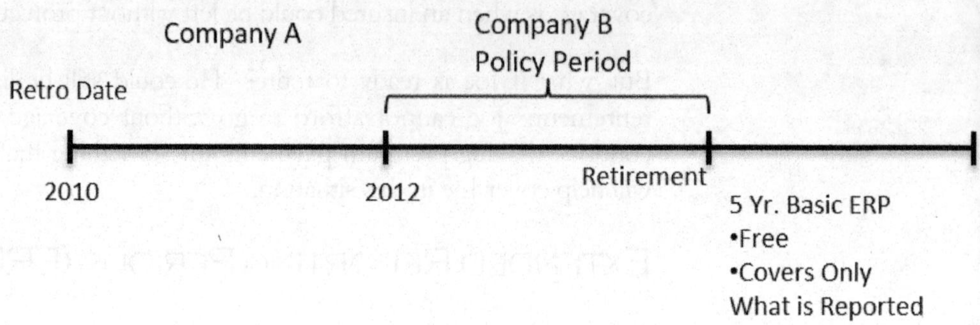

- **Supplemental (Maxi) ERP** – Whereas the Basic ERP's are free, this ERP comes with a cost. If Joe is willing to pay a onetime premium, usually **2 times the annual premium**, then protection will continue indefinitely. Basically, this converts coverage from a Claims Made form to an Occurrence form.

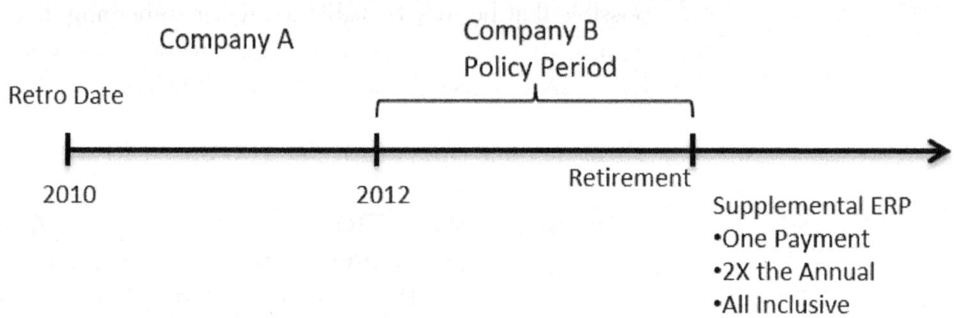

Terms to Know

Liability/3rd Party Insurance

Negligence

Commercial General Liability (CGL)

Coverage A: Bodily Injury and Property Damage Liability

- Premises liability
- Operations liability
- Products
- Completed operations
- Independent contractors
- Contractual liability
    - LEASE
- Fire legal

Coverage B: Personal injury and Advertising injury

Coverage C: Medical Payments

Aggregate limits

Per occurrence limits

Trigger

Occurrence form

Claims made form

Retroactive date

Extended Reporting Periods (ERP)

- Basic (Mini) ERP
- Supplemental (Maxi) ERP

Acronyms to Know

CGL- Commercial General Liability

LEASE- Lease agreements, Easements, Agreement to indemnify a municipality, Sidetrack agreements, Elevator maintenance agreements

ERP- Extended Reporting Periods

Numbers to Know

1 year- Medical payments

Watercraft covered - Less than 26 feet in length

Basic Mini ERP- 60 days

Supplemental Maxi ERP- one time premium of 2 times annual premium amount

Practice Exam

1. The general aggregate limit:

    a) Represents the maximum payout for the policy

    b) Does not include Products and Completed Operations

    c) Represents the maximum payout for the policy year

    d) Does not include Personal and Advertising Injury

2. An Extended Reporting Period:

    a) Extends the time in which a claim may be reported

    b) Extends the time in which coverage is provided

    c) Defines the date in which protection becomes available

    d) Is typically limited to 60 days

3. The Commercial General Liability policy is designed to protect:

    a) Sole proprietors, partnerships, LLC's and corporations

    b) Someone injured by most business establishments

    c) Employees working outside their scope of employment

    d) Stockholders of a corporation for investment purposes

4. Which is NOT under Coverage A: Bodily Injury and Property Damage?

    a) Premises Liability

    b) Completed Operations

    c) Independent Operations

    d) Personal Injury

5. Which of the following is part of Coverage B?

   a) Completed Operations

   b) Advertising Injury

   c) Products

   d) Operations Liability

6. In order for Medical payments to pay, the claim must be reported within ___ year (s) of the date of the accident.

   a) 4

   b) 3

   c) 2

   d) 1

7. Which of these coverages is NOT covered under Supplementary Payments?

   a) Medical payments

   b) Court costs

   c) Loss of earnings up to $250/day

   d) up to $250 of bail bonds

8. John owns a lawn care business. He started his business in 2021. He used a chemical in 2022 that later created some liability concerns. In 2023 a clients pet was killed by ingesting said chemical. In 2024 the client files suit against John. Assuming a different policy each year, under the Occurrence form which would cover John?

   a) 2021 policy

   b) 2022 policy

   c) 2023 policy

   d) 2024 policy

9. Under the same conditions listed in the previous question, if John carried a Claims Made policy, which would have paid?

    a) 2021 policy

    b) 2022 policy

    c) 2023 policy

    d) 2024 policy

10. A retroactive date is:

    a) Available on Occurrence Forms only

    b) What triggers payment of the policy

    c) Triggered due to retirement

    d) Determines when coverage begins

11. There are 5 areas under contractual liability (LEASE). What does the acronym stand for?

    a) Lease agreements, Easements, Agreement to indemnify a municipality, Sidetrack agreements, Elevator maintenance agreements

    b) Liability agreements, Easements, Agreement to indemnify a municipality, Sidetrack agreements, Elevator maintenance agreements

    c) Lease agreements, Exclusions, Agreements to indemnify a municipality, Sidetrack agreements, Elevator maintenance agreements

    d) Liability agreements, Exclusions, Acceptance, Sidetrack agreements, Elevator maintenance agreements

Answer key: 1b 2,a 3,a 4,d 5,b 6,d 7,a 8,c 9,d 10,d 11,a

Chapter 11

Commercial Crime

A business can be exposed to a wide variety of crime exposures. The Crime module offers coverage that will meet the needs of many different businesses and the different exposures that they may be concerned with. The key to this chapter is understanding the terminology used when talking about crime coverage.

There are many different forms of crime from burglary to embezzlement. The Commercial Package Policy provides the opportunity to add coverage within the policy.

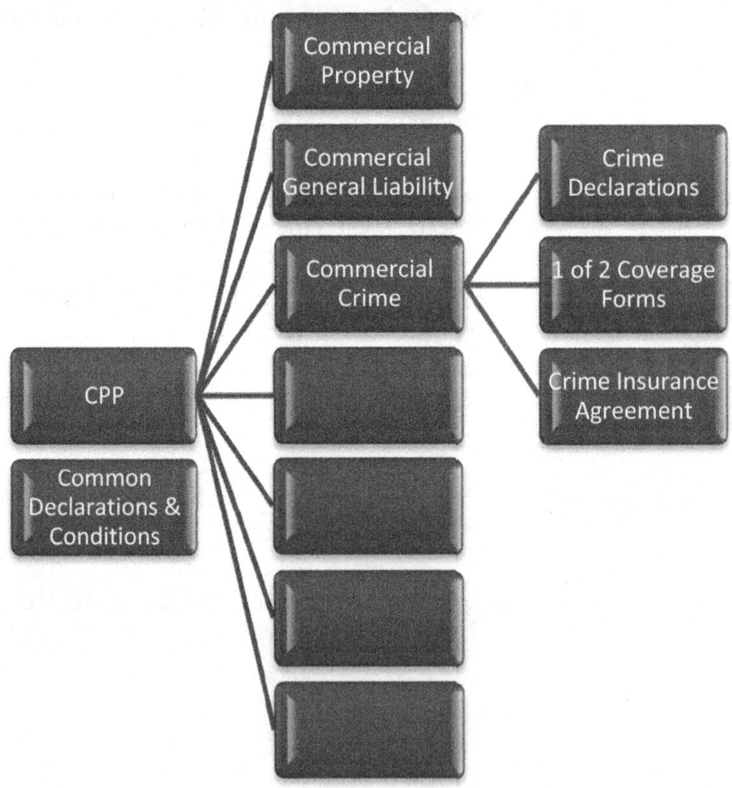

Commercial Crime Form

One of the most important sections of the crime forms will be the definitions. If you understand the definitions, then understanding the coverages comes much easier.

Crime Definitions

Robbery means the unlawful taking of property from the care and custody of a person by causing or threatening to cause **bodily harm**. Robbery is a crime that always involves a threat to another. A bank robber threatens the bank employees and customers in the course of their crime.

Burglary is a crime that always includes **damage to property**. A Cat Burglar cuts the glass and drops through the skylight to steal the diamond. Because the glass was cut, we have damage to property. Burglary means someone is breaking in or out during the commission of the crime. The policy not only covers the item that has been burglarized, but it also includes the damage done as a result of burglary or attempted burglary.

In the case of **Safe Burglary** the policy will also cover the **disappearance** of the safe. Even though there will not be physical evidence of break in or out, if the safe has been taken, we will assume it has been broken into at some point. Disappearance of a safe is considered "physical evidence."

Theft means the unlawful taking of property to the deprivation of the insured. This definition is vague enough to include burglary or robbery; however it would also include stealth. It is the "All Risk" version of crime. A shoplifter would not be covered as burglary or robbery, but they would be covered under the definition of Theft. Theft does have a few exclusions. **Theft by an employee and mysterious disappearance would not be covered.**

A **Custodian** is an individual that has the insured's permission to have the property in their care and custody inside the premises. This might be a sales person. It is not referring to janitors or cleaning staff.

Messengers will have possession of the property off premises. They may be delivering, selling or using the property off premises.

A **watchperson** is hired to watch the property on premises. This person has no other duties but to watch the property inside the premises. This might be a night watchperson. Premium rates may be lowered if a night watchperson is warranted in the policy.

Guards protect the property off premises.

Crime Insurance Agreements

Employee Theft

Employee Theft covers loss or damage to money, securities and other property as a result of theft committed by an employee. Under this form, theft includes forgery.

Forgery or Alteration

This form covers the insured against forged checks and instruments which are drawn upon. This agreement also covers any reasonable expense that the insured must incur to defend themselves for refusing to cover the forged instrument.

Inside the Premises – Theft of Money and Securities

This agreement is designed **specifically to cover cash money** and securities. It provides protection for theft, disappearance or destruction. This means that it not only provides the all-risk version of crime, but would also cover issues like fire, wind and other physical perils that money could be exposed to. It also covers damage to the premises for theft or attempted theft.

Inside the Premises – Robbery or Safe Burglary

This agreement is designed to cover robbery. There must be a threat to do bodily harm. It would not cover burglary unless it was specifically burglary of a safe. The safe must have physical signs of forced entry. If the safe is taken, the disappearance of a safe is considered a physical sign.

Outside the Premises

The Outside the Premises agreement will pay for loss of **money** and securities outside the premises for **theft, disappearance and destruction**. It will also cover other property off premises in the care of a messenger for robbery or attempted robbery.

Computer Fraud

The insurer will pay for loss of or damage to money, securities or other property resulting directly from the use of any computer to fraudulently cause a transfer of that property from inside the premises to outside the premises.

Funds Transfer Fraud

This agreement pays for loss of funds resulting directly from a fraudulent instruction directing a financial institution to transfer, pay or deliver funds from your account.

Money Orders and Counterfeit Money

This will cover loss resulting directly from the insured, having accepted counterfeit money or money orders in good faith, in exchange for merchandise.

Exclusions

Some of the unique exclusions that will be included in the Crime form include: actions committed by the insured or those acting for the insured; acts learned by the insured prior to the policy period; Inventory shortages

Conditions

Termination as to Any Employee

Protection terminates to any employee as soon as the insured becomes aware of any dishonest act committed by the employee. Termination will occur whether the act occurred before or after becoming employed by the insured. Termination will occur with 30 days notice.

Commercial Crime Forms

There are two different Commercial Crime forms available. The first is called the Loss Sustained form. This form is similar to the Occurrence form, discussed in the previous section. The second is called the Discovery form. The Discovery form is similar to the Claims Made form.

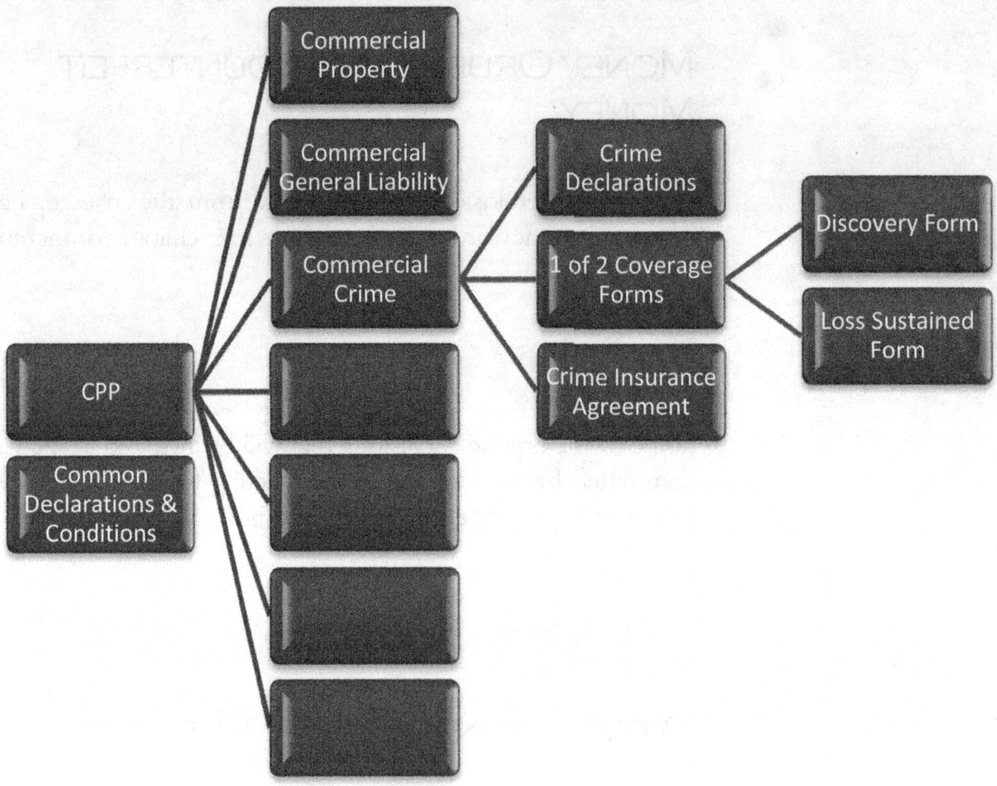

LOSS SUSTAINED FORM

The focus is when the loss is sustained. If the loss occurs during the policy period, the policy will pay, even if the claim is not filed until after the policy expires. The Loss Sustained form works similar to the Occurrence form.

Extended Period to Discover Loss

The insurer will pay for a loss sustained prior to the cancellation date of the policy which is discovered within 1 year from such date. This coverage terminates upon issuance of any other insurance.

Loss Sustained During Prior Insurance Issued By Us or Any Affiliate

If a loss is discovered during the current policy period but it occurred either partially or totally during the previous policy period, then coverage will:

- Be provided as long as it would have been covered under the current policy
- First settle any losses under the current plan and then settle losses under the previous plans
- Pay losses under the current plan according to its limits; Pay losses prior to the current policy effective date according to the previous plans limits

DISCOVERY FORM

The emphasis of the Discovery form is the discovery itself. This form works similar to the Claims Made form. The focus is discovery or the claim itself.

Extended Period to Discover Loss

The insurer will pay for a loss sustained prior to the date of cancelation if discovered within **60 days after cancellation**. This is applicable as long as no other insurance exists. This is a 60 day Basic ERP.

Endorsements

EXTORTION – COMMERCIAL ENTITIES

This is a crime coverage endorsement that is designed to provide protection against loss of money, securities and property which results directly from extortion. Extortion includes a threat of bodily harm against the insured, its employees, directors or those person's relatives who are captured or allegedly captured.

GUESTS' PROPERTY

This endorsement is designed to cover the insured's legal liability for loss of guests' property due to theft.

Terms to know

Robbery

Burglary

Safe Burglary

Theft

Custodian

Messenger

Watchperson

Guard

Loss Sustained Form

Discovery Form

Numbers to Know

Loss Sustained Form- Extended Period to Discover Loss- 1 year

Discovery Form- Extended Period to Discover Loss- 60 days after cancellation

Practice Exam

1. The unlawful taking of property from the care and custody of a person by causing or threatening bodily harm:

    a) Burglary

    b) Theft

    c) Robbery

    d) Forgery

2. Which is FALSE?

    a) With safe burglary, the policy does not cover the disappearance of the safe

    b) A watchperson is hired to watch the property on premises

    c) A custodian is permitted to have property on premises

    d) Burglary always includes damage to property

3. What is the unlawful taking of property to the deprivation of the insured?

    a) Theft

    b) Burglary

    c) Robbery

    d) Custodian

4. What is "crime that always includes damage to property?

    a) Theft

    b) Robbery

    c) Fraud

    d) Burglary

5. On the Loss Sustained Form, the Extended Period to Discover Loss is:

   a) 2 years

   b) 60 days

   c) 1 year

   d) 90 days

6. Mysterious disappearance:

   a) Is defined as a loss from a known place and time

   b) Includes robbery and burglary

   c) Is defined as loss due to stealth

   d) Includes items misplaced or lost

7. Employee dishonesty:

   a) Is included in Money Orders and Counterfeit coverage

   b) Includes loss of money by an employee, and includes forgery

   c) Includes embezzlement but does not include forgery

   d) Protects against computer fraud

8. The Discovery Form:

   a) Emphasizes the date of discovery

   b) Is the same as a Loss Sustained Form

   c) Extends company exposure beyond the policy period

   d) Emphasizes the date when the loss is sustained

Answer key: 1,c 2,a 3,a 4,d 5,c 6,d 7,b 8,a

Chapter

12

Equipment Breakdown

The general rule is that the insurance industry does not insure "inherent vice." Inherent vice is defined as a tendency in physical objects to deteriorate because of instability of the components which they are made, as opposed to deterioration caused by external forces. Mechanical breakdown is a loss that will happen over time. It is not considered a "risk" or "uncertainty." Yet businesses may find themselves dependent upon their machines. If certain machines, within a business breakdown or stop working, the result may be a substantial financial loss to the business. Breakdown can result in loss or damage to property. The Equipment Breakdown policy is designed to protect the business from just such an exposure.

Why Equipment Breakdown

In the mid 1800's, the advent of steam power created a new industrial hazard. The boiler circulated water with great heat and pressure which turned it into steam. This power was used for great advances, but these advances did not come without risk. In 1866, catastrophic boiler explosions were occurring at a rate of approximately one in every four days.

The insurance industry found that this "risk" and the results of this "risk" were not insurable under normal methods. Since these losses were based upon breakdown of machinery, it was a loss that was likely to happen. In other words, it is a form of inherent vice. Based upon the frequency and the amount of damage that could result from these issues, the business owner had a need for help and assistance. In 1866, a group of industrialists and business leaders in Hartford, Connecticut, formed a group to address this problem. Out of their discussions, Boiler and Machinery Insurance was formed. Boiler and Machinery has now become Equipment breakdown, allowing more types of machinery to be included.

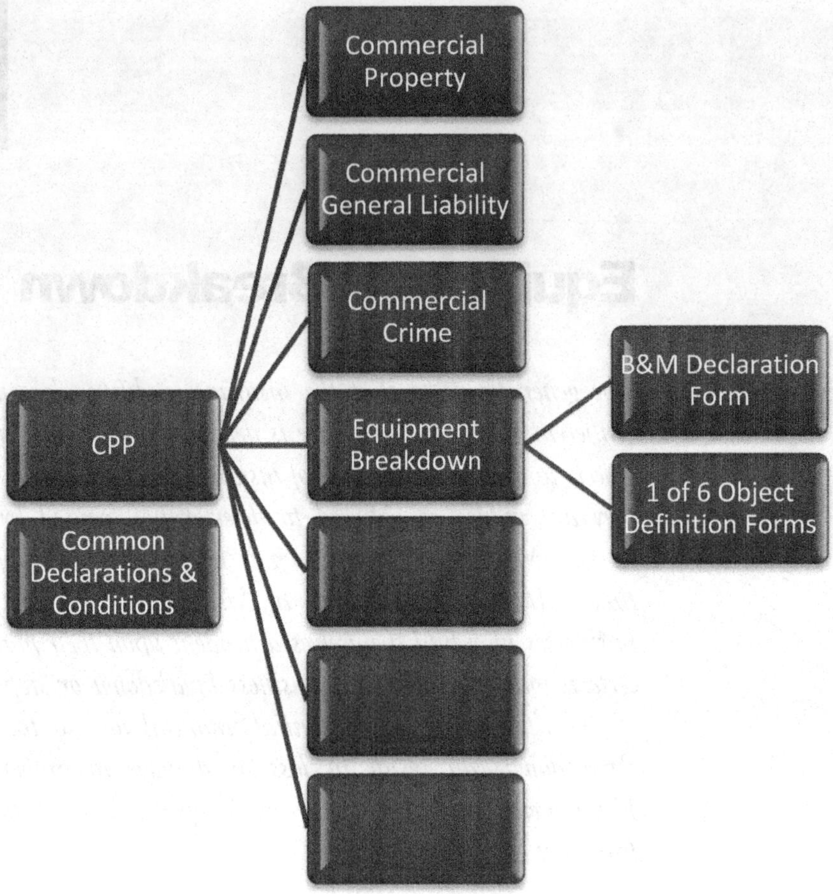

How Does Boiler and Machinery Work?

In order for the insurer to be able to cover a boiler or any other type of machinery for breakdown, the form is going to have to include a few unique elements.

Inspections

It is an **inspection** element that makes this product different than any of the other products we have discussed. Boiler and Machinery insurance is designed to reduce, through periodic inspections, the chance of breakdown. Breakdown is typically excluded on any of the other property forms. Since breakdown is preventable through maintenance and would be considered an inherent vice, it is considered an uninsurable risk. Breakdown is not an uncertainty; it is just a matter of time.

By adding an annual inspection as a condition of coverage, breakdown now becomes the unexpected and thus insurable. If it has been maintained and checked on a regular basis, the breakdown becomes an unanticipated occurrence.

Inspections will typically be required on an annual basis, but the **insurer has the right to inspect at any time.**

Suspension

If as a result of an inspection it is discovered that the insured equipment is in a dangerous condition, coverage may be suspended until the equipment is properly repaired. Once repaired, coverage will continue. With most products, the insurer must give the insured timely notice prior to cancelling or suspending coverage. With this product, the equipment has been found to be dangerous. Any future incidence could and should be avoided simply by shutting down the equipment. For this reason, **suspension will be immediate**. **Notice must still be given, but it will not be advance notice.**

Coverages

Covered Cause of Loss Forms

Unlike most of the other property forms, this form will not have a Basic, Broad or Special Cause of Loss form. The covered cause of loss for Boiler and Machinery is limited to breakdown. **Breakdown** is the peril that this form will insure against.

Breakdown is defined to include **direct** physical loss, which causes damage to covered equipment. It is designed to cover equipment that the business might be dependent upon. Unless otherwise stated, it only covers direct damage done to the equipment. Its definition includes:

- Failure of pressure or vacuum equipment
- Mechanical failure including rupture or bursting caused by centrifugal force
- Electrical failure including arcing

If an initial breakdown leads to another breakdown, then it will all be considered to be one breakdown.

The following coverages would also be covered if indicated on the declaration page. These coverages are only available if chosen. They are not automatically included.

Property Damage

The policy will pay for direct damage to Covered Property located at the premises listed in the Declaration page. Covered Property would be any property that the insured owns (whether building or business personal property) or is in the insured's care, custody and control.

Expediting expenses are also covered under property damage. Expediting expenses are the costs incurred by the insured when making temporary repairs and additional costs associated with repairing the damaged property in a high priority time frame.

Business Income and/or Extra Expense

Indirect coverage is not automatically included in this policy form. If this coverage is indicated on the Declaration page, then one or both of these will be included in the coverage.

Business Income

Business Income is designed to replace lost income because the business is required to shut down as a result of a loss. This coverage replaces lost income during the period of restoration.

Extra Expense

Extra Expense coverage is designed to keep the business open. It will pay the extra expenses required after a loss, in order to stay operational. It is designed to pay throughout the period of restoration.

Both of these coverages are financial losses that result from a direct loss. They can be purchased individually or they can be purchased together.

Spoilage Damage

This coverage would be appropriate for a grocer. It is designed to protect raw materials or finished products from spoilage due to lack of power, light, heat, steam or refrigeration. It will also cover expenses necessary to protect property from spoilage as a result of the lack of power, light, heat, steam or refrigeration.

UTILITY INTERRUPTION

This coverage extends Business Income, Extra Expense and Spoilage Damage. If any one of these is listed in the Declaration page, coverage is extended to include losses resulting from the interruption of utility services.

Other Available Coverages

Other coverages that would be included if designated on the Declaration page would include:

- Newly Acquired Premises
- Ordinance or Law Coverage
- Errors and Omissions
- Brands and Labels

Valuation

This form will provide replacement cost coverage as the standard form of valuation. If an insured wants to reduce coverage, it could be altered to actual cash value with an endorsement. This would reduce premium, as well as protection.

Deductibles

The deductible is the part of the expense that the insured retains. The deductible is first paid by the insured before the coverage under the policy begins. The minimum deductible dollar amount would be $250.

Time element coverages could be expressed as a period of time.

Object Definition Forms

A key element of this form is defining the object which is to be insured. That is accomplished with the "Object Definition Form." Originally this form was created because of the expanded use of boilers and steam related objects. This is where the original name, Boiler and Machinery came from. Once it was determined that with the right type of contract these types of machines could be insured; there became an interest and need to insure other types of machinery. Thus, the name of the product has evolved from "Boiler and Machinery" to "Equipment Breakdown." The equipment breakdown policy is designed to cover a variety of machines that a business may be dependent upon. We now have a need to categorize the type of machinery in order adequately price the product. The risk for boilers is different than the risk for freezers breaking down.

The "Object Definition Form" categorizes the equipment to be insured into one of six categories. One or more must be included in each Boiler and Machinery form. The first four are designed to cover specific types of equipment. The last two cover all four types, one including production equipment and one excluding production equipment.

- Pressure and Refrigeration Objects
- Mechanical Objects
- Electrical Objects
- Turbine Objects
- Comprehensive Objects Including Production Equipment
- Comprehensive Objects Excluding Production Equipment

Terms to know

Inspection

Suspension

Expediting expenses

Spoilage

Utility Interruption Form

Object Definition Form

Numbers to know

$250- minimum deductible

Practice Exam

1. Which of the following is FALSE?

   a) Equipment Breakdown is designed to reduce the chance of breakdown

   b) The insurer cannot inspect at any time

   c) Breakdown is preventable through maintenance

   d) Annual inspections are a condition of coverage

2. Which is NOT a part of the definition of breakdown?

   a) If initial breakdown leads to another breakdown, it is considered 2 breakdowns

   b) Failure of pressure or vacuum equipment

   c) Mechanical failure

   d) Electrical failure

3. Coverage can be suspended. Which of the following is FALSE?

   a) No advance notice is required

   b) Suspension is immediate

   c) Coverage can be suspended until repairs are made

   d) Equipment Breakdown has basic, broad, and special forms

4. What is the purpose of the Object Definition Form?

   a) Categorize the type of machinery covered

   b) List the specific object covered

   c) Define the limits to the object insured

   d) Define the coverage provided

Answer key: 1,b 2,a 3,d 4,a

Chapter

13

Commercial Auto

Businesses can have multiple uses for the auto in their business. There are various vehicles with many different exposures, based upon the type and how the vehicle will be used. We may be talking about concrete trucks, semis, taxi cabs, delivery vans, parking garages, dealerships or many other different scenarios;, each with a different need and each with a different exposure. The commercial auto form is designed to meet these various needs.

Coverage Forms

The business exposure is very similar as our personal exposure when utilizing a vehicle. The main difference is the type of vehicle driven and how it is used. Both will need liability protection to cover their responsibility to the other drivers. Both personal and commercial will need physical damage coverage as well as medical payments. They will also both be exposed to uninsured and underinsured drivers.

There are four different forms that will be explored:

- **Business Auto Coverage Form** – This vehicle is very similar to that covered by the Personal Auto Policy. It may be a car, van or pick up. It may have the same basic exposure as the personal auto. The main difference is that it is owned by the business, not an individual. Insurance must be purchased by the business to cover their vehicle and their exposure. This could be a company car.

- **Truckers Form** – The truckers form is an older form that has basically been replaced by the Motor Carrier Form, described below. It was very specific in its use. A trucker is someone who is hired to haul the goods of others. This would most typically be a semi driver, driver inter or intra state.

- **Motor Carrier Form** – The Motor Carrier Form covers a vehicle that is being used to haul the goods of others or the insureds own goods. The insured vehicle could be a semi, van or automobile. This form is much more versatile than the Truckers Form. It can be used to cover taxi cabs, semi-trucks, delivery vans and a wide variety of vehicles and their uses.

- **Garage Form** – The Garage form is designed specifically for the business based upon the vehicle itself. Examples include; dealerships, mechanics, parking lots or valet parking. In these examples there is a need to cover the vehicles on the lot or on the road. They may be driven by company representatives or customers. This form also provides liability protection against the customer on the business premises.

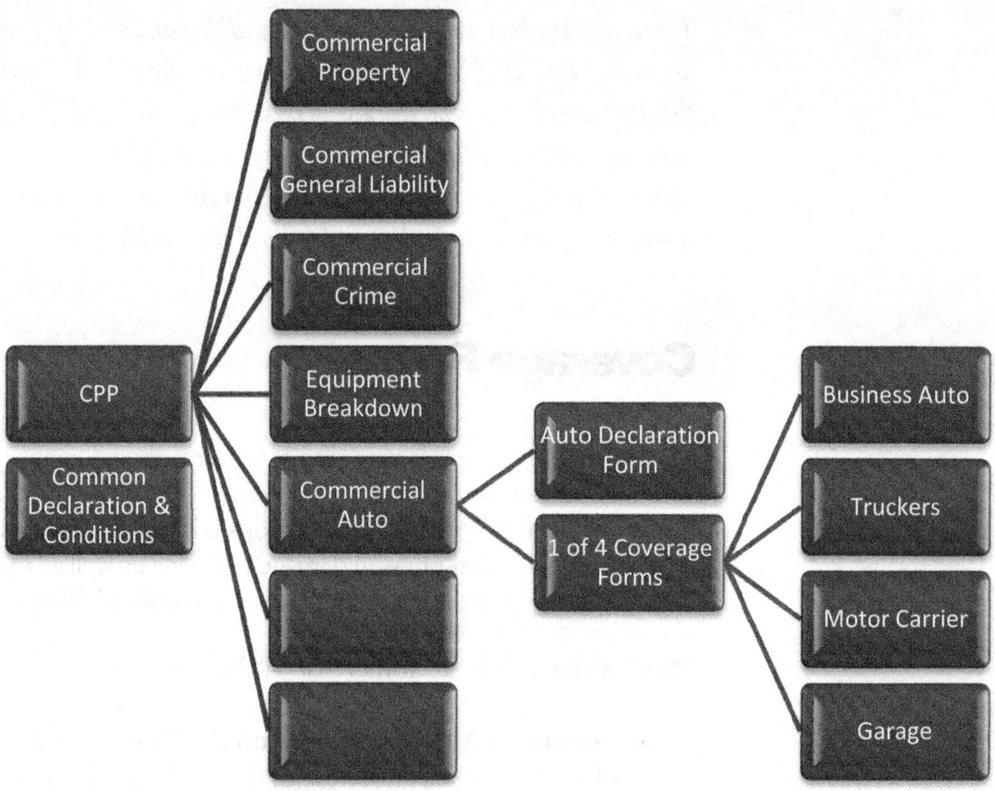

Business Auto Form

The Business Auto Form has several sections in it, the first three sections are:

Section I - Covered Auto

When covering a vehicle under the Business Auto Form, one of the first things that needs to be done is to establish which type of vehicle will be insured. This is done by choosing a symbol and listing it on the declaration page. **A symbol is used to describe the auto** that needs to be covered. The symbols for the Business Auto Form include:

1 • Any Auto

2 • Owned Autos

3 • Owned Private Passenger Autos Only

4 • Owned Autos Other Than Private Passenger Autos Only

5 • Owned Autos Subject To No Fault

6 • Owned Autos subject To a Compulsory Uninsured Motorists Law

7 • Specifically Described Autos

8 • Hired Autos Only

9 • Non Owned Autos Only

19 • Mobile Equipment Subject to Compulsory or Financial Responsibility or Other Motor Vehicle Insurance Law Only

Notice that symbols 1 through 9 are all specific to autos. An auto is defined as a land motor vehicle, trailer or semitrailer designed for travel on public roads or any other vehicle subject to compulsory financial responsibility law. The definition does not include mobile equipment. Symbol 19 is designed specifically to cover mobile equipment on the road.

If financial responsibility is required for mobile equipment on the road, then the policy can cover the equipment. It will need to be listed by using symbol 19.

Section II - Liability Coverage

The liability section of the policy is much like the personal auto liability. It is designed to provide third party liability protection for bodily injury or property damage. It covers any pollution liability as a result of a covered accident.

The policy defines the insured as:

- The insured for any covered auto
- Anyone else while using with the insured's permission a covered auto he/she owns, hires or borrows, or
- Employees

Limits are typically expressed as a single limit policy. This means that all claimants will be paid out of a single pot. The limits are not split into per person or physical damage pots.

The following options are also available. If chosen, the business owner must list them on the declaration page.

- Medical payments – similar to personal auto. It is no-fault, preventive and pro-active.
- Uninsured and Underinsured Motorists – Again, similar to the personal auto coverage. It protects the business against other at fault drivers with no insurance or not enough insurance.
- Employers Non-ownership Liability – This protects the employer when an employee uses their personal auto for business purposes.

Section III – Physical Damage Coverage

The physical damage coverage of the Commercial Auto Policy is also much like the Personal Auto Policy. It provides both comprehensive and collision coverage. Valuation will be on an actual cash value basis.

Coverage Territory

The definition of coverage territory here in the Commercial Auto Policy is slightly different than the meaning in the Personal Auto Policy. The definition will be limited to the United States, its territories, Puerto Rico, and Canada. This is the same as the Personal Auto Policy. But, it will also provide coverage anywhere in the world if:

- A covered auto of the private passenger type is leased, hired, rented or borrowed without a driver for a period of 30 days or less; and

- The insured's responsibility to pay damages is determined in a suit on the merits, in the United States, the territories, Puerto Rico, or Canada.

Business Auto Endorsements

Drive Other Car Coverage

For the employee who is supplied with a company car to drive, this endorsement may allow coverage for them when driving a third party vehicle. Let's say that Joe drives a company car. Since Joe does not own a vehicle of his own, Joe may not feel the need to purchase insurance. He understands that the company that he works for provides insurance when he is driving their car. But Joe finds himself driving other vehicles in his personal time. Perhaps he rents a car, borrows a car, or drives someone else's car when on vacation. Joe carries no insurance for these vehicles since he does not have a Personal Auto Policy. Joe also does not think to ask the owners if they have insurance or how much. Drive Other Car Coverage allows Joe to take the company insurance with him and to treat it much like his own insurance.

Additional Insured – Lessor

When leasing a vehicle or financing one, the finance company may want to be listed as an additional insured to protect their interest.

Mobile Equipment

This endorsement is designed to provide coverage for mobile equipment while being used on the road. Mobile equipment may use the roadways even though it is not licensed for the road. If an accident were to occur, the equipment would not be covered since it is not licensed for the road. This would treat the equipment the same as an automobile.

Auto Medical Payments

This provides medical payments coverage similar to that found in the Personal Auto Policy.

Individual Named Insured

Just because the employee has permission to drive the company car, this does not mean the spouse of the employee has permission. An employee does not have the authority to loan out a vehicle that belongs to his/her employer. If a spouse is driving the company car, without permission from the owner, they will not be covered. If the individual is given permission through the Individual Named Insured endorsement, then coverage would apply.

Motor Carrier Coverage Form

The Motor Carrier Coverage Form was created as an expansion of the Truckers Form. One major difference between the two forms is the Motor Carrier Form expands the definition of covered autos to include private passenger autos.

The Motor Carrier Coverage Form can be used to cover vehicles that are used to transport goods that belong to others or to transport their own goods. Goods could be refrigerated items, livestock, people, merchandise, and just about anything else that one might need to haul. It covers a wide variety of vehicles such as cars, vans, semis, buses and other vehicles licensed for the road.

Section III – Trailer Interchange Coverage

Trailer interchange is a coverage that was available on the Truckers Form and is also included in the Motor Carrier Coverage Form.

A trucker may own his/her personal rig and haul the goods of others, but typically the trailer used to transport the goods will belong to the shipper. They will need to know that the proper trailer is used to ship their merchandise and that it is correctly loaded. It may need refrigeration or other special considerations. The shipper will also use the trailer as their traveling bill board. These trailers can cost a substantial amount of money. Once the trucker takes possession of the shipper's trailer, the trailer is in the truckers' care, custody and control. The trucker will want the trailer properly covered as they are responsible for it.

Once the trailer is dropped off at the delivery point, the trucker may start looking for another trailer to haul on his way back. This second trailer may belong to another shipper.

The Trailer Interchange Coverage is designed to cover the truckers' liability or responsibility to cover the damage done to the trailer that is in the care of the trucker at the time of the accident.

The Motor Carrier Act of 1980

The Motor Carrier Act of 1980 is the financial responsibility law for the trucking industry. The liability exposure of the trucker is much greater than that of the personal auto driver, and as a result, their minimal requirements to drive will also be much higher. Truckers also cross state lines, so a federal requirement makes much more sense.

The three minimal limits are:

- **$750,000** for interstate transport of non-hazardous materials
- **$1,000,000** for transport of oil or hazardous materials
- **$5,000,000** for transport of certain types or amounts of hazardous materials (explosives, compressed gas, radioactive materials, etc.)

The Motor Carrier Act of 1980 was the law requiring the truck driver to provide financial responsibility. **The MCS-90 is the endorsement that provides the insured with the required protection.**

By issuing the MCS-90 endorsement; an insurer is bound to pay according to the terms of the endorsement for public liability "resulting from the negligence in the operation, maintenance, or use of motor vehicles subject to the Act's financial responsibility requirements."

Public liability is defined to include liability for bodily injury, property damage and environmental restoration. Due to the broad nature of the law, the insurer may be required to pay more than the policy would normally cover. For example, environmental restoration would most likely be excluded. The insurer is required to pay the claim, but is entitled to a re-imbursement from the insured. The re-imbursement would be for anything paid that would not be covered by the policy.

Garage Form

Many businesses have a unique relationship with the automobile. It is more than just a means of transportation. It is a much more integral part of the business. With the dealership, mechanic, or parking lots, the automobile is the product or in the insured's care, custody and control. The Garage Form is a form designed to meet these specific needs.

Section I – Covered Autos

Just like any other auto form, a symbol will have to be listed on the declaration page to indicate the type of auto that will be insured.

- 21 • Any Auto
- 22 • Owned Autos
- 23 •Owned Private Passenger Autos Only
- 24 •Owned Autos Other Than Private Passenger Autos Only
- 25 •Owned Autos Subject To No Fault
- 26 •Owned Autos subject To a Compulsory Uninsured Motorists Law
- 27 •Specifically Described Autos
- 28 •Hired Autos Only
- 29 •Non Owned Autos Used in a Garage Business
- 30 •Autos Left with the insured for Service, Repair, Storage or Safekeeping
- 31 •Dealers Autos (Physical Damage Coverages)

Section II = Liability Coverage

The liability section of this policy is a cross between the auto liability coverage and the CGL. It is designed to cover the business for the use of covered autos. But, it is also designed to cover the insured for garage operations.

Garage operations include ownership, maintenance or use of **locations** for the garage business. It includes the ownership, maintenance or use of the **autos** indicated in Section I of the coverage form. It also includes all **operations** necessary for incidentals in a garage business.

Section III - Garage Keepers Coverage

A Garage Keeper would be anyone that has someone else's vehicle in their care, custody or control. For the business that would need the Garage Form this is an expected situation. Section III of the Garage policy provides Garage Keepers coverage. This covers the insured's responsibility for damage to customer's vehicles left with the named insured for service, repair, storage, or safekeeping.

Garage Keepers Form

Garage Keepers can also be sold as a separate form. This would provide coverage for businesses other than dealerships, who have other people's vehicles in their care, custody and control. Examples might include mechanics, parking lots, valet parking and other businesses that may be responsible for the customers' car.

Terms to know

Coverage Forms

- Business Auto Coverage Form
- Truckers Form
- Motor Carrier Form
- Garage Form

Symbol

Endorsements

- Driver Other Car Coverage
- Additional Insured- Lessor
- Mobile Equipment
- Auto Medical Payments
- Individual Named Insured

Trailer interchange

Motor Carrier Act of 1980

MCS-90

Garage Keeper

Numbers to know

Coverage territory- pay anywhere for 30 days

Practice Exam

1. Which is NOT a form on the Commercial Auto Policy?

    a) Claims Made Form

    b) Motor Carrier Form

    c) Truckers Form

    d) Garage Form

2. Which endorsement allows an employee to take their employer's auto insurance with him when he drives other vehicles on his personal time?

    a) Truckers

    b) Driver Other Car Coverage

    c) Additional Insured

    d) Mobile Equipment

3. Which form covers a van being used to haul goods?

    a) Garage Form

    b) Truckers Form

    c) Business Auto Coverage Form

    d) Motor Carrier Form

4. Which form provides coverage for autos under the insured's care?

    a) Motor Carrier Form

    b) Business Auto Coverage Form

    c) Garage keepers Form

    d) Truckers Form

5. Which of the following locations is NOT a covered territory?

   a) United States

   b) Puerto Rico

   c) Canada

   d) Mexico

6. Jim drives his backhoe from one street corner to another. While driving down the street he hits another vehicle. How would he get coverage for this?

   a) Mobile equipment endorsement

   b) Motor coverage form

   c) Trailer interchange coverage

   d) Business Auto Coverage form

7. Which form would be recommended to a car dealership?

   a) Garage keepers Form

   b) Motor Carrier Form

   c) Garage Form

   d) Business Auto Coverage Form

8. A symbol:

   a) Describes the form used in the policy

   b) Describes the vehicle to be insured

   c) Describes the endorsement added

   d) Describes the limits applied to each auto

Answer key: 1. A 2. B 3. D 4. C 5. D 6. A 7. C 8. B

Chapter

14

Commercial Inland Marine

Inland Marine insurance is designed to cover personal property wherever it is located. In commercial insurance, property could be in transit or located off premises. It could be in the process of being moved by train, plane, auto or mail. We might even see things like pipelines, wires and signs. The different exposures are almost limitless. The Commercial Inland Marine Policy is a property policy that is designed to cover most of these types of needs.

The Commercial Building and Business Personal Property Form that we discussed in a previous unit only covered the property within 100 feet of the building. Now, we need a property form to cover the property wherever it is being used or while it is being moved.

Inland Marine insurance is actually an extension of Ocean Marine. The Ocean Marine is designed to cover goods being moved over the waters, whereas Inland Marine has nothing to do with water. Today, the term marine or floater is used to describe insurance that is used to insure property that is either being moved or is at a location off premises. Coverage is designed to be worldwide and on an all risk basis.

Inland Marine policies can be either filed or unfiled. A filed form has been reviewed and approved for use by the State Department of Insurance. The rates, terms and conditions are pre-approved and ready for sale. A filed form is a standardized product.

An unfiled form is one that has been written by the insurer and is designed to meet the specific need of the business. Judgment rating is typically used in this method. Unfiled forms make it possible to meet the variety of exposures and risks in the marine industry. Unfiled are not standardized.

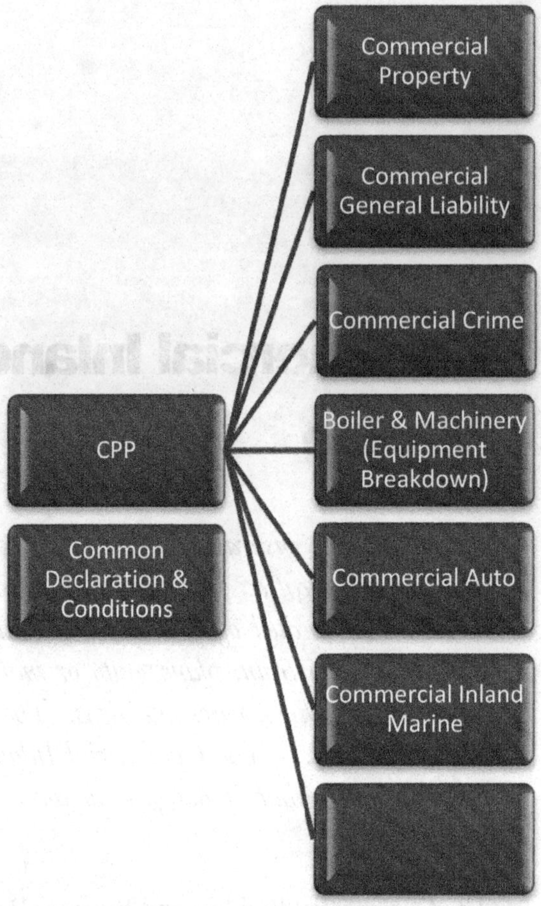

Accounts Receivable

The insurer will pay all amounts due from the insured's customers that they are unable to collect as a result of a covered cause of loss to records of accounts receivable. It will also pay interest on a loan as a result of loss and any collection expenses in excess of normal.

Bailee Customer Floater

A Bailee is defined as someone who has someone else's property in their care, custody and control. Bailee coverage is designed to reimburse the bailor (customer) for damage to property in the care of the bailee (business). Care, custody and control are typically excluded on a liability policy; this is covered as property. Since the policy is a property policy, it will pay regardless of negligence or liability.

Commercial Articles Floater

This works much like the Personal Articles Floater. It allows the insured to schedule difficult to value property and cover it separately on an all risk basis. It is used to insure commercial cameras, musical instruments, video equipment and similar items. It can also be used to cover items of similar description in the insured's care, custody and control.

Contractor Equipment Floater

The Contractor Equipment Floater is used to insure mobile equipment or contractor equipment like bulldozers, backhoes, tools and other machinery. It covers the property worldwide. This means that the property is covered at the worksite, in transit or in storage. Remember, this is a property form. Liability that results from using the property would be covered under the Commercial General Liability form.

Electronic Data Processing Floater

The Electronic Data Processing Floater provides all risk property insurance for electronic data processing equipment. Equipment includes computer programs and data. It also covers computer hardware that has previously been excluded and it also covers some indirect protection. This floater pays extra expense and business interruption coverage as a result of damage to equipment.

Equipment Dealers Floater

Earlier, the Garage Dealers form was discussed and it provided protection for the auto dealerships. The Equipment Dealers Floater provides protection for dealers as well, but is designed to cover equipment dealers selling vehicles other than autos. The Equipment Dealers floater covers the inventory belonging to the business as well as that which is in its care, custody and control.

Installation Floater

The Installation Floater is designed for those businesses which install and test machinery. A common business example for this floater would be the heating and air-conditioning industry. This covers the item while it is in transit, while it is being unloaded, while it is being installed and while it is being tested. Once it is installed and tested, coverage ends. It is now part of the building in which it was installed and as a result, is covered elsewhere.

Jewelers' Block Coverage Floater

The term "block" means all inclusive coverage. A block policy is used to meet the specific needs of that industry. The Jewelers' Block Coverage Floater is designed to cover the jewelers' raw materials used to make their product. Jewelry that is held for sale by the business is covered and those pieces which may be in the jeweler's care, custody and control are also covered.

Signs Coverage floater

At first glance, signs may not seem to fit in this section. Sign coverage under the Commercial Property form was extremely limited by amount and location. There needs to be property coverage available that will cover the sign (which could be very expensive to replace, if damaged). Signs can be found all over, on location and off. This floater will cover the sign wherever the sign happens to be located and for the appropriate amount needed.

Valuable Papers and Records Floater

Coverage for valuable papers and records are limited under the Commercial Property form. Businesses may have a need to properly insure these items and can get them covered by purchasing this floater. Paper and records could include documents, books, maps, manuscripts, abstracts, deeds, mortgages, drawings or films.

Transportation Coverages

The transporting of goods from one location to another is vital to businesses of all types. Insuring the property that is in transit is crucial. It is important to understand the terms that are applicable to the transportation industry. There are three types of carriers of property in the transportation industry:

- **Common Carrier** – A person or company that transports goods or people for any person or company and is responsible for any possible loss of goods during transport. Common carriers offer their services to the general public.

- **Contract Carrier** – A carrier that transports goods for only a certain number of clients for which they have an agreement with. They can refuse to transport goods for anyone else.

- **Private Carrier** – A business that transports its own goods.

The three parties in the transportation industry include:

- **Shipper** – The party that owns the goods and is having it moved to a chosen location.

- **Consignee** – The recipient of the goods.

- **Carrier** – The party transporting the goods.

Common Carrier Cargo Liability

Since common carriers are responsible for the goods or persons in their care, custody and control, they will need protection during their time of responsibility. This coverage is designed to provide the proper liability coverage needed.

Motor Truck Cargo Form

The Motor Truck Cargo form is designed to cover the liability of the Contract Carrier or the Private Carrier. The **Bill of Lading** is the contract between the shipper and the carrier. It will include a list of the merchandise being shipped.

SHIPPERS/OWNERS FORM

The **Shippers Form** or Owners Form is used by private carriers to insure their goods that are being shipped. Since they own the goods and are responsible for their own shipping, they are the ones with the insurable interest. They are shipping their own goods on their own vehicles.

TRUCKERS FORM

The **Truckers Form** is designed to cover the trucking company hauling goods for others. A coverage extension may apply while the goods are in a terminal when they are being loaded and unloaded.

Transit Coverage Forms

TRIP TRANSIT

Trip Transit is a coverage form that is designed to cover a onetime specific shipment. It covers the shipment from the time it leaves the shipper until the time it is received by the consignee.

ANNUAL TRANSIT

Annual Transit is designed to cover the shipment of goods throughout the year. It can be used to cover the interest of the shipper or the consignee.

Terms to know

Inland marine

Filed/Unfiled form

Bailee

Common carriers

Contract carriers

Private carriers

Shipper

Consignee

Carrier

Bill of lading

Shippers form

Truckers from

Trip transit

Annual transit

Practice Exam

1. Which of the following statements is FALSE?

    a) Inland Marine has nothing to do with water

    b) Inland Marine is an extension of ocean marine

    c) Inland Marine is designed to cover property

    d) Inland Marine policies can only be filed

2. Which is NOT a characteristic of Filed Form?

    a) It's a standardized product

    b) Rates, terms, and conditions are pre-approved and ready for sale

    c) Filed form is written by the insurer and designed to meet the specific need of a business

    d) Approval by the State Department of Insurance

3. Which floater allows the insured to schedule difficult to value property on all risk basis?

    a) Commercial Articles Floater

    b) Bailee Customer Floater

    c) Contractor Equipment Floater

    d) Equipment Dealers Floater

4. Which floater is great for heating and air installation or test machinery?

    a) Contractor Equipment Floater

    b) Installation Floater

    c) Bailee Customer Floater

    d) Commercial Articles Floater

5. Which floater is used to insure mobile equipment?

    a) Contractor Equipment Floater

    b) Installation Floater

    c) Equipment Dealers Floater

    d) Bailee Customer Floater

6. A Bailee Customer Floater would cover:

    a) Theft caused by an employee

    b) Property in the businesses care

    c) Liability of property in your care, custody and control

    d) Bailee property in their control

7. What is used to determine the value of property being shipped?

    a) Shippers form

    b) Bill of lading

    c) Motor truck cargo form

    d) Billing and shipping receipts

Answer key: 1,d 2,c 3,a 4,b 5,a 6,b 7,b

Chapter 15

Farms

Farms are unique in their needs because they are the only organization that has a need for every area of coverage which has been previously discussed. The farm needs to be covered for personal property and personal liability. In addition, the farm is a business and will be open to both commercial property exposures as well as commercial liability.

The farm policy is the last of the seven forms available in the Commercial Package Policy. The farm policy is very similar to the homeowners' policy, but the commercial needs of the farmer will be added.

Farm Property Coverage Form

The first part of the policy is designed to meet the property needs of the farmer. It will begin by covering the farmer's personal property needs and secondly, it will meet his/her commercial needs.

Farm Coverages

The personal property side of the farm policy is similar to the homeowners policy. The first four coverages available include:

Coverage A – Dwelling

Coverage B – Other Private Structures Appurtenant to Dwellings

Coverage C – Household Personal Property

Coverage D – Loss of Use

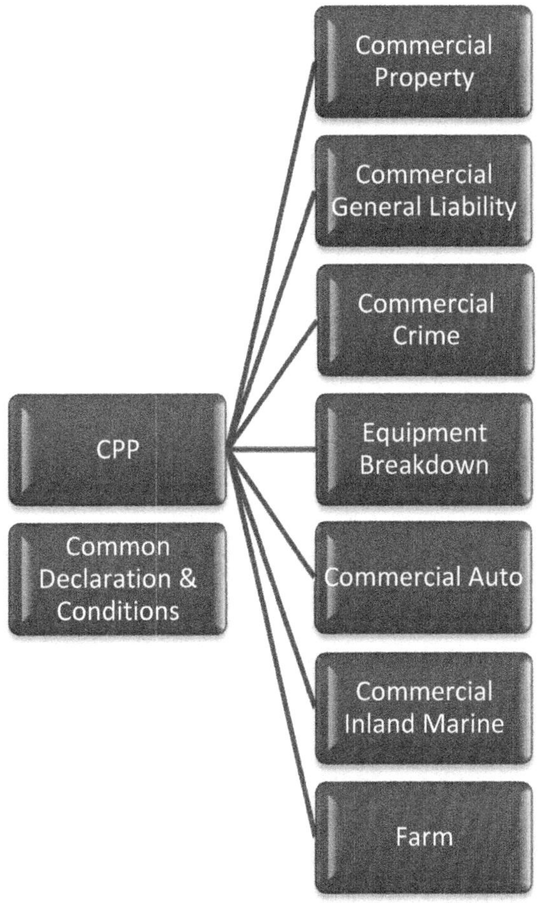

The next three coverages are for the purpose of meeting the farmer's commercial needs.

Coverage E – Scheduled Farm Personal Property

Coverage E will cover property that is described in the declaration page. It allows the farmer to schedule coverage on certain hard to value items. The following items could be scheduled:

- Grain, seed, hay or straw

Note: One of the exclusions of this section is ***growing crops****. Farmers would obviously want their crops insured, but the farm policy does not provide coverage. This is something that is excluded here and covered better elsewhere. It is covered by a* ***crop policy.***

- Poultry (excluding turkeys unless specified), bees and fish
- Computers and software
- Machinery, vehicles and tools usual in operation of the farm

- Farm machinery
- Livestock

Coverage F – Unscheduled Farm Personal Property

Coverage F covers the farm's business personal property that was not scheduled in the previous section (Coverage E). Coverage is provided for:

- Farm personal property
- Livestock (Basic or Broad only)
- Farm machinery, equipment, implements, tools and supplies

Coverage G – Other Farm Structures

Coverage G is designed to cover the commercial structures on the premises. It would include coverage for barns, sheds, fences, silos, and radio/television equipment.

Farm Cause of Loss Forms

The cause of loss forms available on the farm policy includes all the perils of the previous policies. In addition to these perils, the farm policy adds a few unique perils specifically for the farm.

Basic

- Fire or Lightning
- Riot
- Explosion
- Vehicles
- Civil Commotion
- Smoke
- Hail
- Aircraft

- Windstorm
- Volcanic Action (168 hours)
- Vandalism
- Theft

In addition to the previous perils, the Farm policy will also include:

- Sinkhole
- Collision – E and F only causing damage to farm machinery , death of livestock or damage to other farm personal property
- Earthquake and flood loss to livestock

Broad

The broad form includes everything under the basic form plus the broad form perils that we have seen previously:

- Weight of ice, snow or sleet
- Intentional water
- Falling objects

In addition to these standard perils, the farm policy has some specific perils added to meet some common farm exposures:

- Electrocution of covered livestock
- Attacks on livestock by dogs and wild animals
- Accidental shooting of livestock
- Drowning of livestock from external causes
- Loading and unloading accidents

Special

This is the all-risk policy. It covers everything except that which is excluded. The exclusion section will establish what perils are covered and what peril are not.

Farm Liability Coverage

The second section of the policy is the liability coverage. As previously discussed, liability is a third party insurance in which negligence has to be determined in order to establish responsibility. The farm policy has three more coverages under this section. These coverages provide protection for both personal and commercial needs:

Coverage H – bodily Injury and Property Damage Liability

Coverage I – Personal and Advertising Injury Liability

Coverage J – Medical Payments

Practice Exam

1. Which is NOT a coverage under the Farm Policy?

    a) Dwelling

    b) Household Personal Property

    c) Loss of Use

    d) Professional Liability

2. On the Farm policy, which of the following could NOT be scheduled under Coverage E Scheduled Farm Personal Property?

    a) Livestock

    b) Farm personal property

    c) Seed

    d) Grain

3. Since the farm policy is unique, certain perils are added to the standard basic and broad forms. Which of the following is NOT an added peril to the broad form?

    a) Sinkhole

    b) Electrocution of covered livestock

    c) Attacks on livestock by wild animals

    d) Accidental shooting of livestock

Answer key: 1,d 2,b 3,a

Chapter 16

Business Owners Policy (BOP)

The Commercial Package Policy is an excellent policy that is capable of meeting some very specific needs. Its flexibility allows the agent to create a unique product that is designed to meet the needs of a variety of businesses; but, this advantage can also be seen as a disadvantage. The more flexibility and choices available to the consumer, then the more complex the product becomes. The small business owner needs something simple and easy to buy and understand. The Business Owner Policy (BOP) is pre-packaged and designed for the small business owner. If the CPP is the cafeteria line, then the BOP is the number one value meal at the fast food restaurant. It is easy to buy and meets the needs of many small businesses.

The Business Owners Policy is designed to be a **prepackaged** commercial policy that is designed for **small** and **low risk** businesses. It puts together in one policy, the most common needs of a small business. This makes the policy easy for the agent to sell and easy for the business owner to purchase. Many small businesses have the same basic needs. So just like the Homeowners Policy, the BOP product combines these needs for the customer.

Eligibility (Small and Low Risk)

Not every business will qualify for a BOP. In order for a business to purchase a BOP, it first must become eligible. The two rules of eligibility are that the business must be a small business (physically and financially) and a low risk business.

Who is Eligible?

- Apartment buildings
- Office buildings 6 stories or less and less than 100,000 square footage
- Some contractors – dealers, distributors, servicing, carpentry, driveway paving, drywall installation, inside electrical work, interior painting, decorators, etc.
- Convenience food/gasoline stores – gasoline sales must be less than 75% of total gross receipts
- Motels – no more than 3 stories, with eligible restaurant operations
- Processing and service occupancies – bakeries, beauty shops, funeral homes, photographers, printers, TV repairs, jewelry repair, etc.
- Restaurants – no more than $3 million in gross sales. No more than 7,500 in square footage, limited cooking or fast food, beer or wine sales which do not exceed 25% of total sales
    - Limited cooking examples - Cafes, donut shops, coffee bars, sandwich shops, pizza shops, ice cream stores, salad bars
    - Fast food examples – chicken, concession stands, sandwich shops, hamburger shops, pizza, seafood, roast beef, etc.

Who is Ineligible?

- Auto repair, service, parking or dealerships
- Bars, pubs and liquor stores
- Manufacturing risks
- Places of amusement
- Banks, credit unions, savings and loans
- Contractors with payroll over $300,000 or receipts of more than $3,000,000

Coverages

Section I: Property

The property section is designed to cover the **buildings** and the **business personal property,** if designated in the declaration page of the policy. Coverage is provided on an **all risk** or **open** peril basis. The coverages provided and many of their descriptions and limits are similar if not the same as the Commercial Property Form. The difference is that these coverages are prepackaged and built in.

Note: Since this is pre-packaged and designed to give the small business what they will need, certain benefits have been assumed. Two important inclusions would be coverage of perils and the valuation. This policy is sold on an ***all risk*** *basis with* ***replacement cost*** *on property. The policy* ***does not have a coinsurance requirement.***

ADDITIONAL COVERAGES

- Debris removal
- Preservation of property
- Collapse
- Fire department service charge
- **Business income** Period of restoration is now limited to no more than 12 consecutive months
- **Extra expense** Period of restoration is now limited to no more than 12 consecutive months
- Pollutant clean up and removal
- Civil authority
- Money orders and counterfeit money
- Forgery or alteration
- Increased cost of construction
- Glass expense

- Electronic data
- Limited fungi or wet rot

Coverage Extensions

These coverages extensions should also look familiar. The BOP does not create new coverage, it prepackages coverage. The one difference between the BOP and CPP is that the BOP does not make the insured qualify for these coverages with a co-insurance requirement. These coverages are included in the policy automatically. Coverage extensions include:

- Newly acquired or constructed property
- Personal property off premises
- Outdoor property
- Personal effects
- Valuable papers and records
- Accounts receivable

Cause of Loss

The BOP is settled on an open peril or all risk basis.

Loss Settlement

The BOP provides replacement cost for both building and business personal property as long as 80% of the replacement cost is in effect at the time of claim. If not it pays on an ACV basis. Although this sounds like the coinsurance requirement discussed earlier, it is not. It is actually an insured to value clause.

Deductible

The standard deductible for the BOP is $500. Of course, if the insured would want to lower their cost, the deductible could be increased.

Optional Property Coverages

Optional Property Coverages are explained in the policy. To include them, they would need to be listed on the declaration page with their appropriate limits.

Outdoor Signs

This coverage allows the insured to schedule the value of an outdoor sign at the described premises. It covers signs owned by the insured or in his/her control.

Money and Securities

This covers theft, disappearance or destruction of money and/or securities while in transit to, from or at a bank, savings institution or living quarters of those having use or custody of property. It **does not cover** arithmetic errors, money operated devices, or losses due to purchases.

Employee Dishonesty

This covers loss to the business' personal property, money or securities as a result of acts committed by a dishonest employee

Mechanical Breakdown

This coverage provides protection for boilers, pressure vessels or air conditioning units. It will include a suspension clause that allows for immediate cancellation if machinery is considered unsafe.

Section II: Liability

The second part of the policy is the liability section. Any business, large or small, will have a liability exposure. The Business Owners Policy packages in the liability coverage similar to the Commercial General Liability form. The BOP liability coverage packages in **occurrence** form protection.

Endorsements

The BOP has many endorsements available. A few worth noting include:

- Additional Insured
- Earthquake
- Hired Auto and Non-Owned Auto
- Liquor Liability
- Spoilage Coverage
- Utility Services
- Terrorism

Terms to Know

Business Owners Policy (BOP)

Eligibility requirements (Small and low risk)

Numbers to know

Eligible

Office building 6 stories or less and less than 100,000 square feet

Convenience/gas stores- sales must be less than 75% of total gross receipts

Motels- no more than 3 stories

Restaurants- no more than 3 million in gross sales, no more than 75,000 square feet, limited cook/fast food/beer/wine- do not exceed 25% in total sales

Ineligible

Contractors with payroll over $300,000 or receipts of more than $3 million

Practice Exam

1. Which of the following statements about the BOP is FALSE?

    a. The BOP is a prepackaged commercial policy

    b. The BOP is for small businesses

    c. The BOP is for low risk businesses

    d. The BOP is for high risk business

2. Business ABC is interested in purchasing a BOP. What are the two rules of eligibility Business ABC must meet?

    a. Small and low risk

    b. Large and high risk

    c. Small and high risk

    d. Large and low risk

3. Which of the following endorsements are NOT available on the BOP?

    a. Spoilage Coverage

    b. Additional Insured

    c. Debris Removal

    d. Liquor Liability

4. Which of the following statements is FALSE?

    a. The property section of the BOP is All Risk/Open Peril

    b. The insured receives Replacement Cost on property

    c. The BOP does not have a co-insurance requirement

    d. Additional coverages are not built in to the policy

5. Which type of business is eligible for a BOP?

   a. Banks

   b. Apartment buildings

   c. Liquor stores

   d. Auto dealership

6. Which type of business does not qualify for a BOP?

   a. Motels

   b. Apartment buildings

   c. Restaurants

   d. Liquor stores

Answer key: 1,d 2,a 3,c 4,d 5,b 6,d

17

Miscellaneous Commercial Products

The Commercial Package Policy is a policy that is able to meet the needs of many businesses, but it does not meet every single need. This chapter will look at some specific products that are needed to meet the exposures that the Commercial Package Policy is not designed to meet effectively.

Other Liability Products

Commercial Umbrella Policy

The commercial umbrella policy is much like the personal version of the umbrella policy. The main difference is that the commercial umbrella policy is designed to cover the commercial exposures. This policy is designed to provide protection **over and above** the **underlying policies**. It gives the insured higher limits for a **minimal price**. The policy does not pay until underlying policy limits have been reached and more protection is now needed.

This policy may come with a **retention limit**. A retention limit basically works like a deductible, it is the amount of the claim that the insured must pay. It is the part that the insured retains before the umbrella coverage kicks in.

The umbrella policy not only increases coverage over and above the underlying policies, it also picks up coverages in areas that **may not be covered** by the underlying policies.

Excess Liability Policy

The Excess Liability policy is much like the umbrella. It is also designed to provide additional protection over and above the underlying policy limits. It may also come with a retention limit.

The difference between the excess liability policy and the commercial umbrella is that **the excessive liability policy will not pick up the extra areas of protection** that would be excluded by the underlying policies. If it is not covered by the underlying policy, it will not be covered by the excess liability policy.

Professional Liability Policies

Professionals are individuals that have an advanced knowledge or experience in a particular area. As a result of this knowledge, they hold themselves out to assist the public in their particular profession. This means that the public counts on their advice to help them make important decisions. When professionals do not live up to the expectations of their profession or when they make mistakes that affect their clients, they can be held liable.

The Professional Liability Policy is designed to protect the professional against this exposure.

There are many different professions, thus many different types of Professional Liability Policies. Although they have different names, the basic concept and purpose for them are the same. Following are different types of Professional Liability Policies:

- **Errors and Omissions** – This is a policy that protects insurance agents or financial planners against mistakes that affect their client in a financial manner.

- **Malpractice Insurance** – This protects those medical professionals against causing bodily injury as a result of not performing up to professional standards.

- **Directors and Officers** – Directors have a professional responsibility to their stockholders and could be held liable for mistakes and poor decisions that affect the business. This policy is designed to protect them.

Crop Insurance

Growing crops are subject to numerous perils, such as unfavorable weather conditions, hail, fire, floods, insects and disease. The farm policy excluded coverage on growing crops. Yet, this may be one of the most important protections that the farmer may need. Policies can be written covering one or more of these perils, either through the **Federal Crop Insurance Corporation** or private insurers.

Coverage can be categorized based upon the size of the grain. **Large grain** crops include corn, soybean and other physically large grain crops. **Small grain crops** include barley, oats, wheat and other smaller grains.

Limits are reduced as claims are paid and while the crop is harvested. Crop insurance can be sold on a seasonal basis. The insurer will need to know what crops are being planted for each season in order to adequately price the product. When a claim is paid out, payment is based upon the yield.

Bonds

A bond is a three party contract in which a promise is made and backed by a surety. There are three parties to a bond:

- **Principal** – This is the party that is making a promise. The promise that is made will determine the type of bond that is purchased.
- **Obligee** – Is the party that the promise is made to. This is the recipient of the promise. If the promise is not kept, this is the party that would be damaged.
- **Surety** – The surety is the party that financially backs the promise. If the promise is not kept, damages are determined and the surety makes a payment to the obligee.

Fidelity Bonds

A Fidelity Bond is used specifically to protect an employer from a dishonest employee. The word fidelity means faithfulness. When an employee accepts a job, there is an implied promise made that he/she will faithfully perform their job and duties. If an employee steals from an employer, the employer could collect on the bond.

- Principal = Employee
- Obligee = Employer
- Surety = Bonding Company

These bonds could be written one of three ways:

- **Name Schedule Bond** – The name scheduled bond provides coverage for an act committed by one or more employees specifically named.

- **Name Position Bond** - Instead of specific names, the name position bond provides coverage based upon the position held. Coverage would be provided if anyone commits a covered act while holding the named position.

- **Blanket Bonds** – Blanket covers all employees of the business.

The Fidelity Bond is purchased by the Obligee (employer). The employee may not even be aware that the bond exists.

Surety Bond

The surety bond backs a promise that an obligation will be met. Examples of the obligation which may be covered by a Surety Bond would include:

- Bid Bond – Job will be done for no more than the amount bid

- Supply Bond – Supplies will be delivered on time as requested

- Completion Bond – Job will be completed by certain date

- Bail Bond – Promise to show for court appointment

These are just a few examples. Surety bonds are numerous, but most bonds will fall into this category. Surety bonds are commonly used by contractors to guarantee that certain jobs will be done as agreed upon between the contractor and the customer. In a contractor bond the parties would be:

- Principal = Contractor

- Obligee = Customer

- Surety = Bonding company

One difference between the fidelity bond and the surety bond is who pays for the bond. The fidelity bond is paid for by the Obligee (employer), whereas the surety bond is paid for by the Principal (contractor).

Indemnity Agreement – The surety bond will also include an indemnity agreement on the principal. Indemnity means to "make whole." When the principal purchases the bond, they agree to indemnify the surety for any claims that they may become responsible. This means that the bond may need to be collateralized. Unlike insurance which spreads risk, the principal will be fully responsible for the risk. The surety is just fronting the payment.

Workers' Compensation

After the industrial revolution, the manufacturing industry began growing at an extreme pace. Workers were becoming more dependent upon the employer and the job provided. As work related injuries and deaths increased and became more common, employees were finding that they had little recourse or protection.

Prior to the workers' compensation laws, employees would have to sue their employers for damages. This meant that the employee would have to show negligence or fault by the employer. Employers would typically use one of three defenses to avoid responsibility:

- **Assumption of risk** – The argument was that the employee was aware of the danger in the job upon acceptance of the position. In fact, the employee was paid a higher wage because of this high risk position.

- **Fellow servant rule** – The employer would argue that it was not his fault, but it was the fault of the injured employee's fellow worker. As long as the employer could show that he had trained and educated the workers on their responsibilities, the employer had fulfilled their obligation and was not held responsible.

- **Contributory negligence** – The damage incurred was done by the employee who sustained the injury. They did it to themselves and would be held responsible.

As a result of these very effective defenses, employers were very seldom held responsible. So, in 1910 New York established the foundation of our workers' compensation system that we have in place today.

Concept of Today's Workers' Compensation Laws

Today's workers' compensation policy is a compromise between the worker and the employer.

NO FAULT

For the employee, the plan was set up as a "no fault" system. Under today's law the employer will not be allowed to use the above defenses. In fact, liability is not a factor in coverage at all. If the employee's injury was **"arising out of"** and **"in the course of"** employment, then coverage is automatic.

- Arising out of implies that the worker was injured while doing the work that he/she was reasonably expected to do.
- In the course of implies that the injury occurred during working hours, or what was reasonably assumed to be "on the clock."

EXCLUSIVE REMEDY

For the employer, they would be told that payment under the workers' compensation system would be the exclusive remedy for the employee. Each state sets the benefits that would be available for the injured employee. These benefits are predetermined. **Benefits do not include pain and suffering.** Benefits paid for a workplace injury then become the employee's exclusive or only solution. Workers' compensation was intended to avoid the law suit between employer and employee. Money saved from numerous lawsuits could then be paid to injured employees. This would limit the exposure for the employer and save them from excessive legal expenses.

Employer Requirements

REQUIREMENTS BASED UPON STATE LAW

There are different types of workers' compensation laws. Each state establishes their own requirements:

Monopolistic States

If a state is a monopolistic state, then there is only one workers' compensation option. In these states the protection is sold by the agents, but the state sets the benefits and assumes the risk. It is similar to the Flood program, but on a state level.

Competitive States

Most of the states are competitive. This means that the companies can compete for the business. Different companies sell and assume the risk of the coverage. Benefits are still set by the state. The state will typically offer a high risk product for those businesses that have experienced multiple claims. Companies compete with each other and they also compete against the state program.

Compulsory Laws

Most states are compulsory. This means that businesses must provide the workers' compensation protection to all employees, even if the business only employs one person. Coverage is required for part time employees, seasonal employees and even minors. The requirement is based upon the minimum of at least 1 employee.

Elective Laws

Very few states have elective laws. This gives the employer the option to provide the protection or not. If an employer chooses not to subject themselves to the workers' compensation laws, they will lose their common law defenses against liability suits.

EMPLOYEE DEFINED

Employment Relationships that Must be Covered

Most employment relationships must be covered. Minors in particular must be covered. If a minor is injured on the job and coverage is not available, the employer will be penalized. Compensation will be doubled for the minor and the employer will be responsible for half of the compensation.

Part time and seasonal workers must also be covered. In most cases, if the individual is classified or should be classified as an employee by the IRS, then coverage will be required.

Employment Relationships Not Covered

There are a few industries that are excluded from workers' compensation laws. Generally they have established a program for themselves that is industry specific. If not, they may be classified as self-employed.

- Railroad workers
- Real estate professionals
- Independent contractors
- Volunteers for no pay
- Inmates in the penal institutions
- Athletes on scholarships

- Federal employees

Relationships that May Elect Coverage

These are some of the situations where the individual could choose to participate or elect not to participate.

- Self-employed, sole proprietors, and partners
- Farm and agricultural employees
- Casual workers and household employees

Allowable Employer Defenses

Some states will allow the "no fault" rules to be set aside for certain situations. States may allow employer defense due to:

- Injury caused by employee intoxication
- Knowingly self-inflicted injuries
- Knowingly failing to use required safety appliances
- Ignoring posted safety rules
- Commission of an offense, or failure to perform a statutory duty

Part I: Workers' Compensation Benefits

When an employee is injured on the job this is the benefit that most will be eligible for. This is the no fault, exclusive remedy benefit that employers are required to provide. There are four benefits available under this part of the policy;

MEDICAL BENEFITS

Employees who are injured by accident arising out of and in the course of employment are entitled to reasonable and necessary medical treatment, rendered free of charge to the employee. This benefit is with no deductible, co-payments or limit. If it is a qualified claim, all reasonable expenses will be covered.

Medical benefits are also included for "**occupational diseases.**" Occupational diseases are conditions that are tied directly to the job. They are diseases that typically are a result of the work performed. Examples may include: radiation poisoning, asbestos, carpal tunnel and repetitive motion conditions.

DISABILITY INCOME BENEFITS

The disability income benefit is designed to replace lost income as a result of a covered work related accident. Benefits can be for total or partial disability. Disabilities can be permanent or temporary. Most states will replace income based upon **66 2/3** of the AWW (average weekly wage) up to the states limit. Disability income benefits will be paid **tax free**. Benefits may be subject to a waiting period. Waiting periods may be **7** days. If after **14 or 21** days the individual is still disabled, benefits will be paid for the first 7days.

DEATH BENEFITS

If death occurs as a result of an accident which occurred in the course of and out of employment, two benefits may be available. The final expense benefit is designed to assist with burial and other final expense needs. The second benefit that may be available under this section would be a survivor benefit for the spouse and/or children. The survivor benefit would provide an income based upon the AWW.

REHABILITATION BENEFITS

Workers' Compensation was never intended to allow a person to rest easy or get a free ride in society. If a person can work, then he/she should. The rehabilitation benefit is designed to retrain individuals so that they can support themselves. Vocational rehabilitation is good for the individual, the insurer and society as a whole.

Part II: Employers Liability

The workers' compensation law was set up as a "no fault" and "exclusive remedy" concept. It was designed to avoid the expenses involved in a law suit. But, sometimes intentions do not always work the way they were set up to do. Sometimes people find ways around the system.

Even though never intended, lawsuits do arise on occasion. Employers Liability is designed to cover the employer from situations that are not covered under the state Workers' Compensation laws. Coverage is provided for:

- Suits brought by injured employees

- Suits brought by spouses or dependents of injured workers
- Employees not covered by the workers' compensation law
- Legal defense

Remember, the CGL excludes work related injuries. This policy may be the only protection the employer has.

Part III: Other States Insurance

Businesses may conduct business in multiple states. They may have employees working in various states. Since coverage is different state by state, by listing the states in which the employer is doing business on the policy, employees injured in their state would be covered under their state benefit requirements. This allows one policy to provide benefits specific to each employee. Other state coverage is only available if the states are listed in the declarations.

Part IV: Duties After a Loss

If injury occurs on the job, the insured is required to:

- Provide immediate medical care required by law
- Provide names and addresses of those injured and witnesses
- Inform the insurer of any notices of legal action
- Cooperate with the insurer
- Do not make any voluntary payments or settlements
- Allow the insurer to recover from a third party

Part V: Premium

This section will discuss the premium structure and how premiums are calculated. There are several factors involved in determining the workers compensation premium.

Job Classification - Premiums are first based upon the job classification. Some jobs are more dangerous than others and will have a different rate adjustment as a result.

Payroll – Since some benefits are based upon wages, it only makes sense that the higher the payroll, the higher the exposure. High payroll implies more employees exposed to medical payments and more disability benefits.

Experience – An experience modification factor is applied as a method of rewarding those employers with better than average loss experience. It is also used to penalize those with a higher frequency rate.

Obviously, there is no way that an employer can know what payroll is going to be for the coming year. Employees may leave, new hires come in, and raises occur. Insurers charge their premiums in advance. This means that the initial premium payment is an estimate. An audit will be performed at the end of the year to adjust the rate up or down according to precise payroll numbers.

Government Involvement and Programs

SECOND INJURY FUND

The state Second Injury Fund serves three purposes. The first purpose is to protect previously injured individuals from **discrimination in hiring**. The second purpose is to provide appropriate benefits to an employee who has been injured a second time while on the job. The third purpose is to provide **replacement prosthetics** when needed. This fund is supported by all admitted companies selling workers' compensation in the state.

Benefits paid under workers' compensation for permanent disabilities will differ based upon the severity of the injury. As the injury becomes more severe, the payment increases substantially. Each state sets the value for the injury once maximum medical improvement has been established.

Joe injures his arm at the workplace. After it has reached its maximum medical improvement, it is established that he has lost 50% of the use of the arm. This will result in a payment of $40,925. When Joe interviews for a second job, the interviewer can't help but notice Joe's injury. Even though Joe is qualified for the job, the interviewer is concerned about a second injury occurring on the worksite.

If Joe loses 100% use of his arm, it will be worth a total of $101,025. If Joe experiences 50% more damage, he will expect another $60,100 to bring him up to 100%. If the employer hires a healthy person, 50% damage would only cost them $40,925.

The Second Injury Fund limits the new employers' responsibility for a second injury to 50% or $40,925. If Joe is qualified for the position, there is no reason not to hire him. Joe can then apply to the states Second Injury Fund for the balance due him ($19,175).

Assigned Risk Plans

There are times when an employer has difficulty qualifying for the required insurance coverage because of claim frequency. One of the roles of the state is to see that those who need insurance have access to the coverage they are required to carry. In those cases, the state provides a high risk alternative that employers can purchase through the state.

Agents can present the plan and assist the client in obtaining the needed policy. Once the application is received by the state, they will assign the responsibility of providing the protection to one of the insurers selling in the state. Risk will be apportioned to the companies based on the amount of sales that they have in the state. Taking these risks becomes a cost of doing business in the state. If a company wants to be admitted into the state, they will assist in providing insurance protection to the high risk applicants.

Federal Employers Liability Act (FELA)

FELA predates workers' compensation laws and provides similar protection for railroad workers. Since FELA is available to railroaders, workers' compensation policies exclude coverage for those working on the railroad.

U.S. Longshore and Harbor Workers' Compensation Act

For those working on the waterways (except seamen) or around boats and docks, the US Longshore and Harbor Workers' Compensation Act requires that workers' compensation benefits be applied. Those who qualify under this act can be covered by the workers' compensation policy through endorsement.

The Jones Act

Seamen are excluded from the workers' compensation coverage and cannot be added back into it. A seaman is anyone who spends more than 30% of their time on a vessel that is in navigation. The Jones Act is designed to cover the seamen in a similar way as the railroad workers are covered under FELA.

Ocean Marine

Ocean Marine Policies are very specific to the water. These policies are designed to cover ships, boats, barges or any other vessel on the waterway. It also provides coverage for the items that are being transported over the waterways. Inland marine was designed to cover items that are being transported over land or at different locations.

NATIONWIDE MARINE DEFINITION

The primary purpose of this definition is to distinguish the different types of marine risks. It classifies the different risks into six different categories.

Category	Form
Imports	• Ocean Marine
Exports	• Ocean Marine
Domestic Shipments and Transportation Risks	• Commercial Inland Marine Form
Instrumentalities of Transportation and Communications	• Commercial Inland Marine Form
Commercial Property Floater Risks	• Commercial Inland Marine Form
Personal Property Floater Risks	• Personal Inland Marine Fom

OCEAN MARINE COVERAGES

Hull Coverage

Hull coverage provides protection for the vessel itself. With an endorsement (Running Down Clause) it can also cover damage as a result of collision to another vessel. It does not cover damage to passengers or docks.

Cargo Insurance

This provides protection for the cargo in the hold and includes the cargo being shipped. The warehouse to warehouse clause would also extend coverage over land. It covers the merchandise from the time it leaves the warehouse, is loaded on the ship, shipped over the waterway, and delivered to the new warehouse. This allows the insurance company to write one policy instead of multiple policies on the risk.

Freight Insurance

The cost of shipping is quite expensive. The purpose of this coverage is to refund shipping and freight cost which has already been spent. It can be written separately or along with the other coverages mentioned.

Protection and Indemnity

This is the liability portion of the insurance. Not only does it protect the insured from liability claims of a third party, it also covers any lawsuits from the seamen. Under the Jones Act, seamen have the right to sue. Since they have been excluded from workers' compensation coverage, the **insured needs protection against work related injuries.**

PERILS COVERED

The perils covered are unique to the risk specific to travels over the water ways. Perils covered are called the "Perils of the Sea" and include risks like wind, wave action, piracy, running aground, collision, sinking and more. **Jettison** is also covered. This is voluntarily throwing items overboard for the purpose of saving the ship. **Barratry** is covered and this is fraud or criminal acts committed by the ship's master or crew, which results in loss of cargo.

WARRANTIES

A warranty is a statement of fact. It is defined as a condition of coverage. If the warranty is not maintained, then coverage will not exist. **Implied warranties** are warranties that have not specifically been listed. They are expected to be maintained, even though not clarified. They would include seaworthiness of the vessel; legality of the voyage, and cargo is packed appropriately.

Aviation Insurance

Aviation insurance is much like auto insurance. Coverage will be needed for liability, physical damage and medical payments. There may also be hangar keepers insurance. This works basically the same as garage keepers but for airplanes. This would protect the business that keeps the airplane of others in their care, custody or control. This could be the owner of an airplane hangar.

Terrorism Risk Insurance Act (TRIA)

The Terrorism Risk Insurance Act is a federal act providing coverage in the event of a terrorist attack. Since the occurrence of 911, terrorism has been a concern for our society and for the insurance industry. Terrorism and acts of war are typically excluded on most policies. In order to meet the need for this exposure the federal government has created an optional coverage that shares the risk of terrorist acts between the federal government (80%) and the insurance companies (20%). In order for it to be a covered event it must be classified as an act of terror by the Secretary of Treasury with consultation from the Secretary of Homeland Security. An act of terror was defined in 2020 as an act that results in more than $200 million in damages. That number has increased since then to compensate to inflation.

Terms to Know

Commercial Umbrella

Excess Liability

Professional Liability

Federal Crop Insurance Corporation

Large grain

Small grain

Principal

Obligee

Surety

Fidelity bond

Name scheduled bond

Name position bond

Blanket bond

Surety bond

Workers' Compensation

Exclusive Remedy

Monopolistic

Competitive

Compulsory

Elective

Part 1: Medical, Disability (AWW), Rehabilitation, Death

Part 2: Employer's Liability

Second Injury Fund

Ocean Marine

Terrorism Risk Act

Numbers to know

Compulsory- WC is required with 1 employee

Disability- waiting period is 7 days. If still injured after 21 days, the first 7 days are covered

66 2/3- Average Weekly Wage (AWW)

Practice Exam

1. Which commercial policy only pays over and above the underlying policy?

    a) Professional Liability

    b) Personal Excess Liability

    c) Commercial Excess Liability

    d) Commercial Umbrella

2. In a bond, who makes the promise and who is the promise made to?

    a) The promise is made to the Obligee and it is made by the Principal

    b) The promise is made to the Principal and it is made by the Obligee

    c) The promise is made to the Surety and it is made by the Principal

    d) The promise is made to the Obligee and it is made by the Surety

3. What is the difference between a Surety and a Fidelity Bond?

    a) A fidelity guarantees an obligation, surety guarantees faithfulness of an employee

    b) A surety guarantees an obligation, fidelity guarantees faithfulness of an employee

    c) A fidelity includes an indemnity agreement, a surety does not

    d) Surety can be sold on a blanket basis, a fidelity cannot

4. Which of the following is not a professional liability policy?

    a) Employment practices

    b) Errors and omissions

    c) Medical malpractice

    d) Directors and officers

5. In a compulsory workers comp state, what is the minimum number of employees required for coverage to be provided?

   a) 10

   b) 5

   c) 2

   d) 1

6. In regards to the Workers' Compensation policy, which is FALSE?

   a) Part time workers must be covered

   b) Seasonal workers must be covered

   c) Railroad workers must be covered

   d) Minors must be covered

7. Which of the following is NOT included in Part One of Workers' Compensation?

   a) Death benefit

   b) Disability benefit

   c) Employer liability

   d) Rehabilitation benefit

8. Under Part One of Workers' Compensation, there is a benefit for disability. Which of the following is FALSE about this coverage?

   a) Benefits are paid tax free

   b) Benefits are paid for partial or total disability

   c) Benefits are paid based on 66 2/3 of the average weekly wage

   d) Benefits are paid immediately after the injury

9. Workers comp premiums are based upon an initial estimate that is based upon:
   a) The job, payroll and experience
   b) The job and payroll only
   c) Payroll and experience only
   d) Job and experience
10. Under Workers Comp, Other States Insurance is necessary because;
   a) Other states may be competitive and elective
   b) Other states may have different employee requirements
   c) Other states may have different benefit requirements
   d) Other states may be compulsory
11. In order to be covered, an act of terrorism must be declared by:
   a) The president of the united states
   b) The Secretary of State
   c) Governor of state of incidence
   d) Secretary of Treasury
12. Exclusive remedy, under Workers Comp means:
   a) Is intended to limit if not avoid law suits
   b) Allows for compensation for pain and suffering
   c) Allows for the defense of contributory negligence
   d) Is intended to create a path for holding an employer negligent

Answer key: 1,c 2,a 3,b 4,a 5,d 6,c 7,c 8,d 9,a 10,c 11,d 12,a

Chapter

18

Practice Finals

Practice Final I

1) The transfer of risk is:
   a) Insurance
   b) Hazard
   c) Peril
   d) Risk
2) If the insurer cancels a policy, how will unearned premium be refunded?
   a) Pro rata
   b) Short rate
   c) Non-renewal
   d) Retroactive
3) When the insurance company makes the insured whole, no more, no less, this is the concept of:
   a) Insurable Interest
   b) Adverse Selection
   c) Insurance
   d) Indemnification
4) Which of the following is not included in the definition of insurance?
   a) Subrogation
   b) Indemnification
   c) Spreading of risk
   d) Law of large numbers

5) Which type of risk is insurable?

a) Strict

b) Absolute

c) Speculative

d) Pure

6) Which of the following would define an increase of risk due to a the careless maintenance of a home?

a) Physical hazard

b) Moral hazard

c) Morale hazard

d) Speculative hazard

7) If an insured experiences a loss due to a peril covered by the policy, the claim will be paid by the insurance company. A peril is defined as:

a) The chance of a loss

b) Increases the chance of a loss

c) The cause of a loss

d) The chance and cause of a loss

8) Ice on the road increases the chance of an auto accident. The ice is an example of:

a) Peril

b) Risk

c) Exposure

d) Hazard

9) What are the essential components of a contract?

a) Competent parties, Legal purpose, Offer + Acceptance = Agreement, Consideration

b) Competent parties, Legal purpose, Offer, Counteroffer

c) Counteroffer, Legal purpose, Agreement, Consideration

d) Consideration, Legal capacity, Agreement, Counteroffer

10) The answers the applicant gives on the application are called:

a) Misrepresentations

b) Representations

c) Warranties

d) Concealment

11) Which of the following questions could result in a concealment that could lead to voiding the policy?

   a) Have you had any speeding tickets lately?

   b) How many tickets have you had in the last 12 months?

   c) What is your full name?

   d) How far is your drive to work?

12) A warranty is defined as:

   a) Truth to the best of your ability

   b) The truth as you know it

   c) A statement that is a condition of coverage

   d) A fact, promise or guarantee

13) In the law of agency, the agent represents:

   a) The insured

   b) The broker

   c) The principal

   d) The insurance agency

14) Underwriters use which law to accurately predict losses?

   a) Law of Adverse Selection

   b) Law of Large Numbers

   c) Law of Underwriting

   d) Law of Accurate Predictions

15) Of the following perils, which is listed on the Basic Form?

   a) Weight of snow

   b) Water pipe burst

   c) Volcano

   d) Collapse

16) When one party passes on his right of recovery to another party, it is called:

   a) Subrogation

   b) Arbitration

   c) Liberalization

   d) Legal Action

17) A type of coverage that is designed to cover a variety of items without listing any specific items, is called:

a) Blanket coverage

b) Specific coverage

c) Replacement cost coverage

d) Market value coverage

18) The formula for Actual Cash Value (ACV) is:

a) Replacement Cost + Depreciation

b) Stated Value – Depreciation

c) Replacement Cost – Depreciation

d) Agreed Value – Depreciation

19) Which concept is designed to reduce over utilization?

a) Coinsurance

b) Deductible

c) Arbitration

d) Appraisal

20) Which of the following statements is FALSE?

a) After a loss, the insured is required to protect the property from further damage

b) Coverage territory is the location where coverage is in force

c) With No Benefit to the Bailee, payment is made to the bailee

d) The policy period begins on the effective date

21) Which Property Provision is free, automatic, and pays above and beyond the policy's limits?

a) Co-insurance

b) Right of Salvage

c) Extensions of Coverage

d) Additional Coverages

22) A liability policy provides protection for the ________ and pays a benefit to the __________.

a) Insured, insured
b) Injured 3rd party, insured
c) Insured, injured 3rd party
d) Insured, insurance company

23) Which of the following types of damage coverage pays for the pain and suffering of the injured 3rd party?

a) Special
b) Specific
c) General
d) Punitive

24) Which of the following statements about Medical Payments is FALSE?

a) Commercial claims must be filed within 1 year
b) Personal claims must be filed within 3 years
c) It guarantees that all charges against the insured will be dropped
d) It is used as a preventive measure

25) Which of the following is necessary in order to establish negligence?

a) Assumption of risk
b) Proximate cause
c) Punitive damages
d) Intervening cause

26) ______ is products liability and provides coverage for bodily injury and property damage but does not pay for the recall itself.

a) Strict liability
b) Vicarious liability
c) Absolute liability
d) Intervening cause

27) Which type of policy pays over and above and expands protection?

a) Umbrella
b) Excess liability
c) Strict liability
d) Vicarious liability

28) Sue owns her own condo. Which type of form fits Sue's needs as a condo unit owner?

a) HO-3

b) HO-4

c) HO-5

d) HO-6

29) The Dwelling Policy gives coverage for:

a) Only property insurance

b) Basic perils

c) Property and casualty

d) Liability only

30) Bob's home is worth $200,000 and he carries a limit of $120,000. How much will Bob's policy pay for his kitchen fire that results in $10,000 in damage?

a) $10,000 minus his deductible

b) $6,000 minus his deductible

c) $6000

d) $10,000

31) If Joe has a $300,000 limit for Coverage A, how much coverage is available for Coverage B?

a) $30,000

b) $1,000

c) $10,000

d) $300,000

32) Coverage C provides coverage for:

a) Medical payments

b) Other structures

c) Personal property

d) Loss of use

33) Homeowners coverage F provides protection for?

a) Umbrella

b) Personal Liability

c) Personal Property

d) Medical Payments

34) Insurers give an incentive to encourage insureds to carry adequate limits. Which term describes this concept?

a) Coinsurance

b) Deductible

c) Arbitration

d) Appraisal

35) Joe owns his own condo. Which of the following statements is FALSE?

a) The condo association owns the complex

b) Joe only has insurable interest in his unit

c) Joe is not a renter

d) The condo association owns Joe's unit

36) Which two policies do not have coverage for Coverage A and B?

a) HO-3 and HO-5

b) HO-4 and HO-6

c) HO-4 and HO-5

d) HO-5 and HO-6

37) The Dwelling policy is an ideal product for:

a) A homeowner needing to save premiums

b) A condominium association

c) An owner of rental property

d) A tenant insuring the building

38) The Homeowners policy contains Additional Coverages. Which of the following is FALSE about these Liability Additional Coverages?

a) For loss of earnings, the insurer pays up to $250

b) Pays above the limit of liability

c) Free and automatic

d) Pays legal defense only if the insured is at fault

39) Which of the following perils is only included on the Broad Form?

a) Falling objects

b) Theft

c) Fire

d) Volcano

40) Volcanic eruption within __ hours is considered one volcanic eruption in personal lines.

a) 148

b) 72

c) 75

d) 48

41) Which form is unique in that it uses All Risk coverage only on Coverage A and B?

a) HO-2

b) HO-3

c) HO-5

d) HO-8

42) Which of the following would be required in order to insure a mobile home?

a) Actual Cash Value and a permanent foundation

b) Permanent foundation only

c) Stated value with a permanent foundation

d) Stated value only

43) Coverage D is Loss of Use. Which of the following characteristics describes Coverage D?

a) Direct loss

b) Physical loss

c) Indirect loss

d) Coverage D is only available to condo owners

44) The Personal Articles Floater is a separate policy. Which of the following characteristics is FALSE?

a) There is no deductible

b) Agreed value is used

c) Open peril coverage

d) Provides blanket coverage

45) Which statement is FALSE about Coverage C? Coverage C provides coverage :

a) On personal property worldwide

b) On a replacement cost coverage basis

c) With an automatic limit is 50% of A

d) For the HO 4 and HO 6 as a primary limit

46) Coverage B provides protection for Other Structures. Which of the following statements is FALSE about Coverage B?

a) The limit is automatically 10% of Coverage A

b) Land is excluded

c) Coverage is provided for a detached garage

d) Includes coverage for a structure being used for business purposes

47) On the Homeowners policy, Section I is ________ and Section II is _______.

a) Property, Liability

b) Property, Personal

c) Personal, Casualty

d) Personal, Commercial

48) The PAP insures all of the following EXCEPT:

a) More than 10,000 lbs

b) Autos with 4 wheels

c) Trucks and vans

d) Trailers

49) Joe's truck is in the shop and is driving another vehicle while his truck is being repaired. This vehicle is called a:

a) Temporary substitute

b) Acquired auto

c) Replacement auto

d) Additional auto

50) In a split limit, the second number is:

a) The total BI and PD for the accident

b) Property damage

c) BI per accident

d) BI per person

Use the following information for 51 -54

Joe carries the following limit: 25/50/25

Joe is at fault in an accident with the following damages:

Driver BI= $10,000

1st Passenger BI= $30,000

2nd Passenger BI= $40,000

PD= $30,000

Legal defenses=$50,000

51) What is the most that Joe's policy could pay for the 2nd passenger's BI?

a) $50,000
b) $30,000
c) $40,000
d) $25,000

52) How much will Joe's policy pay for the total BI?

a) $80,000
b) $50,000
c) $25,000
d) $30,000

53) How much will the policy pay for legal defense?

a) $50,000
b) $30,000
c) $25,000
d) $40,000

54) How much will the policy pay for property damage?

a) $30,000
b) $10,000
c) $25,000
d) $20,000

55) A comparable single limit policy for a split limit of 250/500/200 is:

a) $500,000
b) $700,000
c) $250,000
d) $600,000

56) In personal lines a medical payments claim must be filed within __ year(s) of the accident.

a) 1
b) 2
c) 3
d) 4

57) Under Part D, collision and other than collision definitions provide coverage for different perils. Which of the following is covered under collision?

a) Theft
b) Flood
c) Car overturns
d) Contact with an animal

58) If the insured's vehicle is stolen, the PAP will provide coverage for temporary transportation within __ hours.

a) 48
b) 24
c) 40
d) 22

59) Which endorsement provides coverage for a vehicle over 10,000 pounds?

a) Towing and Labor
b) Trailer and Camper
c) Extended Nonowned Coverage
d) Miscellaneous Type Vehicle

60) Which of the following is NOT a part of the definition of flood?

a) Mudslide

b) Landslide

c) Collapse

d) Overflow of tidal waters

61) In regards to the FAIR Plan, which of the following statements is FALSE?

a) Insurer participation is voluntary

b) It is a high risk program for personal and commercial

c) The FAIR Plan is for those who have been denied a homeowners policy due to risk

d) The insurer cannot deny coverage due to location or neighborhood

62) Which type of policy only pays over and above the limit on the underlying policy?

a) Umbrella

b) Excess liability

c) Personal articles

d) Personal effects

63) Which of the following statements is FALSE?

a) Excess liability and Umbrella policies may require a retention limit

b) The umbrella policy pays over and above underlying limits

c) The excess liability policy kicks in only after coverage has been exhausted by the underlying policy

d) The excess liability policy is designed to pick up coverages not provided by the underlying policies

64) Which components make up a Commercial Package Policy?

a) Common Declarations Page, Common Conditions, 2 or more modules.

b) Common Declarations Page, Common Conditions, Interline Endorsements

c) Cafeteria policy, Common Conditions, 2 or more modules

d) Farm, Crime, Inland Marine, Commercial Auto

65) Choose the FALSE statement concerning the Commercial Package Policy from the following:

a) Each business can build its own policy to meet its individual needs

b) Any one module can be sold on its own

c) A mono-line policy requires one policy

d) A package policy requires at minimum 3 modules

66) There are some exclusions on the Commercial Property Form. Of the following, which is NOT an exclusion?

a) Animals boarded by the insured

b) Money

c) Things ground level or below

d) Autos for sale

67) How many hours between quakes must transpire before a new earthquake claim may be filed on a personal policy?

a) 120

b) 72

c) 48

d) 24

68) Often, commercial buildings are left vacant. Certain losses are not covered if a building is vacant for more than ___ days.

a) 90

b) 50

c) 30

d) 60

69) The Business Owners Policy is ideal for a:

a) Independently owned business

b) Small low risk business

c) High risk business

d) Small home business with no employees

70) If vacant for more than 60 days, the insurer will not pay for certain losses. All of the following are excluded EXCEPT for:

a) Fire

b) Vandalism

c) Theft

d) Water damage

71) Which form is designed to keep a business open after a loss?

a) Period of restoration

b) Business income

c) Builders risk

d) Extra expense

72) For a volcanic eruption to be considered as a new claim on a commercial policy, it must be free from activity for:

a) 132 hours

b) 90 hours

c) 168 hours

d) 60 hours

73) Which would be included as part of a commercial building?

a) Attached signs, not worth more than $10,000

b) Foundation of the building

c) Fire extinguishers

d) Large machinery

74) Which term includes both of these definitions: Net income that would have been earned and continuing normal operating expenses incurred?

a) Extra expense

b) Period of restoration

c) Business income

d) Inflation guard

75) In the construction of a building, coverage begins when there is something to insure, while coverage ends when all of the following occur EXCEPT:

a) Policy expiration or cancellation

b) The insured no longer has interest in the property

c) After 30 days if occupied

d) The property has been accepted by a purchaser

76) Under the Commercial General Liability, which claims would not reduce the general aggregate limit?

a) Premises and Operations

b) Advertising and Personal Injury

c) Products and Completed Operations

d) Fire Legal and Contractual Liability

77) All of these are exclusions under Coverage A of the Commercial Liability policy EXCEPT:

a) Workers Compensation

b) War

c) Recall of Products

d) On site mobile equipment

78) There are 5 areas under contractual liability (LEASE). What does the acronym stand for?

a) Lease agreements, Easements, Agreement to indemnify a municipality, Sidetrack agreements, Elevator maintenance agreements

b) Liability agreements, Easements, Agreement to indemnify a municipality, Sidetrack agreements, Elevator maintenance agreements

c) Lease agreements, Exclusions, Agreements to indemnify a municipality, Sidetrack agreements, Elevator maintenance agreements

d) Liability agreements, Exclusions, Acceptance, Sidetrack agreements, Elevator maintenance agreements

79) How far back an Insurer will consider an occurrence for a claim is based on:

a) Retroactive date of the Claims Made policy

b) Retroactive date of the Occurrence Form

c) The Extended Reporting Period on the Claims Made form

d) The Extended Reporting Period on the Occurrence Form

80) Which is NOT under Coverage A: Bodily Injury and Property Damage of the Commercial General Liability policy?

a) Premises Liability

b) Completed Operations

c) Independent Operations

d) Personal Injury

81) Which of the following is part of Coverage B, Commercial Liability?

a) Completed Operations

b) Advertising Injury

c) Products

d) Operations Liability

82) In order for Medical payments to pay in a commercial policy, the claim must be reported within ___ year (s) of the date of the accident.

a) 4

b) 3

c) 2

d) 1

83) Which of these coverages is NOT covered under Supplementary Payments?

a) Medical payments

b) Court costs

c) Loss of earnings up to $250/day

d) up to $250 of bail bond

84) The unlawful taking of property from the care and custody of a person by causing or threatening bodily harm:

a) Burglary

b) Theft

c) Robbery

d) Forgery

85) What is "crime that always includes damage to property?

a) Theft

b) Robbery

c) Fraud

d) Burglary

86) Under equipment breakdown, which of the following is FALSE concerning the suspension provision?

a) No advance notice is required

b) Suspension is immediate

c) Coverage can be suspended until repairs are made

d) Notice does not have to be provided

87) Which endorsement allows an employee to take their employer's auto insurance with him when he drives other vehicles on his personal time?

a) Truckers

b) Driver Other Car Coverage

c) Additional Insured

d) Mobile Equipment

88) Which of the following is FALSE?

a) Boiler and Machinery is designed to reduce the chance of breakdown

b) The insurer cannot inspect at any time

c) Breakdown is preventable through maintenance

d) Annual inspections are a condition of coverage

89) Which form provides coverage for autos under the insured's care?

a) Motor Carrier Form

b) Business Auto Coverage Form

c) Garage keepers Form

d) Truckers Form

90) Which floater allows the insured to schedule difficult to value property on all risk basis?

a) Commercial Articles Floater

b) Bailee Customer Floater

c) Contractor Equipment Floater

d) Equipment Dealers Floater

91) On the Farm policy, which of the following could NOT be scheduled under Coverage E Scheduled Farm Personal Property?

a) Livestock

b) Farm personal property

c) Seed

d) Grain

92) Since the farm policy is unique, certain perils are added to the standard basic and broad forms. Which of the following is NOT an added peril to the broad form?

a) Sinkhole

b) Electrocution of covered livestock

c) Attacks on livestock by wild animals

d) Accidental shooting of livestock

93) Which of the following statements about the BOP is FALSE?

a) The BOP is a prepackaged commercial policy

b) The BOP is for small businesses

c) The BOP is for low risk businesses

d) The BOP is a small cafeteria business policy

94) Business ABC is interested in purchasing a BOP. What are the two rules of eligibility Business ABC must meet?

a) Small and low risk

b) Large and high risk

c) Small and high risk

d) Large and low risk

95) Which of the following endorsements are NOT available on the BOP?

a) Spoilage Coverage

b) Additional Insured

c) Debris Removal

d) Liquor Liability

96) Which policy might a business buy to provide added protection over and above their underlying policies?

a) Professional Liability

b) Personal Excess Liability

c) Commercial Excess Liability

d) Commercial Umbrella

97) The party that makes a promise in a bond is called:

a) Principal

b) Obligee

c) Surety

d) Insurer

98) In regards to the Workers' Compensation policy, which is FALSE?

a) Part time workers must be covered

b) Seasonal workers must be covered

c) Railroad workers must be covered

d) Minors must be covered

99) Which of the following is NOT included in Part One of Workers' Compensation?

a) Death benefit

b) Disability benefit

c) Employer liability

d) Rehabilitation benefit

100) The arbitration clause requires each to get an arbitrator. Who pays?
a) Each pay for their own arbitrator and they split the cost of the third
b) The insurer pays the cost of all arbitrators
c) Each pay for their own arbitrator, but the insurer pay the third
d) The insured pays all costs

Test I Answer Key

1) A
2) A
3) D
4) A
5) D
6) C
7) C
8) D
9) A
10) B
11) A
12) D
13) C
14) B
15) C
16) A
17) A
18) C
19) B
20) C
21) D
22) C
23) C
24) C
25) B
26) A
27) A
28) D
29) A
30) B
31) A
32) C
33) D
34) A
35) D
36) B
37) C
38) D
39) A
40) B
41) B
42) A
43) C
44) D
45) B
46) D
47) A
48) A
49) A
50) C
51) D
52) B
53) A
54) C
55) B
56) C
57) C
58) A
59) D
60) B
61) A
62) B
63) D
64) A
65) D
66) A
67) B
68) D
69) B
70) A
71) D
72) C
73) C
74) C
75) C
76) C
77) D
78) A
79) A
80) D
81) B
82) D
83) A
84) C
85) D
86) D
87) B
88) B
89) C
90) A
91) B
92) A
93) D
94) A
95) C
96) C
97) A
98) C
99) C
100) A

Practice Exam II

1) Which term is defined as "the chance of a loss?"
   a) Risk
   b) Peril
   c) Hazard
   d) Loss
2) Which of the following statements is FALSE?
   a) Insurance companies insure only pure risks
   b) Pure risk is the chance of loss only
   c) With a speculative risk, the insured has the chance to financially gain or lose
   d) Insurance companies insure both pure and speculative risks
3) An insurance company is able to insure:
   a) A pure risk only
   b) A speculative risk only
   c) Either a pure or speculative risk
   d) Neither the pure or speculative risk
4) Which best represents the concept of insurance?
   a) The financial interest one has in their property
   b) The chance of winning or losing
   c) A contractual agreement protecting the insured from physical hazards
   d) The spreading of risk among a large number of people
5) In Property & Casualty insurance, when must insurable interest exist?
   a) At the time of the sale and at the time of the loss
   b) At the time of the sale
   c) At the time of the loss
   d) At the time of the beneficiary's death

6) A sudden unexpected event is defined as:
   a) Occurrence
   b) Accident
   c) Liberalization
   d) Inherent vice
7) What is the "law of large numbers?"
   a) A legal requirement for insurers to justify premiums
   b) Is not used to establish premiums for insurance policies
   c) The more numbers in a statistic, the more accurate
   d) The larger the premium, the less the loss ratio
8) What is the definition of a "hazard?"
   a) The chance of a loss
   b) The cause of a loss
   c) Making the insured whole, no more or less
   d) Something that increases the chances of a loss
9) What is the difference between a "direct" and "indirect" loss?
   a) A direct loss is consequential, an indirect loss is financial
   b) A direct loss is financial, an indirect loss is consequential
   c) A direct loss is financial in nature, an indirect loss is physical
   d) A direct loss is physical in nature, an indirect loss is financial
10) Which of the following is not an essential component of a legal binding contract?
   a) Competent Parties
   b) Consideration
   c) Agreement
   d) Incompetent Parties
11) Who typically makes the offer in an insurance transaction?
   a) The applicant
   b) The agent
   c) The insurer
   d) The policyholder

12) In order for agreement to occur, both parties must exchange consideration. What is the applicant's consideration?

a) Promise to pay

b) Premium

c) Information on the application

d) Premium and information on the application

13) A promise or guarantee is defined as:

a) Representation

b) Misrepresentation

c) Warranty

d) Concealment

14) When a client withholds important information crucial to the underwriting process, it is called:

a) Misrepresentation

b) Concealment

c) Fraud

d) Representation

15) Which of the following statements is FALSE?

a) Binders can only be issued in written form

b) Binders are temporary immediate coverage

c) Binders can end by being cancelled, replaced by policy, or they can expire

d) The insurer has the right to cancel the binder

16) Falling objects is a named peril on which form?

a) Broad

b) Basic

c) Special

d) All Risk

17) Which type of policy covers everything except what is excluded?

a) Named Peril

b) Basic Form

c) Broad Form

d) Open Peril/ All Risk

18) After a small house fire, the insurer replaces the personal property items but pays after accounting for depreciation. Which form of valuation was used?

a) Replacement cost

b) Functional Replacement Cost

c) Actual Cash Value

d) Fair Market Value

19) If a building is vacant over __ days, coverage may be limited or cancelled.

a) 60

b) 30

c) 90

d) 120

20) Which Property Provision gives the insurer the right to claim ownership of the damaged property?

a) Arbitration

b) Abandonment

c) Right of salvage

d) Additional coverages

21) Someone who has temporary custody of another person's property is called:

a) Bailee

b) Bailor

c) Insurer

d) Umpire

22) Liability coverage includes protection for different types of damages. Which of the following is NOT covered by the liability policy?

a) Punitive

b) General

c) Special

d) Specific

23) Legal defense is an Additional Coverage on the liability policy. Which of the following statements is FALSE? Legal defense…

a) Is free, automatic and pays over and above

b) Will only pay if the insured is not at fault

c) Will pay as long as the insurer has money at stake

d) Is not a part of aggregate or occurrence limits

24) Which defense is used to point the blame at someone other than the insured?

a) Contributory negligence

b) Comparative negligence

c) Proximate cause

d) Intervening cause

25) ______ is products liability and provides coverage for bodily injury and property damage, but does not pay for the recall itself.

a) Strict liability

b) Vicarious liability

c) Absolute liability

d) Intervening cause

26) If the city zoo brings in a tiger and it breaks out of the zoo and does property damage around the city, the zoo is responsible for the damages. This is called…

a) Vicarious liability

b) Strict liability

c) Excess liability

d) Absolute liability

27) The purpose of the "Arbitration Clause" is to:

a) Provide a method to come to an agreement outside of a court of law

b) Provide the means of a settlement through use of the court system

c) Allow the insured to challenge the insurer at the expense of the insurer

d) Provide a method to come to an agreement with the use of the Department of Insurance

28) Jim rents a two bedroom apartment. Which type of Homeowners form does Jim need since he is a renter?

a) HO-3

b) HO-4

c) HO-5

d) HO-6

29) In a Homeowners policy, a dwelling can have up to ___ units.

a) 2

b) 4

c) 6

d) 8

30) Under the Homeowners policy, who is NOT an insured?

a) Joe's daughter who lives in a college dorm

b) Joe's father-in-law who lives in Joe's basement

c) Joe's 20 year old son who lives in his own home across the street from Joe's house

d) Joe's 2 year old foster child

31) Homeowners Section I, Coverage A provides coverage for the dwelling. Which of the following statements is FALSE about Coverage A?

a) An attached garage is covered

b) Permanently installed fixtures are covered

c) Land is covered

d) Covers structures attached to the dwelling

32) In the Homeowners policy, the limit of liability on Coverage B is automatically:

a) 10% of A

b) 10% of C

c) $1,000

d) 20% of A

33) What is the coverage territory of personal property under the Homeowners policy?

a) United States and US territories

b) United States, US territories and Canada

c) North America excluding Mexico

d) Worldwide

34) The HO-2 Broad Form uses _______ for Coverage A and B and __________ for Coverage C.

a) Replacement Cost, Actual Cash Value

b) Actual Cash Value, Replacement Cost

c) Fair Market Value, Actual Cash Value

d) Replacement Cost, Replacement Cost

35) Which of the following perils is not a part of Extended Coverages?

a) Volcano

b) Vandalism

c) Wind

d) Vehicles

36) Which two policies do not have coverage for Coverage A and B?

a) HO-3 and HO-5

b) HO-4 and HO-6

c) HO-4 and HO-5

d) HO-5 and HO-6

37) Which of the following covers the residence with the Basic Form?

a) HO-3

b) HO-5

c) HO-6

d) HO-8

38) Statements on the application are referred to as:

a) Warranties

b) Representations

c) Concealments

d) Notices

39) Which of the following uses Open Peril for Coverages A, B, C, and D in the Homeowners policy?

a) HO-3

b) HO-4

c) HO-5

d) HO-6

40) As an additional insured, the mortgagee has all the following rights except:

a) The right to pay a premium

b) The right to file a claim

c) The right to cancel the policy

d) The right to be notified prior to cancellation

41) The "Other Insurance Provision:"

a) Protects against over indemnification

b) Protects against subrogation

c) Establishes insurer payments on a primary secondary basis

d) Establishes multiple coverages from different companies

42) Under Homeowners Section II, Coverage E is _____ and Coverage F is ______.

a) Personal, Commercial

b) Personal Liability, Medical Payments

c) Personal Property, Medical Payments

d) Medical Payments, Personal Liability

43) Where would you find the parties and the promise to pay in the insurance policy?

a) Insuring agreement

b) Declaration page

c) Definitions section

d) Conditions section

44) When an insured gives up their right to sue to the insurer, this is called:

a) Subrogation
b) Indemnification
c) Warranty
d) Speculative risk

45) What is the purpose of the "Fair Credit Reporting Act?"

a) State legislation designed to protect consumer information
b) State legislation protecting state information
c) Federal legislation designed to protect consumer information
d) Federal legislation protecting federal information

46) If an insurer cancels an insured mid term of the policy

a) The full premium must be refunded
b) No refund is required
c) Non earned premium may be refunded on a short rate basis
d) Non earned premium must be refunded on a pro rata basis

47) The Dwelling Policy is similar to Section I of the Homeowners policy, however one difference is the _____ peril is not automatically included on the DP.

a) Earthquake
b) Fire
c) Theft
d) Vandalism

48) Which part of the PAP policy has a description of the vehicle such as the auto's make and model?

a) Conditions
b) Declarations
c) Definitions
d) Insuring clause

49) Which of the following is Part A of the PAP?

a) Physical damage
b) Uninsured
c) Medical payments
d) Liability

50) Which of the following provides coverage for collision and other than collision in the Personal Auto Policy?

a) Part A

b) Part B

c) Part C

d) Part D

51) In the PAP, who would NOT be an insured?

a) Joe's wife Laura

b) Joe's son who is away at college

c) Joe's mother in law who lives 2 blocks away

d) Joe's foster son

52) What single limit amount would be comparable to 100/300/100?

a) $400,000

b) $500,000

c) $100,000

d) $300,000

53) Which is NOT a definition of uninsured?

a) No insurance

b) Insurer denies coverage

c) Insurer becomes insolvent

d) Legal limits, but not enough coverage for this accident

54) Joe borrows his neighbor's car to pick up pizza for the guys. From a coverage perspective, the vehicle is described as a:

a) Covered vehicle

b) Non owned vehicle

c) Temporary substitute

d) Newly acquired vehicle

55) In a split limit, the second number is:

a) The total BI and PD for the accident

b) Property damage

c) BI per accident

d) BI per person

56) In order for a medical payments claim to be paid, it must be filed within __ year(s) of the accident in the PAP.

a) 1

b) 2

c) 3

d) 4

57) Under Part D, collision and other than collision definitions provide coverage for different perils. Which of the following is covered under collision?

a) Theft

b) Flood

c) Car overturns

d) Contact with an animal

58) Which of the following is considered to be underinsured?

a) Legal but not enough

b) Less than legal

c) Hit and run driver

d) Bankrupt companies

59) Which of the following would not be an example of a "covered auto."

a) Temporary substitute

b) Newly acquired auto

c) Auto listed in the declaration page

d) Borrowed auto

60) Concerning the Flood Policy, which of the following is FALSE?

a) The agent sells the policy, but the government assumes the risk

b) A building does not have to be in a flood zone to be eligible to purchase a flood policy

c) The agent does not have binding authority

d) The deductible on the emergency program is $500 and the deductible on the regular program is $1,000

61) If a boat is over 26 feet in length, which type of policy provides coverage?

a) Boatowners

b) Homeowners

c) Yacht

d) Warranty

62) In order to insure mobile homes, insurers will require:

a) ACV and permanent foundations

b) Market value and permanent foundations

c) ACV and an enhanced deductible

d) ACV without foundation requirements

63) Which Personal Inland Marine Policy schedules a specific item?

a) FAIR Plan

b) Personal effects

c) Personal articles

d) Personal property

64) Which of the following is NOT a Common Condition?

a) Cancellation

b) Examination of First Named Insured

c) Inspections and Surveys

d) Changes

65) Which is NOT a module of the Commercial Package Policy?

a) Ocean Marine

b) Farm

c) Commercial General Liability

d) Equipment Breakdown

66) Which form is used to provide coverage to a building during the construction process?

a) Extra Expense Coverage Form

b) Builders Risk Form

c) Legal Liability Coverage Form

d) Condo Coverage Form

67) Which coverage would you recommend to a plumber?

a) Extra expense

b) Business income

c) Equipment breakdown

d) Builders risk

Co-Insurance Math Questions, 68 &69

Property value= $400,000

Co-Insurance= 80%

Loss= $80,000

Deductible= $500

Customer carried= $200,000 of insurance

68) How much insurance should the customer carry to qualify for replacement cost coverage on partial losses?

a) $320,000

b) $80,000

c) $400,000

d) $200,000

69) How much will the insurer pay on this claim?

a) $39,500

b) $40,000

c) $64,000

d) $49,500

70) Which business would you recommend "Business Income" to:

a) An insurance agency

b) A restaurant

c) A Landscaper

d) A handyman

71) Which of the following would be included in the definition of business personal property in the Commercial Property policy

a) Copy machine

b) Lumber for remodeling purposes

c) Fire extinguishers

d) Lawn mowers to maintain premises

72) Proof of coverage is provided by the insurer through a/an:

a) Binder

b) Surety bond

c) Occurrence form

d) Certificate of insurance

73) Which of the following would you recommend Errors and Omissions coverage to?

a) An accountant

b) A manufacturer

c) A grocery store

d) Any employer concerned with employers liability

74) In the event of a loss, the insured has duties. Which of the following is NOT a duty of the insured?

a) Notify police when appropriate

b) Cooperate with the insurer

c) Allow the insurer to inspect the property

d) Repair the property

75) In regards to Loss Conditions, which of the following statements is FALSE?

a) In the event of loss, the insured must contact the insurer

b) The fee of an umpire's appraisal is paid in full by the insurer

c) If the property has been recovered after a loss, the insurer has the right to salvage the property at the insured's option: amount paid or property

d) After a loss, the insurer has the right to pay the cost to repair or replace

76) In the Commercial General Liability policy which coverages are provided under Coverage B:

a) Products and Completed Operations

b) Personal and Advertising Injury

c) Medical Payments

d) Bodily Injury and Property Damage

77) The purpose of the Extended Reporting Periods is to:

a) Allow claims to be filed after the policy period

b) Extend coverage after the policy period

c) Determine how far back coverage is extended

d) Report extensions as needed

78) The Occurrence Form of the CGL requires that:

a) The event must happen during the policy period to be covered

b) Notification must happen during the policy period

c) Focus be on the claim and its time period

d) Occurrences must happen after the retro active date

79) Which is NOT under Coverage A: Bodily Injury and Property Damage of the CGL policy?

a) Premises Liability

b) Completed Operations

c) Independent Operations

d) Personal Injury

80) Which of the following is part of Coverage C, under commercial liability?

a) Completed Operations

b) Legal expenses

c) Products

d) Operations Liability

81) Which is FALSE?

a) With safe burglary, the policy does not cover the disappearance of the safe

b) A watchperson is hired to watch the property on premises

c) Theft is the unlawful taking of property to the deprivation of the insured

d) Burglary always includes damage to property

82) The robbery definition includes:

a) Damage to property

b) Mysterious disappearance

c) Threat of violence

d) Employee dishonesty

83) Which is NOT a part of the definition of breakdown?

a) If initial breakdown leads to another breakdown, it is considered 2 breakdowns

b) Failure of pressure or vacuum equipment

c) Mechanical failure

d) Electrical failure

84) An Auto Dealers Form would probably include:

a) Garage Keepers Coverage

b) Transportation Expense

c) Newly Acquired Autos

d) Utility Interruption

85) Which form covers a van being used to haul goods?

a) Garage Form

b) Truckers Form

c) Business Auto Coverage Form

d) Motor Carrier Form

86) A new claim occurs on the earthquake when free from events for over:

a) 48 hours

b) 72 hours

c) 120 hours

d) 168 hours

87) What could be used to insure bull dozers used and multiple locations?

a) Business Personal Property

b) Personal Article Floater

c) Commercial Property Floater

d) Business Owners Policy

88) Workers Compensation was designed to cover injuries:

a) Work and non work related injuries

b) Employment practices liability

c) For which employers are found responsible for

d) Out of and in the course of employment

89) On the Farm policy, which of the following could NOT be scheduled under Coverage E Scheduled Farm Personal Property?

a) Livestock

b) Farm personal property

c) Seed

d) Grain

90) Which of the following statements is FALSE?

a) The property section of the BOP is All Risk/Open Peril

b) The insured receives Replacement Cost on property

c) The BOP does not have a co-insurance requirement

d) Additional coverages are not built in to the policy

91) Which type of business is eligible for a BOP?

a) Banks

b) Apartment buildings

c) Liquor stores

d) Auto dealership

92) Which type of business does not qualify for a BOP?

a) Motels

b) Apartment buildings

c) Restaurants

d) Liquor stores

93) The party in a bond that financially backs the promise is:

a) Principal

b) Surety

c) Obligee

d) Insured

94) Surety bonds differ from fidelity bonds because they:

a) Include an indemnity agreement

b) Cover employee dishonesty

c) Are purchased by the obligee

d) Do not have to be collateralized

95) Which of the following bonds is NOT a surety bond?

a) Bid bond

b) Bail bond

c) Completion bond

d) Fidelity bond

96) Under Part One of Workers' Compensation, there is a benefit for disability. Which of the following is FALSE about this coverage?

a) Benefits are paid tax free

b) Benefits are paid for partial or total disability

c) Benefits are paid based on 66 2/3 of the average weekly wage

d) Benefits are paid immediately after the injury

97) In regards to the Workers' Compensation policy, which is FALSE?

a) Part time workers must be covered

b) Seasonal workers must be covered

c) Independent contractors must be covered

d) Minors must be covered

98) Which of the following statements concerning Workers Compensation premiums is FALSE?

a) Premiums are estimated up front

b) Premiums are based on payroll

c) Premiums are based upon job classification

d) Premiums may be passed on to the employee

99) All of these are exclusions under CGL Coverage A, liability EXCEPT:

a) Workers Compensation

b) War

c) Unintentional acts

d) Criminal Act

100) There are 5 areas under contractual liability (LEASE).What does the acronym stand for?

a) Lease agreements, Easements, Agreement to indemnify a municipality, Sidetrack agreements, Elevator maintenance agreements

b) Liability agreements, Easements, Agreement to indemnify a municipality, Sidetrack agreements, Elevator maintenance agreements

c) Lease agreements, Exclusions, Agreements to indemnify a municipality, Sidetrack agreements, Elevator maintenance agreements

d) Liability agreements, Exclusions, Acceptance, Sidetrack agreements, Elevator maintenance agreements

Test II Answer Key

1) A
2) D
3) A
4) D
5) C
6) B
7) C
8) D
9) D
10) D
11) A
12) D
13) C
14) B
15) A
16) A
17) D
18) C
19) A
20) C
21) A
22) A
23) B
24) D
25) A
26) D
27) A
28) B
29) B
30) C
31) C
32) A
33) D
34) A
35) B
36) B
37) D
38) B
39) C
40) C
41) A
42) B
43) A
44) A
45) C
46) D
47) C
48) B
49) D
50) D
51) C
52) A
53) D
54) B
55) C
56) C
57) C
58) A
59) D
60) D
61) C
62) A
63) C
64) B
65) A
66) B
67) A
68) A
69) D
70) B
71) A
72) D
73) A
74) D
75) B
76) B
77) A
78) A
79) D
80) B
81) A
82) C
83) A
84) A
85) D
86) D
87) C
88) D
89) B
90) D
91) B
92) D
93) B
94) A
95) D
96) D
97) C
98) D
99) C
100) A

Glossary

Accident - a sudden and unexpected event, not under the control of the insured, resulting in injury or damage

Adhesion - one party (the insurer) is responsible for the wording of the contract

Adverse Selection - selection of risks that is higher or more likely to have a claim

Agent - one who represents the insurance company (principal)

Agent/Producer Report - report that allows the agent to share information and observations with the insurance company concerning the applicant

Aleatory - a contract of unequal exchange; one party stands to receive more than the other

Alien Insurer - an insurer organized under the laws of another country

Apparent Authority - the appearance of authority created by the insurance company; not official authority

Application - the starting point of the application process

Assignment - to give the rights of the policy to another party

Authorized (Admitted) Insurer - an insurer who has been approved by the Indiana Insurance Commissioner to do business in the state of Indiana

Binding Receipt (Binder) - provides temporary, immediate coverage

Broker - one who represents the client

Cease and Desist Order - an order to stop

Concealment - the hiding or withholding of the truth

Conditional Contract - certain events must occur (sickness or death) before the insurance company will pay its claims

Conditional Receipt - states that coverage will begin either on the date of the application or the date of the physical (if required), whichever is last, **if** the applicant was insurable on that date

Consideration Clause - specifies what each party to the contract has exchanged in order to validate the contract

Consideration - the something of value exchanged between the two parties of the contract

Consultant - a person who for a fee, offers advice, counsel, opinion, or service with respect to the benefits, advantages, or disadvantages promised under any policy of insurance that could be issued in Indiana

Contract - an agreement between two parties

Controlled Business - insurance written on the interests of: the applicant or licensee, the applicant's or licensee's immediate family, or the applicant's or licensee's employer

Deductible - the amount of the risk that the insured retains full responsibility for

Dividend - a return of premium

Domestic Insurer - an insurer organized under the laws of Indiana

Effective Date - the date the policy goes into effect

Entire Contract - includes the policy itself, the application and any attachments

Estoppel - to be legally stopped from being able to enforce one's legal right

Expenses - load; cost of doing business

Exposure - an area in which a loss could occur

Express Authority - powers and authorities expressed in the agency agreement

Fair Credit Reporting Act - federal legislature designed to protect consumer information

Foreign Insurer - an insurer organized under the laws of another state

Fraternal - non-profit entity that offers insurance to its members and is organized under a lodge system

Fraud - an intentional misrepresentation for the purpose of benefiting

Gross Premium - the total amount paid by the policyholder. Risk- Interest + Expenses

Hazard - a situation that increases the chance of a loss

Implied Authority - powers allowed by the insurance company but not expressed in the agency agreement

Incontestable Clause - the period of time the company has to challenge the information the insured gave on the application (2 years)

Indemnity (Indemnify, Indemnification) – to make whole, no more no less

Inspection - a report concerning the financial, moral, physical or any other relevant information concerning the applicant

Insurability - the ability to be insured

Insurable Interest - financial or emotional interest one has in another's life or health

Insurance Guaranty Association - protects policyowners, insureds, and beneficiaries of life, health, or annuity contracts when these insurers fail to perform their contractual obligations due to financial impairment

Insurance - transference of risk from an individual to an insurance company, which then spreads it among its policyholders

Insured - the policyholder

Insurer - the insurance company

Insuring Clause - clause stating the parties to the contract and the company's promise to pay under the conditions stated within the policy

Interim Insuring Agreement - an agreement for the insurance company to provide coverage for the client while still completing the underwriting process

Law of Large Numbers - more numbers used to establish a statistic the more accurate the statistic will be

Lloyd's - a company that insures risk by spreading risk over a group of investors; not an insurance company

Material Statement - something that had the insurance company been aware of, the information would have affected how or if the policy would have been issued

Misrepresentation - mistruth or a lie

Moral Hazard - a hazard based upon a person's values and ethics

Morale Hazard - a hazard that deals with carelessness or irresponsibility

Mutual Company (Participating) - an insurance company owned by its policyholders

Net Premium - the true cost of insurance; Risk-Interest

Nonparticipating - product or company that does not pay a dividend to its policyholders

Owner - the party that controls the policy

Ownership Clause - the owner has all of the rights in a policy

Partial Assignment (Temporary Assignment) - the owner gives up some of his/her ownership rights for a temporary period of time

Participating - product or company that pays a dividend to its policyholders

Peril - an event that causes the loss to the insured

Physical Hazard - hazards that are physical in nature; you can see, touch or smell them

Preferred Rating - better than average risk

Premium Mode - the frequency of payment (Annual, Semi-annual, quarterly, monthly)

Producer - the insurance agent

Pure Risk - a possibility of loss; insurable

Rate up - when the insured charges a higher premium to cover a higher risk

Reinsurance - when one insurer, for consideration, assumes the risk or part of the risk of another insurer

Representation - the truth to the best of one's knowledge

Retained - a way to manage risk by being willing to pay for a loss when and if it occurs

Rider (Endorsement) - a change in the original policy

Risk - the chance or possibility of a loss

Speculative Risk - a possibility of loss or gain; not insurable

Standard Rating - average or normal rating

Stock Company (Non-Participating) - an insurance company owned by stock or shareholders

Substandard Rating - higher than average risk

Temporary Producer - a license that allows an individual to service, not sell, existing insurance

Transferred - a way to manage risk by taking the risk and transferring it to another party, who then assumes the risk

Twisting - when one party misrepresents the truth for the purpose of replacing business

Unauthorized (Non-Admitted) - an insurer that has not been approved by the Commissioner to do business in the state of Indiana

Unilateral - only one party in the contract is held to a promise

Valued Contract - contract that pays a specified amount that may or may not be related to the extent of the loss

Waiver - to voluntarily give up a known right

Warranty - a promise or guarantee

Index

Made in the USA
Monee, IL
14 September 2026

63198313R00184